'You hear the stories all the time at work: how everyone is struggling to pay their bills, what an awful experience they have if they get ill, if they fall out with a manager who can then mess with their hours. **They don't see us as humans, or workers'** Ali Waqar

'**Something has to change. I don't care what it is, but something has to change**' Sara Bryson

'I know it sounds really small and stupid, but no one normally comes up to you and just asks, "**How are you doing?** Is your money situation OK, is your living situation OK, are you getting by, what's happening?"' Shen Batmaz

Now We Have Your Attention

Also by Jack Shenker

The Egyptians: A Radical Story

JACK SHENKER

Now We Have Your Attention

The New Politics of the People

THE BODLEY HEAD
LONDON

1 3 5 7 9 10 8 6 4 2

The Bodley Head, an imprint of Vintage,
20 Vauxhall Bridge Road,
London SW1V 2SA

The Bodley Head is part of the Penguin Random House group of companies
whose addresses can be found at global.penguinrandomhouse.com.

Penguin
Random House
UK

First published by The Bodley Head in 2019

www.vintage-books.co.uk

A CIP catalogue record for this book is available from the British Library

ISBN 9781847925404

Typeset in 11.5/15 pt Sabon LT Std
by Integra Software Services Pvt. Ltd, Pondicherry

Printed and bound in Great Britain by Clays Ltd, Elcograf S.p.A.

Penguin Random House is committed to a sustainable future for our
business and products made from

For Amy,
and making maps together

'We're happy, surely?' He pressed his presumption just a little. 'Shouldn't we be sensible, too?'

But the disturbance that had come did not give up its ground.

—William Trevor, 'An Idyll in Winter'

Contents

Prologue

This book is a journey across a country in crisis, although not the crisis we usually read about in the papers or hear about on the news. In a weird, disorientating age marked by political earthquakes and volcanoes – shock election results, constitutional chaos, new parties, new leaders, new governments – it tries to go below the surface and look instead at what is animating all this turmoil; at the movements of the tectonic plates underneath. Over the past few years, while most journalists were converging on Westminster to understand why things are falling apart, I've found myself going the other way: seeking out not the symptoms of the breakdown, but the causes. I ended up sitting in franchised coffee outlets and nondescript office blocks all over Britain; climbing over mammoth construction sites and factory ruins; wedging myself into basements, squats and the shadows of glitzy conference halls; walking along fields, rivers, football pitches and far-flung business parks, searching all the while for clues. What I discovered was the opposite of what we've been led to expect: not an anti-politics, but a fierce and liberatory engagement with the way that power, money and privilege mould our lives. There is mass disillusionment, certainly, with the organs of the state that are supposed to mediate and regulate these forces – in 2019, polling suggested that three-quarters of the population believe politics 'is not fit for purpose' – but it is accompanied by a hunger for new forms of agency, representation and action, both within the conventional political arena and beyond it.[1] What path those new forms take, and the disturbances they produce, will have a revolutionary impact on us all.

As the long, late twentieth century draws messily to a close, we are witnessing – for better or for worse – the end of a particular paradigm, one that has shaped our world for about forty years. For many, including myself, it spans an entire lifetime or more. That period has not been uniform: it has encompassed great changes to the ways in which we work, play and communicate, to the technologies we use and to the tales we tell about ourselves. But there is a constant thread running through it, namely an organising principle based on free markets, movable money and competition – on an ever-growing rivalry between people, companies, cities and regions. The economic system that was built around that principle imploded during the financial crash of 2008, with spectacular global consequences. In Britain, our political leaders tried to carry on as if nothing had really changed; the grammar and syntax of institutional power remained the same, as did the lens through which the press evaluated and reported it. But although liberal capitalism has so far endured, superficially at least, something important did change, and that was the logic behind the economic system, the justification it offered up for its existence. After 2008, that logic contradicted the lived reality of millions. In the gap between the mentality of a sclerotic governing class and the way things felt to those outside of it, rebellions began to take root. They came from the left and the right, from the young and the old, and they manifested themselves at the ballot box, on the street, and in a vast array of different forms. They went off haphazardly, in multiple directions, and political pandemonium ensued. Now, although the economic system staggers on for the time being, the infrastructure around it is crumbling. We don't yet know what will emerge from the rubble, but in this book I identify the shoots of something altered, something new.

Historical paradigms do not end neatly and tidy up behind them as they leave; nor do new ones arrive fully formed, ready to fill the void. What we can say is that we are living simultaneously through the slow-burn decline of a still-present past, and the birth pangs of contested futures: it's a churn that fills the air around us, and seeps into all the cracks. This churn has left many of those who traditionally navigate the political terrain on our behalf – pundits, columnists and politicians – scratching their heads, and staring at outdated maps in confusion. 'I feel completely lost,' admitted David Runciman, head of politics at Cambridge University, in 2019.[2] 'I'm not sure I fully understand politics right now,' said former prime minister Tony Blair three years earlier.[3] The political writer John Harris describes the predicament of his colleagues as akin to that of Joan Didion, who documented the American cultural revolutions of the late 1960s.[4] 'I was supposed to have a script, and had mislaid it,' wrote Didion. 'I was meant to know the plot, but all I knew was what I saw: flash pictures in variable sequence, images with no "meaning" beyond their temporary arrangement, not a movie but a cutting-room experience.'[5]

Most journalists continue to fixate on the personalities, parties and parlour games of Parliament, as if the answer to where the turmoil comes from must lie somewhere within its limits. It's a category error that has contributed to an epic disconnect: the breathless frenzy of Westminster on the one hand, where things seem to change at a thousand miles a minute but are actually mired in stasis, and real life on the other, where we continue to go about our days as normal, even as, gradually, many of the political, economic and social building blocks of the country around us are transformed. 'What a funny, contained emergency it is,' observed the economics commentator Aditya Chakrabortty, on the means by which our current bedlam is routinely presented to us. 'It is as if the revolution of 1789 was being covered entirely from inside the Versailles court of Louis XVI.'[6]

And so in these pages I'm attempting to do something very different. While most news coverage is sped up, this book slows down – to give time and space to the stories of individuals and communities about how we got here, and where we might be going next. While most news coverage feels weightless and free-floating, curiously disembodied from the physical places that frame our lives and inform our politics, this book is grounded in tangible geography – in concrete, metal, grass and water. And while most news coverage is ahistorical, landing with instant razzmatazz but little context, this book interrogates the reckonings, and unreckonings, of the past that run right through us. It illustrates the ways in which the tone of most news coverage reflects the outlook of our formal politics, a formal politics that is failing in our midst. And it travels into the crevices where an alternative politics is beginning to mate-rialise – from a dank club night in Brighton to a cleaner's store cupboard near the House of Commons and a shabby shopfront in Scotland, almost 400 miles north.

What follows is not objective, or anything like exhaustive. It is an entirely personal snapshot of Britain at a unique moment of flux, one that inevitably overlooks great swathes of the country and its fluid, fractious political debate. It is coloured throughout by my own perspective, one that I share with most of the young people whom we meet in Chapter 1, which is that in our post-crash era it is those fighting for radical change who are the realists; the fantasists are those who believe that the pre-2008 world can somehow be resurrected and continue. But I hope that people with different perspectives also read the book and discover something in it that is thought-provoking, or even convincing. I hope that although they may disagree with some of its arguments, they find that it still sheds some light upon the origin of all those earthquakes and volcanoes, and on the driving forces behind ruptures that are yet to appear. Right now, we all need as much hope as we can get.

In the American South of the 1930s and 40s, legions of baseball correspondents filed dutiful and scrupulously balanced articles detailing the twists, turns and dramas of their sport: the highlights of each match, the transfers from one team to another, the battles for supremacy that formed the backbone of every season. With very few exceptions, none of them ever commented on the fact that US baseball leagues were racially segregated, or that the informal 'Baseball colour line' was being progressively undermined by a nascent civil rights movement that would go on to change the country's history. The correspondents operated within the boundaries of the system they reported on, and rarely questioned its underlying structure or the wider social forces that were rendering it an anachronism.[7] Albeit in a different context, something similar has characterised political journalism in Britain over recent years. The UK media is sometimes described as suffering from a lack of diversity, and the charge is a fair one – but it does not only apply to the racial, gender and class backgrounds of its personnel. Crucially, the media has also failed to diversify its thinking; to move beyond the narrow confines and limited horizons of the political assumptions that came before. This book aims to provide a corrective, and in the process uncover some of the people and movements that have long been marginalised by those assumptions, and robbed of the attention they deserve. Their struggles will play a critical role in determining what tomorrow looks like for all of us, a tomorrow that is fraught with danger and possibility. As the author Rebecca Solnit puts it, 'The future is dark, with a darkness as much of the womb as the grave.'[8]

1

Youth

Ancoats, Manchester

It will unravel.

—Stuart Hall

When Layla first arrived in Britain, at the age of three, a gust of wind caught her unexpectedly and sent her flying.[1] She landed in a tangle on the floor. 'I was so used to hot weather,' she told me, 'and the combination of rain and cold and gales was something I'd never experienced before. I was small and skinny, and I just went "whoosh" into the air.'

Layla's father had left the Democratic Republic of Congo a few years earlier, at the outset of a war that would go on to claim hundreds of thousands of lives. He made his way to Manchester, found a job and a home, and then brought the rest of the family over to join him. He was relieved to have them out of harm's way – far from the military dictatorship he had spent much of his life resisting, settled now in a country where life seemed calm, predictable and secure. Not that things were easy, of course. As asylum seekers, they were moved continuously from one form of temporary accommodation to another, and survival depended on an exhausting, convoluted dance: through the bureaucracy of the benefits system, through the worlds of formal and informal work, through the grey zones in between. But despite all the upheaval – from Moston to Openshaw, Clayton to Longsight – the ground beneath the family's feet felt solid. It was the early 2000s, New Labour were at the height of their powers, and Britain's second city was undergoing a glitzy urban rebrand which promised to transform the fortunes of its citizens. 'The story was that Manchester was becoming more and more global, more and more successful,' remembers Layla.

She struggled with English at first, even while translating for her parents: she could understand the words in her head, but they got muddled up with French and Lingala when she tried to form them in her mouth. Moving from neighbourhood to neighbourhood meant that social connections were always transient, and there was rarely enough money spare for the bus ride back across town to visit old classmates. Layla wasn't fazed. She pored over books in local libraries to improve her language skills, and became adept at making new friends, again and again and again. She studied for her GCSEs at a school where kids set fire to the bins at break time and police regularly patrolled the corridors, but she got the results she needed to make it to sixth-form college and from there she won a place at university. Her parents were overjoyed; they dreamed of her becoming a civil servant, or a teacher. There was a path, they knew, that ran from university to a graduate job, and from a graduate job to a home of one's own, and from a home of one's own to a family, and Layla was now on it.

But as Layla neared adulthood, something strange began to happen: that path began to blur and warp. For a hundred years in Britain, each generation had been more prosperous than their parents; Layla and her cohort were about to break the mould. 'The summer after I turned sixteen, just before I started college, I had an awakening,' she explained. 'I was looking around at the school I'd come from, which was so poorly funded, and at the futures we had waiting for us, and it all felt wrong. I just thought, I can't ignore this any more.'

Some of Layla's friends expected to live in social housing after leaving school, but waiting lists had grown so long that they were worried about being shunted towards homelessness instead. At the same time, those in her social circle planning on higher education no longer saw it as a gateway to dependable middle-class employment; now it seemed more like a guarantee of crippling debts, and entry into a jobs market that was delivering the longest period of wage stagnation and falling incomes in recorded economic history.[2] By the time Layla started her degree in 2017, the average student in England owed more than £50,000 upon graduation – a fifteenfold increase in her lifetime – and for those like her from poorer backgrounds, who are afforded extra maintenance loans, that figure was higher still.[3] 'I was stressed,' she told me. 'About whether I'd ever pay it back, about how commodified it all felt, and about how I'd ever afford a home on the other side.' For Layla, the thought of eventually buying her own place was an increasingly wild fantasy: by this point, twentysomethings in Manchester were spending almost half their pay on rent, three times more than their grandparents did, and although the city's horizon was restless with cranes hardly any of the new apartments they were building were affordable.[4] That once-solid ground beneath her feet no longer slanted upwards towards progress.

'There's worry, all the time, and that produces an anger,' said Layla. 'It comes out in different ways, but you notice it. And it takes people in different directions.' For Layla, it took her here: to the top floor of a former textiles mill on the banks of the Ashton Canal in Ancoats. At the far end of the room in which Layla and I were talking, somebody had pinned up a map of Manchester's city centre with protest sites and surreptitious approach routes marked out; around us lay crisp packets, mobile-phone chargers, and a casual, convulsive disregard for the status quo. Young people talking in low voices began to gather their things together, preparing to descend the stairs and head out on to the street. Layla pulled her jacket tight, and I did the same. These are the days when we all feel like the wind could blow us down, or maybe, just maybe, lift us into something new.

*

The Ashton Canal was dug in the late eighteenth century to ferry coal from the great mines at Oldham and Ashton-under-Lyne into eastern and central Manchester, where the clothing and hat-making industries were concentrated. Upon its completion, a dense cluster of wharves, warehouses and industrial buildings sprung up along the waterway, many of which are still standing. Some have been converted into high-end flats for aspirational professionals, while others have been abandoned, or are stuck somewhere in the middle. One has been completely demolished with the exception of its original facade, which keeps watch over an acre of rubble; it looks out over its inverse, a building site where a recently constructed steel and concrete skeleton has been left without a skin. The canal wends its way out from the chain stores and franchised coffee outlets around Piccadilly station and past a former retail park on the inner ring road, where a collection of colossal grey boxes once stuffed with consumer goods for the very young – Mothercare, the Early Learning Centre, Toys R Us – now lie empty: prefab squares of silence, encircled by a rush-hour traffic roar. Further east, the roads that run alongside the towpath become quieter, and the spaces they border more piecemeal. There are miles of metal fences here, screening off car parks and guard dogs and yawning scrubland on the other side. Scattered among them are iron gas holders and half-broken outhouses. Walk past at the right time of day and you'll hear the discordant sounds of evangelical church congregations and illicit teenage band rehearsals mingling as they seep into the sky.

At almost any point in its history, Manchester has provided two things simultaneously: a window on to the prevailing economic orthodoxy, and a case study in the flaws and fightbacks that threaten it. Free Trade Hall on Peter Street was built to celebrate the repeal of the Corn Laws in 1846, a move celebrated by its supporters as fulfilling the natural 'destiny' of competitive markets; it was constructed on the site of the Peterloo Massacre, in which landowning yeomanry charged at crowds who had assembled to demand parliamentary representation, and swung at demonstrators with their sabres. The Royal Exchange next to St Ann's Square was designed as a mart in which mill owners could buy and sell their wares, but it's also where factory hands held demonstrations and disaffected cotton workers attacked symbols of Manchester's moneyed elite. Friedrich Engels' father sent him to work in the family's thread-manufacturing plant in Salford so that the young man might better appreciate the wonders of industrial modernity; instead he and Karl Marx commandeered a corner desk at Chetham's library and began writing *The Communist Manifesto*. 'Capitalism was born here,' observed Layla, 'and, in a way, I guess socialism was too.' A city forged from the violence of the cotton industry and slavery, Manchester has always played host to competing notions of identity and solidarity. During the American Civil War, for example, local business leaders lobbied for British military intervention on behalf of Southern plantation owners, while cotton workers – despite facing hunger and unemployment themselves on account of the Union blockade – mobilised to support the north. Seven decades later, working-class neighbourhoods in the city sent aid and volunteers to wage war with Franco in Spain; at the same time, the Blackshirts of Oswald Mosley – holder of the hereditary baronetcy of Ancoats – were attempting to march through nearby streets. When nations are in flux and fog, Manchester brings their fault lines into the light. Today, the Ashton Canal and the city beyond it are emblematic of an interregnum once again.

This one concerns a deep unravelling: the breakdown of a long-prevailing economic logic, and of the political principles and social norms that developed with it. We've been through similar implosions before. The 'Long Depression' of the late nineteenth century brought an epic Victorian era of globalisation to an end, and culminated eventually in the horrors of the First World War. A generation later the Great Depression led to yet another global conflict. In the decades that followed the Second World War, a new era of industrial capitalism in Western Europe and the USA shaped the lives of billions, until widespread economic stagnation in the mid-1970s resulted in political transformation once again. We have been living with the economic orthodoxy that replaced it – a late, aggressive form of capitalism – ever since; at least, that is, until 2008, when a financial crash of almost unparalleled magnitude exposed and intensified a whole series of interconnected crises that had been bubbling below the skin, both in Britain and abroad. Some of these crises were directly related to the functioning of the existing economy, such as the proliferation of unsustainable debt, a collapse in confidence in the global banking system, and the growing disconnect between zippy, rootless, financialised capital and widespread economic stagnation and inequality as experienced by real people in real places on the ground. Others were sparked by deeper questions about the future: how demographic changes and increased automation would rewire the labour force; which regions, classes and generations would gain from rapid changes to the way the economy reproduced itself, and which would lose out. These were all part of a meta-crisis regarding our ability as individuals, communities and even nation states to check or influence such developments – a crisis of agency itself, within a system that seemingly recognised no decisions and no authority other than those determined by aggregated market forces. In the decade or so since the crash, none of these crises has been dealt with; on the contrary, in its aftermath they have all raged fiercer than ever, overlaid by the ultimate, existential crisis, which is the catastrophic damage being wrought by that very same economic orthodoxy to our living planet and the looming possibility of our slow-burn extinction as a species. The result has been political uproar in countries across the globe.

Like all paradigm shifts, the one we are living through will be lengthy, complex and tortuous, and its outcomes will appear inevitable only with hindsight. In the meantime, we exist in one of what the historian Robert Darnton calls 'moments of suspended disbelief': those rare, fragile conjunctures in which anything seems conceivable, and – far from being immutable – the world around us appears ready to be redesigned.[5] That kaleidoscopic sense of pieces being thrown up in the air, with no clear sign yet of where they might land, is especially acute because of the nature of this particular paradigm shift. At the heart of late capitalism is the conviction that ever-increasing areas of human activity could and should be walled off from politics itself. This ideology – sometimes referred to as market liberalism or neoliberalism (though all of these terms are used to describe a wide range of overlapping phenomena, and their definitions are furiously contested) – rests on the notion that market activity is most efficient and productive when it is protected from political interference, and that the world can be made more efficient and more productive, more extensively liberated from grubby political bickering, by the extension of market principles into as many spheres of life as is viable, with states making active interventions to achieve this where necessary. For better or for worse, we have all seen this tendency manifest itself in the places we live and work. Ancoats is no exception: the transformations wrought by the introduction of new markets over several decades are visible everywhere, from the once-public and now-privatised trains that run along the Calder Valley railway line to the neighbourhood's north and the Hope Valley line to the south, to the business-sponsored academy school on Blossom Street designed to replace the state provision of education in the area (subsequently mired in scandal and shut down), and the former council homes of the Cardroom estate that have been demolished to make way for fresh housing units available to buy or rent at eye-watering prices on the open market.

Neoliberal ideology works by invisibilising itself and claiming to transcend politics altogether; its dictums are presented not as political choices to be tested and debated alongside other, rival political choices, but rather as a set of natural laws. It's simply what works, the argument goes. With the delegation of decision-making over so many areas of our lives to the market, the spaces in which *politics* can play out have shrunk in the late-capitalist era, leaving vacuums in their wake. By politics, I mean not only those policy matters that are subject to democratic oversight via politicians who, in theory at least, are responding to collective demands, but also the mental realms, both private and public, in which different ideas are contested about how power and resources should be understood, structured and distributed. However, after the 2008 financial crash, neoliberalism's claim to 'legitimacy by results' was torn to shreds in many people's eyes and ideological combat has returned with a vengeance. Opinion polls show that popular faith in our existing economic structures is foundering. In 2016 YouGov found that more Brits favour socialism than capitalism, and the following year the pro-market Legatum Institute published a study showing that the words most strongly associated with capitalism by nearly every socio-economic group were 'greed', 'selfishness' and 'corruption'; they concluded that the general public 'instinctively view capitalism negatively'.[6] Theresa May, when prime minister, was forced to defend the very idea of markets in her conference speeches; the *Sun*, Britain's bestselling tabloid newspaper, has published panicked editorials reminding readers that capitalism is the 'best system of wealth-creation mankind has yet invented', while in 2018 the *Daily Telegraph*, the right-of-centre broadsheet widely considered to be the 'in-house' newspaper for Britain's political establishment, launched a campaign to save capitalism and free markets from ruin.[7] Before 2008, there was no need for the *Daily Telegraph* to run any such campaign, and the *Sun* rarely mentioned capitalism at all; the general nature of our economic system was taken for granted. Now, as popular justification for the current orthodoxy collapses, politics – motley, capricious and disorderly – is surging in to fill the gaps.

The defining feature of our age is that politics itself is being reanimated, drawing an era of mass, passive spectatorship to a close. That process is enchanting politics with all kinds of things – place, culture, nationhood, race and dogma, to name but a few – and opening up possibilities that are both emancipatory and revanchist; imaginative horizons are being stretched in ways that are thrilling but that are also capable of inflicting untold pain and suffering, pain and suffering which will not be shared equally. In Ancoats, as in every corner of the country, history is tilting – and many of those who wielded control and influence in days gone by are scrabbling to find a foothold. 'There are times, perhaps once every thirty years, when there is a sea change in politics,' remarked Jim Callaghan, the premier who presided over the last great metamorphosis in the late 1970s. 'It then does not matter what you say or what you do. There is a shift in what the public wants and what it approves of.'

Layla, who couldn't stay up to watch the 2017 general election results roll in because she had to sit an A-level exam on the Tudors the following day ('I love Henry VII,' she admitted to me, 'but for the life of me I couldn't remember anything about Henry VIII'), understands all this far better than most of the professional politicians or lobby journalists 200 miles from her whose lives revolve around the Palace of Westminster. Rather than trying to explain away our present commotion with reference to cults of personality, or conspiratorial Russian bots, or as a paroxysm of 'anti-political' sentiment among an apathetic electorate, Layla views the contemporary moment as intensely political. 'Just look at our reality: it's a political education in its own right,' she told me once. 'All these experts say that people are "anti-politics" right now, but what we're seeing is the epitome of politics.' A couple of years before, just as she was beginning to seriously contemplate life beyond school and her family home, Layla began paying more attention to the things her friends and other people she followed on social media were saying about race and class, about economic opportunities for the young or lack of them, and about the worthy life advice handed down by the comfortably-off to insecure millennials – advice which quickly became fodder for derision, satire and memes. 'Twitter started my political awakening,' she grinned. 'My dad is a Blairite; he'd roll his eyes when I talked about some of the stuff I was reading. The thing is, the ways that generation expect us to think, the things they say to us: they don't work any more. So jokes about that, they become part of your life.'

We compared social media posts that we had come across in recent months, most offering ironic comment on news headlines or major events. 'Reminder: there's alternatives to capitalism,' read one, linking to a media report entitled 'Analysis: Millennials should be willing and able to work longer than their parents and grandparents did'. 'Can't wait for £800k homes in London to suddenly only be worth £20,' stated another, attaching a graph showing the value of sterling plummeting after the EU referendum. There is an entire social media subgenre dissecting the preposterous charges made against young people for supposedly ruining beloved things, be they food items, forms of language or social norms (a sample exchange – Bloomberg: 'Millennials have killed again. The latest victim? American cheese'; response: 'yeah ok but baby boomers killed liberal democracy and the social safety net so can we call it even'). After a former UKIP MEP tweeted a condemnation of teenagers who complain about the economic system, insisting that 'as young people grow up, and have jobs, and mortgages, and children, and obligations, they tend to change their views', one reply from a young person – 'What if those people don't get the jobs, the mortgages, can't afford children or caring for their parents? What if all of these things were contingent on a political settlement which has now completely disappeared?' – went viral. '7 years ago i joined twitter to keep up with one direction on x-factor and now i'm a communist,' posted a woman called Stephanie in late 2017. Her tweet has so far been 'liked' by nearly 300,000 people.

It was against this backdrop – a sense that the politics of the past had failed her, and a resolve to struggle against the cancellation of her future – that Layla came along to 'Demand the Impossible' at Bridge 5 Mill, a radical education programme that had already hosted several courses in London and was now expanding beyond the capital. This series of workshops is the brainchild of Ed Lewis and Jacob Mukherjee, two former secondary-school teachers who became disillusioned with the politics and sociology A-level syllabuses, which they believe leave students spiritless and stymied. 'Everyone talks about the stress and the paperwork of being a schoolteacher, all of which is true,' says Jacob, 'but more depressing is just how boring some of it is. Anything interesting, really interesting, has to be shoehorned in because so much of the course is prescriptive: the taxonomy of electoral systems, the number of hereditary peers, and so on.' The two friends were politicised as students by protests against the Iraq War in the early 2000s. By the early 2010s, when they were settling in to their teaching careers, there were new forms of social unrest that felt urgent and worthy of interrogation: the fallout from the financial crash, austerity, a huge student movement against tuition fees that brought tens of thousands on to the streets of London in 2010, and nationwide riots in 2011. And yet, as Ed puts it, 'The things we were told to teach were so decontextualised. It's not that big ideas like conservatism, liberalism, anarchism and fascism weren't in the syllabus, it's that they were presented in such a simplified and theoretical manner, as just another set of categories to memorise ahead of exam season, that the kids didn't have any way of connecting them to their lived experiences.'

In February 2012, with the streets blanketed in snow, the pair made a plan to go sledging on Hampstead Heath; at the last minute, they decided to duck into a pub instead. It was there that they came up with the idea for a free, extracurricular course for students which would run during the summer holidays and be open to anyone interested in exploring politics beyond their official A-level modules. The inaugural Demand the Impossible was staged a few months later, in a hired room at Goldsmiths University in south-east London. 'We didn't have any money so we held a fundraising party at Ed's flat and encouraged people to give us donations in exchange for portions of themed salads,' said Jacob. 'One was called "Bread" and the other "Roses",' a reference to a slogan that originated in the women's suffrage movement and has become an anthem for working-class struggle: 'Bread for all; and roses, too.' '"Roses" was the fancy one,' explained Jacob, 'as it had halloumi in it.' The budget for that first course was so small that they had to go dumpster-diving to cater for participants; each day they microwaved hastily cobbled-together risottos in the student-union kitchen and served it up for lunch.

The initial Demand the Impossible lasted for five days and included debates and workshops on big oil, feminism, the Egyptian revolution and activist tactics. It culminated in the students conducting a short-lived sit-in of a Sainsbury's outlet in south London, to protest against the retail giant's refusal to pay its staff the living wage. 'We tried to put attendees in different groups, each of which would tackle the issue from a different strategic perspective: some handed out leaflets to shoppers, others tried to collect signatures on a petition, others formed a flash mob inside the store,' said Ed. 'It wasn't entirely successful. After that, we made sure that on subsequent courses the students themselves took the lead in formulating any actions, and that they all did it together.' Over the following years Demand the Impossible grew in scope and size, offering evening sessions staggered across a period of many months as well as intensive week-long programmes. With each new cohort, Ed and Jacob refined the course structure and content, attracted a wider range of guest tutors, and watched on as the young people attending became more fired up, more ambitious. Some of the teens ended up wanting to occupy an HSBC bank branch; others launched demonstrations inside Westfield shopping centres which made the local news. One of the student groups conducted a march through Bishopsgate, at the heart of London's financial district, to oppose government cuts to state services. They were shocked at the aggressive reaction they got from City workers. 'The reception was so hostile, and often racist as well,' remembers Ed. 'Many of the kids later said it was the first time that they had been made to feel like strangers in their own town.'

Most of the teens who sign up for Demand the Impossible tend to be economically disadvantaged to some degree: frustrated at the world they see around them, but so far unable to reconcile their experience with the neatly delineated concepts and terminology of their textbooks. Like Layla, their looming adult lives appear to them almost impossibly precarious. 'When I was being brought up, there was a sense that there was a ladder you could get on,' Neil McInroy, chief executive of the Centre for Local Economic Strategies think tank and a Manchester-based economics commentator whose offices are located just north of the Ashton Canal, told me. 'Now there are no rungs on half of these ladders, there's no such thing. You've got to jump across from one ladder to another all the time, and often you end up further down than when you started. And sometimes there's nowhere to go at all.' The data backs McInroy up; in the post-crash era, according to the Equality and Human Rights Commission, young people have lost out more than any other age group and face the 'worst economic prospects for several generations'; when asked about social mobility, eighteen-to-twenty-four-year-olds are the most pessimistic in the country.[8] Those attending Ed and Jacob's courses already know all this; they want to understand why, and what they can do about it. 'We had one student who studied economics for two years at A level and yet had never once discussed the word capitalism, despite that being the context of everything in her official course,' observed Jacob. Demand the Impossible tries to highlight those unspoken framings, and offer participants the opportunity to think about not just the way things are, but also other ways they could be. The majority have never joined any sort of protest or direct action before, and for many, doing so can be a transformative experience. 'Actually doing something like that, not just talking about it, changes you – it's how you get politicised,' Jacob concluded. 'You think, "wow, this collective thing, this rush of energy … this is intoxicating". And when you unpack that later on, it raises more questions, inspires more curiosity.'

*

Kyle works the phones by day and flies pteranodons by night: feet in stirrups, body half upright to take the reins, surface noise fading to zero. Up high, there's nothing to thud against your eardrums but the soft grunt of the creature's breath, the rhythmic flapping of its wings. When Kyle speaks of the things he sees from a pteranodon – the crags and overhangs of great granite mountains, sweeping waterfalls throwing up huge clouds of water vapour, troglodyte cave systems, vines and tendrils strung across shadowy gorges, mottled plains so vast that it's impossible to tell where or if they come to an end – his eyes shine and his frame slants forward, bobbing with excitement. It looks as if a part of him is launching into flight, even as we talk.

One of the reasons Kyle is so enraptured by computerised life in the air – as generated by an Xbox video game called *Ark* – is that he has spent too much of his physical life on the ground. Some of that ground lies at the western end of the Ashton Canal: on the pedestrianised ramp that leads down from the Piccadilly station concourse to Ducie Street; in half-crevices dotted along the edge of the concourse itself; in the elevator that ferries passengers between platform level and the trams. 'It was the only place I could find where the floor had a bit of warmth, everything else was freezing,' he said. 'Benches are the best, and air vents too. Then anywhere flat and sheltered where you can lay a blanket. But finding a spot is competitive, so if other places are taken you don't have much choice. The problem with the elevator is that security won't let you stay there, so it's only brief. Then you have to go back outside.' There were times, during the two-year period in which he was homeless, when Kyle had to get by on a single meal a day. At one point, he lost a stone in the space of a fortnight. 'It's weird,' he told me. 'Being on the streets was kind of a relief, because I felt like I could finally be myself and do what I wanted. I was still attending school, so I hadn't stopped caring. But I wasn't looking forward to growing up.' The first time we met, Kyle had just been placed in temporary accommodation by social services. He was seventeen years old.

Kyle is from Oldham, a town on the outskirts of Greater Manchester that once spun more cotton than all the spindles in France and Germany combined. Today, it is the most deprived urban community in Britain.[9] Kyle took me on a tour, pointing out his old schools, the takeaway place in Rippenham Road where he used to work and that nearly everyone agrees is the best chippy in town, the beautiful and expensive homes nestled into the foothills of Saddleworth that seem forever distant and out of reach, and the streets around Sholver, St Mary's, Shaw Road and Derker that he knows much more intimately, and now tries to avoid. We wound up at the estate where he grew up, staring out at the grassy fields that played host to his childhood football games, and up at the window on to what was once his bedroom. Kyle's mother still lives there, but we didn't knock on the door. 'It's fine, it's life,' he said, when I asked if he was OK. 'It's what makes you who you are.'

When Kyle was eleven, his mother was diagnosed with a mental health condition and suffered a series of breakdowns. Kyle became the primary carer for his sister, who was nine, taking her to and from school each day and cooking her tea. Their older brother ran away, and so did the family dog. 'My dad was in and out of the picture,' remembers Kyle. 'Sometimes he'd be there, sometimes he'd promise to appear and then not show up, leaving us crying on the sofa.' By the time he was in his mid-teens, Kyle's mother's condition had deteriorated; she was taking drugs, lashing out, and verbally abusing Kyle on a regular basis. The two remaining children shut themselves away in their bedrooms to protect themselves, and became increasingly isolated. One day, when Kyle was fifteen, things reached a tipping point; he fled from the house, and didn't come back. 'With my mum and my sister, I felt like I'd already seen everything and been through so much, so the idea of getting out there on my own wasn't as scary as it should have been,' he said. In common with most people who experience homelessness, Kyle's journey didn't take him directly from his own room to sleeping on pavements in a single, straightforward tumble. Instead he was batted about between different realms of insecurity: long stretches where he sofa-surfed between friends and family members; others where he found a short-lived bed in a squat or shelter; hard nights, cold nights, where the only thing available was the station elevator at best and the ground outside at worst. Sometimes, he found himself pressed up against the hoardings of one of the new housing construction sites that are everywhere in Manchester, advertising 'The best of UK buy-to-let!', 'Sophisticated design and high-end finishes' and 'Be Original! Live Original!'

Manchester has one of the highest levels of homelessness proportionate to its overall population in the country.[10] Thirty new households in the city are forced into emergency accommodation every week, while the number of rough sleepers has risen thirteenfold since 2010.[11] Over the same period, thanks to heavy financial and regulatory support from the council, tens of thousands of high-end apartments have been built in Manchester by private developers, who have been rewarded by a jump in sale prices of 150% since 2012 and rental yields of more than 6% per annum.[12] 'It's official – Manchester is at the very centre of Britain's property boom' announced one *Manchester Evening News* headline in 2017.[13] 'How to win on Manchester's booming property market' promised another.[14] So many luxury flats have either already been built in Manchester or are currently in the pipeline that the *Financial Times* has warned of oversupply in the top echelons of the market.[15] How did it come to pass that in one of the richest cities of one of the richest nations on the planet, in a place boasting such a glut of investment and more units of living space than there are people able to fill them, a child such as Kyle could end up sleeping on the street? The answer lies, at least in part, with the reinvention of places like Manchester across the globe to take advantage of a new epoch of financialisation, one in which towns, cities and regions competed against each other on the global market to capture some of the money that late capitalism encourages to flow unencumbered between them.

In the early 1990s, Manchester's Hulme Crescents were torn down. The Crescents – huge social housing estates that had dominated the city's southern skyline since their construction – were initially heralded as modernist masterpieces, but by the time they were bulldozed they had become a byword for urban decline. Richard Leese, who became leader of Manchester council in 1996, later pinpointed the Crescents' demolition as the moment when the new, modern Manchester was born.[16] In keeping with New Labour's turn towards market logic, he and his chief executive Howard Bernstein saw in Hulme the fresh start from which a better city – entrepreneurial, cosmopolitan, competitive and global – could finally rise. Over the next two decades, the pair oversaw a regeneration programme that transformed the city beyond recognition, carpeting the centre with new businesses, jobs and residents, and sending privately owned home and office towers soaring into the sky. The project was unapologetically property-driven and geographically concentrated. There was little attempt to distribute economic growth to parts of the city beyond the ring road, never mind to outlying towns in Greater Manchester, such as Oldham, which had been devastated by deindustrialisation. 'Spreading money thinly and evenly is not the solution,' concluded Mike Emmerich, who ran an economic think tank supported by Leese and Bernstein's council. The pair were proud to have sloughed off the city's older traditions of municipal socialism, which in their opinion erected barriers to wealth creation and discouraged capital investment. 'There was no understanding that successful cities are really about how you attract people who have got money,' observed Bernstein.[17] 'Investors have a great liking for our leadership.'[18] What mattered above all else was the pragmatism of getting things done, things that could be measured in the form of numbers and percentages, and how those numbers and percentages stacked up against those of other cities, regions and rivals. 'Everyone sings from the same hymn sheet in Manchester,' said Jim O'Neill, a former chief economist at Goldman Sachs. Leese and Bernstein were venerated by governments and corporations alike for having overseen an audacious millennial renaissance.

To entice investment, Leese and Bernstein's council did everything they could to render property construction in Manchester an attractive proposition to global capital. The planning process became geared towards waving applications through at all costs, largely dismissing any concerns about heritage preservation or neighbourhood impact.[19] Section 106 contributions – the funding which developers normally have to provide for the benefit of the local community who live in the vicinity of big building projects – were drastically reduced, and in most cases completely scrapped; in 2018, not a single new property development in Ancoats had a Section 106 contribution attached to it. The national target of ensuring that 20% of new housing units should be within reach of those who could never meet the market price for sale or rent was effectively abandoned altogether; one recent report revealed that out of more than 25,000 homes currently under construction in central Manchester and neighbouring Salford, only five (less than 0.02%) could be considered affordable, none of which were in Ancoats. Meanwhile, the council lavished public money on developers: on just over 5,000 of those new, non-affordable homes alone, £265 million worth of state financing in the form of loans was provided to the private sector – an average of nearly £30,000 per housing unit.[20] That shared wealth, which had been produced and collected locally, had now been put to work for property investors based in London, Abu Dhabi, Saudi Arabia and the Far East. Property seminars in Singapore and China were held to encourage smaller-scale investors to put their savings into bricks and mortar 7,000 miles away on the Ashton Canal. Sometimes the entire housing stock of a new development project would be sold off-plan, primarily to international investors, before a single foundation stone had been laid.

'This city has played a certain game, and it's won at that game to some extent,' says Neil McInroy. 'It chose to play that game because of the wider context it was operating in, which is all about financialisation and return, and because in that context the global investment model seemed like the most reliable route to growth and generating some economic va-va-voom in a city that was on its knees. And the story that was then told about Manchester, this international success story, is itself part of the marketisation process – it's a tool designed to leverage yet more investment. But it's a selective story; it leaves out the bad bits. It leaves out the fact that there has been no trickle-down.' On the nights when he tried to evade security and sleep in the Piccadilly station elevator, Kyle was just yards away from great swathes of empty new housing units piled up in developments like Cotton Field Wharf, part-owned by an investment vehicle backed by sovereign wealth funds in the Gulf and headquartered in the tax haven of Jersey; or Crusader Mill, a new private housing block that received £25.5 million in state aid and boasts a secluded courtyard 'complete with fire pits, barbeques, Wi-Fi and Bluetooth speakers'.

When in 2008 the countless, impenetrable layers of securitisation, speculation and debt that were fuelling the global economy collapsed, the British government decided that most of the financial institutions involved were too big to fail; profits from their risk-taking were private but the losses, it turned out, were to be socialised. Two years later, the Conservative Party came to power promising a new era of 'fiscal responsibility' and implemented a programme of national austerity in a supposed effort to 'balance the books'. Most of the cuts demanded by the Treasury were implemented at the local level, using a formula that proved preferential to already-prosperous communities in the south-east but calamitous for those councils with high levels of poverty and demand for public services. Oldham, Kyle's home town, had already been weakened by central Manchester's property-driven growth model, which sucked in jobs and resources from communities on its periphery without redistributing the proceeds back out again. Now it had to confront the austerity programme as well; across the following decade, it was one of the top ten hardest-hit local authorities in England.[21]

Since austerity began, Oldham has been forced to cut a total of £208 million in public spending – 42% of its total budget – and that cut has directly impacted Kyle at every stage of his path into homelessness.[22] The year his mother was first diagnosed with a mental health condition, the mental health charity Mind – which was responsible in Oldham for delivering many of the council's mental health support services – had its funding in the town slashed by 80%.[23] The following year, a local initiative specifically designed to tackle youth homelessness by mediating between families and runaway teenagers was shut down completely.[24] As Kyle prepared to spend his first nights in Piccadilly station, Oldham's council leaders were announcing a further £843,000 reduction in mental health spending, a £613,000 reduction in adult social services spending, and a £1.2 million reduction in children's care spending – all to be implemented over the following twelve months alone.[25] Across the whole of Greater Manchester, children's services budgets now face a total shortfall of at least £25 million a year; nationwide, councils are set to confront £10 billion of unfunded costs by 2020.[26] 'What we now have is a perfect storm: more people depending on public services than ever, but significantly less money to support them,' Oldham's council leader, Sean Fielding, has explained.[27] 'We need solutions to the severe pressures on adults' and children's services. Councils can't just keep dipping into reserves or selling buildings and land to stay afloat. We truly are at breaking point.' Had a different decision been taken – to insulate people like Kyle from the fallout of the financial crisis rather than to protect the institutions and systems that created the crisis in the first place – Oldham might have been able to intervene at the various stages in which Kyle's family life got harder, preventing him from having to leave his mother in the first place.

The bailout of banks in 2008 and the drastic cuts to public services were accompanied by a third major intervention in the economy by Britain's government: quantitative easing, essentially a massive injection of new money into the financial system by the state in order to get banks lending and investing once more. In the seven years following the start of the Bank of England's quantitative-easing programme, the stock market grew by 87% and homeowners, aided by historically low interest rates, saw the value of their property soar.[28] For Layla and Kyle, and almost anyone their age, the prospect of ever getting on to the housing ladder receded even further into the distance. Combined with an ongoing shift towards low-wage, precarious labour (explored more fully in Chapter 3), the effect of these various attempts to buy more time for our stricken financial system has amounted to an epic transfer of wealth, benefits and opportunity from one umbrella social class – predominantly younger wage-earners, private renters, social housing tenants and benefit recipients – to another, predominantly older one, comprising property owners, shareholders and those already invested in financialisation. Since 2009, the wealth of the richest 1,000 families in the UK has doubled; meanwhile young people are on course to be poorer than their predecessors at every single stage of their adult lives, and those currently in their thirties are half as financially secure as those currently in their forties were at the same age.[29] The political significance of this is hard to overstate. As the economics commentator Aditya Chakrabortty puts it, 'No ideology can survive unless it has something to offer the young and almost young. You can't keep winning elections if you can't promise reasonable jobs, wage rises, affordable groceries and housing. Put another way, you can have neoliberalism but you can't have democratic validity.'[30]

Kyle has had it rough of late. Attempts to reconnect with his mother have foundered, and he's been wrestling with extended periods of depression. 'I'm hashtag optimism,' he once said to me, a wide smile breaking across his large, open face. And there is some cause for optimism: Oldham's overburdened social services department has finally found him a permanent place to live, and he's been getting work – first a warehouse job at a car-parts retailer, then a gig at a local telecoms centre, cold-calling mobile-phone customers and trying to persuade them to upgrade their contracts. The minimum wage is welcome, but it's not enough. 'The pay is liveable, because you can physically live on it, just about,' Kyle told me. 'But it's not enjoyable. You can't enjoy a life on it.' And of course his job is fundamentally insecure: of utility at the moment, but easily disposed of as and when the market turns. Kyle dreams of joining the army: he likes the idea of service, of feeling like he's truly valued by something bigger and stronger than himself, and when I last saw him he was waiting to hear back about his application. In the army, he points out, you are part of a community whose worth is measured by something other than money, and you always have a place to sleep. His ultimate fantasy, he confided, is to settle down in a pretty seaside village called Hornsea, situated on the east coast just north of Hull. Kyle has never been to Hornsea, but a friend of his comes from the area and has mentioned it to him in the past. 'It sounds nice and quiet, and it's not here,' he said, when I asked him what the appeal was. 'I think it's got healthy scenery, healthy people, you know, that sort of thing. It's the sort of place old people retire to, so I guess it must be safe.'

Meanwhile he's doing his best to make his small one-bedroom flat – the first place of his own he's ever known – into a home. 'It's not the friendliest neighbourhood,' he said ruefully, pointing out a shattered windowpane in the apartment below his. 'This is supported accommodation so everyone in here has been homeless before and a lot of people are messed up, there's always trouble. Sometimes I wonder if I'm the only one who is sane.' The flat came furnished but Kyle has added mirrors and decorations on the wall to make it feel more personal, and he and his new girlfriend have adopted two kittens – Coconut and Peanut – who bound about with glee and shred toilet roll whenever Kyle's back is turned. 'I'm just taking life as it goes,' he shrugged.

Debi Blanchard, a housing campaigner who works with homeless youth in Greater Manchester, believes that chronic insecurity, combined with a ruinous overhaul of the state benefits system, has helped to traumatise an entire generation of young people. 'The face of poverty, homelessness and destitution in Britain is increasingly a young one,' she told me. 'And we are doubly hit by that because we are a young city.' A few years ago, Manchester was chosen as a testing ground for one of the government's flagship and most controversial reforms – the introduction of universal credit, which rolls a series of separate benefits into a single payment and is supposed to help incentivise recipients back into work. A close study of the city's official statistics indicates a direct correlation between the implementation of universal credit and levels of homelessness.[31] As he lacked parental support, Kyle should have been eligible for universal credit from the day he turned sixteen, but as per the official policy it took many weeks for his first payment to come through, despite the authorities being aware that he had nowhere to live. 'I got let down,' he says, bitterly. It's an experience shared by nearly all of the young people who Debi works with; many have also suffered from the strict application of benefit 'sanctions', which kick in if universal-credit recipients trip up in any way whilst jumping through a long set of bureaucratic hoops, including a requirement to show evidence that they have spent at least thirty-five hours per week searching for jobs and never to be late for a Jobcentre appointment. 'The way they've rolled this out – it's a deliberate choice, and it indicates that in these crazy times nothing is considered politically unconscionable any more,' says Debi. She used to live in the Hulme Crescents and can remember the bad days of the early 1980s, when riots broke out across Moss Side and Manchester's skyline grew thick with sirens and smoke. She had mixed emotions when she watched the Crescents being demolished, but she never thought that the city which rose in their place would look or feel quite like this. Now she spends most of her days touring Manchester's homeless squats – the ones that are left, that is, after a series of violent evictions carried out by police and private security forces – and is continuously checking in on dozens of young people for whom she is a source of everything from legal advice to toothpaste. 'They call me the crazy auntie: I know their shoe sizes, I know their histories, I know that someone has to keep battling for them,' she says. 'Young men and boys, teenage girls … In a way that you simply would not have thought socially possible even just a decade ago, these groups are increasingly disconnected, destitute and targeted on all policy fronts for collective punishment. It's a tearing of the social fabric. And it's left many of these kids with a kind of PTSD.'

One chilly winter's evening, a few months after the council first managed to secure accommodation for him, Kyle walked out of his flat, purchased a packet of paracetamol from the nearest shop, returned home, and overdosed. 'I just didn't want to do it any more,' he said softly, averting his eyes. 'My mind was just a blur: I was struggling with money, with no family support, I was feeling really alone, and that's what happened.' After swallowing the pills, he wandered downstairs in confusion; an ambulance was called, and doctors worked overnight to save his life. He still struggles with loneliness, and with that sensation that can creep up on you at the strangest moments – of there being no one who cares, and nothing out there which values you at anything more than £4.20 an hour.

But Kyle is hashtag optimism, most of the time anyway, and he's discovered novel ways to fight back. Recently, at work, he found himself chatting on the phone to a young woman doing a philosophy degree at university; Kyle was intrigued, and in between pitching a monthly text bundle and data package he smuggled in a whole string of questions: about philosophy, and her studies, and the ideas contained within them. 'If you get to a part of the conversation where you've stopped selling, you can get in trouble with the supervisor,' he said. 'But this call went on for absolutely ages, it was brilliant.' And then of course, he has *Ark* – the Xbox video game populated by fantastical animals that allows you to team up with strangers from around the world and build an alternative universe. When he's not working, Kyle will sometimes play *Ark* for more than ten hours at a stretch: curtains drawn, lights off, a headset over his ears and a microphone angled towards his mouth. Participants form alliances and share resources, organising their nascent societies however they see fit. The in-game rules are accompanied by an informal etiquette among players, one that Kyle takes very seriously; breaches of honour infuriate him. He described his current game to me in detail: he and some of his regular *Ark* friends had built what sounded to all intents and purposes like a delicate but vibrant democracy, with resources for all and plenty of space to fly around peacefully and reconnoitre. 'In the real world there are people who look for confrontation, but here it's different,' he said. 'People are generally friendly and co-operative.' *Ark* offers Kyle a universe in which there are no limits to what can be created other than those imposed by your own imagination, a universe regulated by a shared set of rules that provide everyone with an equal chance. 'It's a safe haven,' he explained. 'When I'm in *Ark*, I can't hear reality – that's my reality now.'

After Kyle takes off the headset, what surrounds him is much more complex. According to the political scientist Helen Thompson, 'The post-2008 world is, in some fundamental sense, a world waiting for its reckoning,' and for Kyle, that reckoning cannot come soon enough.[32] That's why he has now returned to the Ashton Canal – not to the stacks of buy-to-let homes, among whose hoardings he once sheltered, but to Bridge 5 Mill, where he has teamed up with Layla and Ed and Jacob; all people from very different backgrounds, all convinced they can assemble a different universe for real. 'I've lived politics,' Kyle told me. 'Anyone who thinks this, all this, can carry on is mad.'

*

Hannah is a shapeshifter. She knows exactly what people think when they first meet her and in many ways they're right: she does have a trust fund, she does have friends who hold shooting parties on their country estates, and she does occasionally run into Jacob Rees-Mogg. When she applied for a place at Jesus College, Oxford and stayed overnight ahead of an admissions interview, she found herself sharing a room with a fellow applicant who had flown over from India. 'Being the idiot loudmouth that I am, I mentioned to her that I am a descendant of Robert Bulwer-Lytton, who was viceroy of India in the 1870s,' she recalled. 'As soon as I said his name, she told me never to open an Indian history textbook because he's not very popular there.' Earl Lytton took up his posting in Delhi just as the Great Famine began to devastate the south and west of the country, but insisted on continuing with trade policies that saw hundreds of thousands of tonnes of grain exported from India even as starvation spread. Lytton, who was also Queen Victoria's favourite poet, believed in social Darwinism and adopted a laissez-faire attitude towards the crisis; it went on to claim between 6 million and 10 million lives.

But in other ways, Hannah has nothing in common with the stereotypes that are often projected on to her. 'I was one of those weird children who stayed up for the ten o'clock news, mainly because it was an excuse to go to bed late,' she remembers. 'But I also took an interest because so many people in our family's social circle seemed to have a superiority complex, and I wanted to understand why. Once I was old enough, I started reading newspapers.' She has always been fascinated by structures of power – whether operating in a single room or across an entire nation – and tried to be conscious of her own privileged position within them. The latter hasn't always been easy. 'Private girls' schools like mine train you to be a good housewife, not to think critically about the world around you,' Hannah said. 'In our business class we were once given a talk by one of the teacher's friends at her bridge club, and it was about how to cultivate a positive appearance: literally, how to hold a handbag, what sort of perfume and lipstick to wear, how to match your colours. I made a fuss, said that it was offensive – it's the sort of thing my grandma would have been taught as a debutante in the 1950s. I was sent to the headmistress for that.' Hannah told me that trying to map out the flow and balance of authority in any given situation, and identify the material and psychological factors that have caused person x to say thing y to person z, helps her to make sense of her own mental flow and balance – or lack of it. 'Understanding people and politics helps me understand me,' she explained. 'It helps me understand my own brain.'

In this urge to unpack what is happening within her mind, Hannah is not alone. 'I've been on Facebook since I was ten,' she said, checking her phone compulsively as we talked. She went on to depict an existence in which daily life is inextricably entangled with the need to capture and present it flatteringly online. For many of Hannah's generation, there is nothing unusual about the tired drinks table at the end of the night being revived for someone's all-important Instagram shot, or the worth of a moment on the dance floor or a holiday sunset being largely dependent on its reception on social media. These digital spectacles are not distinct from 'real' life; the two are indivisible. But a ceaseless performance in pursuit of likes, retweets and followers cannot help but blur the line between the personas we enact online and the messier images we privately hold of ourselves.[33] The question 'Who am I?' demands a continuous response, even as it becomes harder to answer. The danger is not just that we end up jealous of our friends, and their friends, and the airbrushed lifestyles of legions of social media celebrities and influencers; it is that we can be afflicted by self-jealousy too. 'We look at the lives we have constructed online in which we only show the best of ourselves, and we feel a fear of missing out in relation to our own lives,' explains psychologist Sherry Turkle.[34] 'We don't measure up to the lives we tell others we are living, and we look at the self as though it were another, and feel envious of it. We feel inauthentic, curiously envious of our own avatars.' A culture of competitiveness that demands constant self-evaluation applies not just economically, but socially too, and late capitalism has provided us with the perfect measuring tools: the panopticon of social media platforms, which serve as a personal shop window to our fellow humans and offer us real-time feedback on what everyone else thinks of the display behind the glass. 'The important thing is that you will never ever see a double chin on my feed,' Hannah told me, with something like pride. 'I keep it meticulously clean.'

She showed me her Snapchat profile, which includes a mapping feature indicating the current location and activity of her contacts. At that particular moment one friend was on a train, another at an airport, a third in Block C of her university accommodation building. Hannah raised an eyebrow at the latter, then fired off a quick barrage of WhatsApp messages. 'It's so in your face, because you know you're being tracked and so your instinct is to track everyone else. I don't just mean where people are, but what people are saying and thinking, who is chatting shit about who.' Perhaps the most disturbing thing is that the majority of photos on Hannah's phone are actually not holiday sunsets at all, but rather screenshots of other people's status updates and group chats: a permanent record, perpetually citeable, of arguments, alliances and gossip. 'We all interact in this way, so nothing is private,' she grimaced. 'Everything I say might be screenshotted and used against me in the future, and that makes me paranoid enough to do the same to everyone else.' She talked of people she knows who live in terror of old social media posts featuring offensive language or compromising images resurfacing, but also of the ways in which this normalised collective surveillance can lend mundane social dramas a lasting and disproportionate significance. 'Everything gets heightened and sensationalised,' she explained. 'Back in the day, if you messaged a guy you fancied and he didn't reply you could convince yourself that he'd got a new number or something, but now you can see that he's read your message, that he was online two minutes ago, that he's chosen to ignore you.' She told me about a recent falling-out among her university friendship group over living arrangements for the following year. 'That sort of bitchiness is probably always there in people's heads, but I think it used to be easier to move on and forget about it. Now it goes through fifteen different phones in an instant. It's our worst emotions made public, and put on replay.'

Hannah has grown up in the age of the self as enterprise, one in which each of us is subject throughout our lives to a permanent economic tribunal. It's a thread that runs from childhood – where early teaching is increasingly focused on the 'core competencies' demanded by future employers – to a university environment in which faculties are encouraged to think like businesses and students to think like customers, all the way through to a world of work in which, for many, success is increasingly dependent on the maintenance of a personal brand that is being constantly tested, validated, or rejected by market forces. For millions, the popularity of a Twitter handle or the star rating of one's Uber driver profile will help determine the outcome of some of life's most critical junctures. The moral psychology of social media reinforces the notion that, just as financialisation has turned homes into commodities, we ourselves are tradeable assets with the metrics to prove it; dating apps, for example, are now beginning to reveal their users' algorithmically determined 'attractiveness score'.[35] And in an economic system that insists that we are the captains of our own fate and that almost anything – be it a new iPhone or a different sexual partner – is attainable if we desire it, that is proving to be a corrosive cocktail for mental health, especially among the young. Never has more (consumer) choice been available to us, and never have we borne more responsibility for the outcome if those choices are wrong. Stoked aspirations combine with heightened expectations of fulfilment, personal responsibility for failure and an awareness that, even when we are ahead, there are always countless competitors just behind us, ready to overtake if we stumble. Around half of young people in Britain now say that comparing their lives to others on social media makes them feel inadequate, increases their anxiety about the future, and creates an overwhelming pressure to succeed.[36]

Loneliness is now more common among sixteen-to-twenty-four-year-olds than any other age group; anxiety, depression and conduct disorder are all on the rise.[37] Research carried out in 2018 by Action for Children found that one in three young people in the UK suffer from a mental health problem; a survey for the Prince's Trust that same year revealed that three in five young Brits are regularly overwhelmed with stress, and one in four feel hopeless.[38] 'It should ring alarm bells for us all that young people are feeling more despondent about their emotional health than ever before,' declared the charity's chief executive. 'This is a generation rapidly losing faith in their ability to achieve their goals in life, who are increasingly wary of and disillusioned with the jobs market and at risk of leaving a wealth of untapped potential in their wake.' According to the United Nations, economic insecurity and austerity policies have played a key role in driving a decline in mental health.[39] Ellen Key, the Swedish writer, famously proclaimed the twentieth century to be the 'century of the child'; Paul Verhaeghe, a Belgian professor of clinical psychology and psychoanalysis, asserts that the following one, our own, is the 'century of the disturbed child'. Shortly before taking his own life, the cultural theorist Mark Fisher warned that we cannot hope to meaningfully address today's mental health crisis without acknowledging its political dimension; psychological stress, he argued, was increasingly being 'privatised' as a personal, individual problem, hyper-medicalised and divorced from its social context. 'It is not an exaggeration,' he concluded, 'to say that being a teenager in late-capitalist Britain is now close to being reclassified as a sickness.'[40]

For Hannah, who has been diagnosed with attention deficit hyperactivity disorder (ADHD) – 'Either I'm inattentive or super-focused on something,' she explained to me, 'so sometimes I can work for ten hours straight without realising it, but if I look at my phone for two minutes my attention will completely shatter and it's impossible to get back on track' – all this adds up to something feeling very wrong, an uneasiness that has penetrated the many layers of economic advantage which have cushioned her life to date, and brought her all the way from her home in Buckinghamshire to Bridge 5 Mill in order to learn more about Demand the Impossible. 'I didn't come here with an ideology,' she said. 'I think I just looked around. And for people my age, nothing is working for us. I know how lucky I am personally, but a lot of my friends, they just think "damn, what's the point". It's not working for middle-class young people, the kind of people who were expecting to do alright before, and it's not working for my cousins, who come from a really ordinary background and they don't have a fucking chance. One is doing bricklaying and the other wants to be a vet, but how will she ever afford the training fees? How will she get a home?' And so Hannah shapeshifts: she hangs out in the corridors of the *Sunday Express* on a work-experience placement and is told by family friends that she'll make a great leader of the Conservative Party one day, all the while convinced that the politics these institutions represent is bankrupt, and that nothing can remain the same. 'All this,' she said, waving her hand vaguely in the air as if to encompass everything we could see, and everything we could not, 'it does nothing for us.' Strikingly – completely independently of each other, and of Hannah – I had previously seen both Layla and Kyle make the same nebulous gesture: the same attempt to indicate something that was difficult to pin down and articulate, precisely because it was simultaneously so fragile and so amorphous. 'We've lived through this as fifteen-year-olds, sixteen-year-olds, seventeen-year-olds and now I'm an eighteen-year-old, and I can see it offers us nothing: nothing as we go into higher education, nothing as we go into the workplace,' said Hannah, shaking her head. 'I think that disillusionment is irreversible.'

Of course Hannah, like Layla and Kyle, found out about Demand the Impossible on social media; one of the many ways in which some of the building blocks of late capitalism are being turned against it. Experts have suggested that at the 2017 general election, the propensity of young people to tell positive stories about themselves on Facebook, Snapchat, Instagram and Twitter helped Labour's campaign messages – which focused on optimistic visions of an alternative future, in contrast to doom-laden warnings about the consequences of tinkering with the present – spread faster and to far bigger audiences than those of their Conservative rivals.[41] A short while after I first met Hannah on the banks of the Ashton Canal, she emailed me to say that she was about to join her first ever picket line at Edinburgh University, where she had wound up doing her undergraduate degree; lecturers and support staff were participating in a national strike to defend their pensions. One of the most interesting aspects of what turned out to be the longest sustained industrial action in UK higher-education history was the way in which students around the country chose to express their solidarity with the strikers: by demanding refunds of their tuition fees for lost days of teaching – purposefully turning the transactional makeover of academic life back against the university managers. Hannah was excited. 'I am no longer a pedestrian,' she wrote.

In 1944, the Austro-Hungarian intellectual Karl Polanyi published a book entitled *The Great Transformation*, in which he traced the acceleration of market relations within society. He predicted that the more completely efforts were made to free markets from social oversight, the more social dislocation would follow, leading ultimately to a point in which society reacts by attempting to forcibly subordinate and re-embed markets within a system of social relations. He called this spasm of societal self-protection a 'double movement', or 'counter-movement', and believed that at a certain stage of ever-greater economic liberalisation, such a response becomes inevitable. Polanyi also warned that, among the unpredictable energies unleashed by citizens attempting to re-anchor capital, dangers lurked. 'This is a hell of a time to be alive,' Nick Dearden, the director of Global Justice Now – a social justice campaign group – told Hannah and her fellow Demand the Impossible participants in Bridge 5 Mill. 'It's also an incredibly frightening time to be alive. Great monsters walk among us; in some cases they have seized the seats of power. What is clear is that out of the instability and volatility that we see all around us in the world, there is certainly more opportunity for change – good change, bad change – than I have ever known in my lifetime. Quite simply, there is a fully-fledged rebellion under way against an economic project that sees the whole world as a gigantic marketplace, and which has dominated our society for forty years.'

Those liberal revivalists who wring their hands at the state of things around them, bemoaning contemporary politics as merely irrational, emotional or populist, have missed the point of all this. Their voices loom disproportionately large in both the mainstream media and formal political discourse, and yet this yearning for a return to 'grown-up politics' and a redemptive centrist saviour in the mould of French president Emmanuel Macron – someone who could turn back the clock to an imagined golden age of late-capitalist technocracy – takes no account of the fundamental ways in which tensions between markets and society are reaching their limits. The political and economic circumstances that gave a Bill Clinton or a Nick Clegg their appeal in the 1990s and 2000s simply no longer exist. The prolonged reluctance to acknowledge this fact by so many of those whose job it is to mediate between citizens and power – from official economists to political pundits and reporters – has only increased their mutual alienation. And yet recognising the fallacy of Third Way ideology today does not mean that fears of what a new paradigm shift will bring are unfounded; as Polanyi cautioned, today's possibilities are also fraught with menace. A failure by generations of political leaders to offer any meaningful critique of the rise and rise of markets has left the door open for the far right to offer other explanatory narratives about what has gone wrong and who is to blame. An appetite for economic protectionism has become entwined with a desire for cultural protectionism as well: more borders, more walls, more delineations between those who belong and those who do not. Some of those who benefit most from late capitalism are finding ways to harness these ethnocultural narratives and blend them with a muscular and authoritarian renewal of market forces. What is happening at Demand the Impossible, however, is something altogether different: neither denial of the present nor wistfulness for the past, but rather a collective struggle for an alternative future.

In fact, it's happening all over Ancoats, all around Manchester, and throughout the country beyond. You can find it in Chorlton, south-west of the area where the Hulme Crescents used to stand, where a new club is reinventing what politics looks like and who it is for. 'We organise football tournaments, film clubs, karaoke sessions, northern soul and Italo-disco nights,' says Beth Redmond, one of the co-ordinators. 'It doesn't look like the professional politics that came before. That was all about the centre, and the centre has collapsed. This is something else.' You can find it in Preston, thirty miles north of Manchester, where a daring new council administration is attempting to haul the town out of post-industrial deprivation using a very different development strategy to the global investment model pursued by Richard Leese and Howard Bernstein. Local-authority leader Matthew Brown drove me around in his battered Kia Rio and pointed out the many techniques they are using to flip the normal pattern of financial extraction by international capital hubs on its head, instead rooting wealth within the Preston community: worker-owned co-operatives, local investment of public assets, a relentless focus on economic democracy. 'Decline here has fuelled an anger towards the political class, and our choice was between saying "well, it's been this way for as long as anyone can remember and so this is the way it must continue to be", or deciding that is was more viable to think of something radically new,' he told me. And you can find it among that small group of teenagers, tired, wired and hopeful – part of a generation afflicted and liberated by what the anthropologist David Graeber has labelled 'despair fatigue' – now making their way slowly along the Ashton Canal from Bridge 5 Mill towards the heart of Manchester, ready to break some rules.

*

By the time the Demand the Impossible protesters had arranged themselves into a circle in the middle of Manchester's Piccadilly station concourse, the police were already upon them. Security is tight at a major railway terminus and unauthorised gatherings illegal; cameras had tracked the group's approach long before they had even made it to the top of the pedestrianised ramp that Kyle, in his old life, had come to know so well. Like most of the other participants, he had taped his own mouth shut: it was a visual symbol of the exclusion of young people from contemporary political debate, he explained to me, especially when it came to youth homelessness. 'Ignored, Abused, Isolated – Invisible', read a handwritten sign clutched in his hand; other signs, held by other people, made reference to benefit cuts, low wages and the impossible cost of housing. As the cops began harrying the teenagers out the doors, cajoling and shoving in equal measure, Layla, the gang's dedicated press officer, flitted between them, snapping pictures on her phone and filming on Facebook live. Once outside, I was worried that these young people would feel despondent: their demonstration had lasted less than a minute, and it was doubtful that anything more than a handful of busy commuters would have noticed their presence or had time to absorb the moving, albeit somewhat unfocused, messages scrawled on their various placards before the whole endeavour was unceremoniously put to an end. I was wrong. They whooped and cheered and high-fived, frantically swapping stories in the way we all do when something unexpected and seismic has just happened, throwing us off-balance in a gripping, giddying way. 'First day of many,' beamed Kyle, his heart pounding. 'We should give ourselves a cheer.'

Later, when I looked back through my own photos of the protest, one image stood out. In it, a thicket of hi-vis jackets and walkie-talkies swamp the foreground. One policeman has his arm on someone's shoulder, and another is holding his finger to his ear. Through the middle of them, unnoticed, one of the young protesters remains in their original position in front of a pasty shop and a Burger King: hood up, head bowed, sitting silently on the floor. They are holding a square of corrugated cardboard, bigger and bolder than the others, its words crisp and clear amid the madness. 'Can you see me?' it reads.

2

Community

Tilbury, Essex

We unrolled history. We made history. We cast history in iron
and the train shat it out behind it. Now we've ploughed that up.
We'll go on, and we'll take our history with us.
                                        —China Miéville, *Iron Council*

On Saturday afternoons, twenty short miles to the east of central
London, Tilbury Football Club comes alive. Players drive up to
the stadium's clubhouse and knock the mud off their boots on to
the grass outside. Fans squeeze through the old turnstiles and
line up for quarter-pounders and cups of tea. Flags are hung
under the faded Carlsberg billboards, and kids skitter along the
sidelines of the pitch. Maggie bustles around the boardroom,
putting out biscuits and making drinks for the referees. The
loudspeaker pumps out Coldplay, then Sean Paul.

'The Dockers', as the team and its followers are known, are
about as old as the nearby docks themselves. You can get the
history from Mavis Billinghurst, who is eighty-four years old
and the club's longest-serving fan. Over one of her home-made
sausage rolls, she'll tell you about the night the floodlights were
switched on for the first time, and the legendary cup run in
the 1970s that carried Tilbury into a third-round clash with

Stoke City. She'll tell you about the times – long gone, of course, because things are always changing and it's hard to keep up – when hundreds of supporters would tumble out of the port at the end of a shift and walk right across town to cheer on the boys. These days, the Dockers are in the Isthmian Northern Division, the eighth tier of English football, and generally only a few dozen people attend matches. But they are a tight-knit and raucously loyal bunch who put on ska nights at the bar, make you drop a penny in the swear jar if you mention Grays (Tilbury's hated local rivals) and are generous with the pints. 'Hello, hello, we are the Tilbury boys,' they chant. 'We're the famous Tilbury Town, the hardest team in the land.' There is a mountain of shared experiences here, massive enough to hold you safe in an untethered world, or perhaps to pin you down and break your back.

Leaning up against the railings that separate spectators from the action, in between muffled curses and sharp intakes of breath, Charlie Lawrence conjures up one such memory. It was the first day of February in 1953, the morning a great flood churned up the ground and separated tens of thousands from their homes, and Charlie can still picture the dogs. His family had two of them, a pair of scruffy mongrels named Wag and Prince. When the seven-year-old rose that Sunday from the bed he shared with his brother and peeked out the window, he was dumbfounded to see both floating past on a piece of driftwood. Later – after he and his six siblings were evacuated by American soldiers, after the funerals for the victims and the long, messy clean-up of the streets – dignitaries began making their way to this little corner of Britain, where the narrow kinks of the River Thames begin to straighten out, and the water widens fast toward the sea. Famous and important folks came to sympathise with locals and pose for photo ops; Charlie, the young tearaway who stole sherbets from the penny sweet shop and spent his holidays pulling up potatoes in the field, got to shake hands with the queen. But almost seven decades later, it's that image of his pets, rather than his brush with royalty, that remains with him: how comic they looked, how confused, as the world spun giddily around them.

'There was a Sunday joint in the oven, and my dad, God bless him, swum down to get it so we could feed them something,' Charlie grins. 'It was pandemonium. There were rats and snakes everywhere.' He pauses to watch one of Tilbury's forwards break through on goal, before tumbling in the mud. 'It was the glory days,' he says, turning back to me. 'I loved it. I want to go back there now.'

*

Tilbury, the most storied town you've never heard of, lies almost equidistant between England's eastern coast and the heart of London. Sail inland from the North Sea on to the Thames and you'll find yourself navigating an eerie, beautiful mash-up of ocean and river, past the relics of 1940s Royal Navy towers perched on squat concrete pillars or slender stilts, and the occasional beluga whale. It's hard to pinpoint where exactly the open water ends and the inlet begins, until you round the final bend of the Hoo peninsula and see the fields of Kent to the south and Essex to the north closing in. Humans have built settlements here for over a thousand years, taking advantage of the natural contraction of the river to establish transport links and military defences against any foreign marauders, and it's served as the backdrop to some of Britain's greatest historical milestones. It was near Tilbury Fort on the north bank, a beautifully preserved complex of moats and bastions now run by English Heritage, that Queen Elizabeth I made her famous speech to the troops as they prepared to face down the Spanish Armada in 1588, declaring: 'I know I have the body but of a weak and feeble woman, but I have the heart and stomach of a king, and of a king of England too, and think foul scorn that Parma or Spain, or any prince of Europe, should dare to invade the borders of my realm.' More than a century later, the writer Daniel Defoe – who operated a tile and brick factory in the area – wrote that Tilbury was still 'the key of the river ... and consequently the key of the City of London'.[1]

It was only in the nineteenth century, though, that the modern town – home these days to about 13,000 people, with several thousand more living in a cluster of surrounding villages – really began to take shape. The railway arrived in 1854, and the docks three decades later. This was the start of the steamship era – for the first time, commercial boats could ferry goods all the way from China and the Far East in a single voyage. Before long, the tally clerks, scrubbers and shipwrights of Tilbury were processing everything from crates of Madeira wine to sausage skins packed in brine and bales of jute. Ramsay MacDonald, Britain's first Labour prime minister, opened a cruise terminal in 1930, which remains London's only deep-water passenger wharf. It became the staging point for two great waves of migration: the departure of the 'Ten Pound Poms' – Brits who left England for Australia in the aftermath of the Second World War – and the arrival of the *Empire Windrush* in 1948, a passenger ship carrying one of the first large groups of Caribbean immigrants, which became synonymous with a new period of multiculturalism in the UK. Today, Tilbury port serves as one of the country's key links to the rest of the planet, a site where money, goods and people find their way across borders – usually officially, sometimes illicitly. It is the backstage of the capital, home to the pipes, wires and storerooms that few people see, but which everyone front-of-house relies on to keep the show alive.

'When you go out and speak to people, no matter where they live or where they're from, you can almost always find a connection somewhere to Tilbury,' says Lucy-Emma Harris, who works with the port and local community organisations to showcase the area's heritage. 'There are so many important markers of history here, and they all make Tilbury quite fundamental.' Tilbury's street names bear witness to its global reach: Bermuda Road, Toronto Road, Malta Road, Auckland Close. The docks and associated industries used to employ thousands of locals, and many can still remember the good times when the stevedores might purloin a slab of prime imported steak and a bottle of whisky from the crates and go for a riotous crawl through the town's countless drinking holes. 'We were honest thieves,' Charlie remembered. 'We lived through the best years there ever was.'

In 1967, Pink Floyd played the Railway Club on Calcutta Road, Tilbury's main thoroughfare, and brought the house down. Back in those days, an annual carnival paraded through the town, featuring floats, folk songs and the crowning of a carnival queen in Anchor Fields Park. On the Tilbury and Chadwell Memories website, where residents upload photos of their old haunts and reminisce, you can scroll through sepia pictures of schoolkids and dockers and dancers garlanded in flowers and lining the pavements for the procession. Those images are all that are left of the carnival – or, for that matter, the Tute, the Athlone, the Anchor Inn and all the other pubs, working-men's clubs and traditional social centres that once gummed Tilbury together. In the late 1960s, containerisation transformed the port's operations: where it once took dozens of people several days to unload sacks of barley from a ship, now a pair of skilled crane operators could finish the job in under an hour. Over the next two decades, just as social housing was ushered out of collective ownership, so too were the town's major industries parcelled up and sold to private companies.

Today, almost every large employer or local institution that Tilbury might once have claimed as its own has been privatised, shut down or both. The huge coal-fired power station that overlooks the Tudor fort is being dismantled, wall by wall, chimney by chimney. The Bata shoe factory just north of the river stands idle and empty. The docks were sold off to a company in Edinburgh in 1992. The local fire station closed in 1997. The Railway Club, once the focal point of Tilbury social life, is a charred ruin, its debris shielded from view by thick black boards that have been scrawled with graffiti. 'The rot set in, and it started a downward spiral,' says June Brown, a sixty-eight-year-old retired civil servant who spent time as a child helping her grandmother clean the bathrooms at the cruise terminal. First-class passengers had one set of toilets, she remembered, and third-class passengers another. 'What's left of the Railway Club is at the end of my street, and it's a sorry sight. I can't wait for it to be knocked down, to be honest.'

With the erosion of secure homes and the disappearance of the town's most dependable source of jobs, instability became the new norm. Today, according to figures provided by the local authority, Tilbury's two council wards are by some margin the most deprived in the region. Nearly one in five working-age people are without employment, close to double the regional average; income levels, education levels, skilled qualifications and health indices in Tilbury are all lower than almost every other administrative unit in the area, and crime rates are higher. Almost half of Tilbury's children grow up in poverty, more than double the national figure, and the average resident can expect to die around eight years earlier than someone from the more affluent settlement of Corringham just a few miles up the road.

Wedged between the cruise terminal and the outer edges of Tilbury Fort stands the World's End, the last proper drinking hole in the entire town. To reach it from Calcutta Road, you have to drive almost a mile to the west, navigate a busy roundabout, cross the train tracks and then head back down in the opposite direction for two more miles. The route is dark, on account of the steep port walls that line the verge, and smoggy, thanks to the ceaseless cavalcade of trucks making their way between the docks and the nearby motorway. Many people in Tilbury told me they felt cut off from the rhythms of the port and the water it looks out on, particularly the younger generation, for whom any connection with the area's riverside – past or present – is tenuous. 'I don't look at it,' said one seventeen-year-old, before gesturing around at the town centre. 'I just live here.'

Towards the back of the pub, at an old wooden table lacquered in varnish and framed by maritime paraphernalia on the wall, Charlie sipped at a pint and served up his account of Tilbury's history. It's a story that superficially embodies some of the clichés surrounding Britain's post-industrial 'left behind' communities, and also critically refutes them; one that explains much about why this was among the country's top 1% Brexit-voting regions in the 2016 EU referendum, and how our political landscape has mutated as a result. 'Tilbury is the connection point to the world,' argues Polly Billington, a recent – and defeated – Labour parliamentary candidate for the area, 'but the winds of globalisation have blown harshly through this community, and so its residents have turned away from those winds.' Anyone who wishes to make sense of the bigger picture could start by thinking about what has happened to this small, precariously positioned dock town, and what it might do next.

Like many older men in Tilbury, Charlie has worked at one point or another for almost every big employer in town, and – he related with mischievous pride – he was a rabble-rouser at every one of them. 'I left school at fifteen, and I wasn't really educated. But although I weren't that political, I've always stood up for myself,' he said. Charlie's father was a shop steward at the Ford motor plant in nearby Dagenham, and it was from him that Charlie inherited a strong notion of trade union solidarity and a willingness to fight for one's rights. It was an instinct reinforced by Tilbury's illustrious record of labour agitation, which stretches back to the earliest days of the port and the great waves of unrest that roiled the shipping industry in the late 1880s. Workers' leader Ben Tillett was a docker in Tilbury and founded the Dockers Union here, which would later go on to lead a victorious national strike for better pay. Strikes continued to be frequent throughout the twentieth century, especially in the 1960s, 70s and 80s as port jobs gradually gave way to mechanisation. In the past few years, those who remain at the docks have walked out on strike again, most recently over attempts by a logistics company to force workers on to zero-hours contracts.

That legacy of working-class political organisation rendered Tilbury a Labour fortress for most of the modern era, even during the 1980s, when the rest of Essex became a poster child for Britain's lurch to the right. 'We kept this area a red island under Thatcher,' recalled Vincent Offord, a local Labour Party activist. 'And in terms of state investment, we paid a price for it.' The town's economic decline put a strain on its residents but also fostered a sense of communal defiance. As Charlie put it: 'We're Labour men because we look after each other when no one else does.' By 1997, when Tony Blair ended eighteen years of Tory government and Labour secured almost two-thirds of the entire vote in Tilbury's parliamentary constituency of Thurrock, the prevailing sentiment was that Tilbury was down, but not out.

New Labour, however, failed to instigate the metamorphosis that many in Tilbury had been counting on. Yes, investment in public services increased, but above the Isle of Dogs – Thatcher's citadel of financialised capital that lies just fifteen miles west from Tilbury – new skyscrapers continued to grow, jostling for space in the clouds. From the cranes at Tilbury's port, you could see their glass and steel facades glimmering across the gulf between; after dark, the aircraft warning lights on the roofs at Canary Wharf crowded a corner of the night in a thicket of blinking red. Of course, as a focal point for rising trade, Tilbury's docks and cruise terminal were part of London's growing success story. But amid all the talk of a newly cosmopolitan 'cool Britannia' and growing GDP, the rest of Tilbury continued to stagnate. Grand regeneration plans for the surrounding Thames Gateway region were drafted, debated and forgotten. Unemployment persisted and social institutions continued to be shuttered. For many Tilbury residents, a sense that something was being snatched away from them – that they were being locked out of a widely trumpeted voyage to prosperity passing by their very doorstep – became more entrenched. It takes forty minutes to travel by train from Tilbury to London's Fenchurch Street station. Even today, there are people in Tilbury who have never made that journey.

Just as painful as the economic exclusion was the moralising that justified it. Thatcher's political imperative was to replace class identity with individual aspiration. In place of a distinctly working-class respectability, one had to choose between being either an affluent striver – those well versed in a new entrepreneurial language who shrugged off their social housing and dreamed of being homeowners – or a welfare dependent, whose financial failures were by implication personal and selfish. New Labour sought to soften rather than reverse the trend. Britain, according to Blair, was now part of a global economy that was 'indifferent to tradition', rewarding only those 'swift to adapt, slow to complain, open, willing and able to change'.[2] The role models were city centres like Manchester under the transformative leadership of Richard Leese and Howard Bernstein; there was not much time to worry about how fairly the fruits of late capitalism were being distributed, or the devastation it might be wreaking on communities who struggled to change fast enough. Indeed, the very idea of 'communities' was cast as economically backward when compared to the frictionless financial networks and new multiculturalism championed by Third Way ideologues. 'Settled, stable communities are the enemies of innovation, talent, creativity, diversity and experimentation,' claimed New Labour adviser Charles Leadbeater in 2000.[3] 'Community can too quickly become a rallying cry for nostalgia; that kind of community is the enemy of knowledge creation, which is the wellspring of economic growth.'

Charlie's old-school conception of Labourism in Tilbury, based around the power-station canteen and the local working men's club, began to feel wildly out of sync with Labour's new age. As the writer Lynsey Hanley argued, Britain had entered a period in which 'To feel discomfort about constant change – an emergent feature of globalisation – was to be inherently right wing; yet equally, to believe in the strength of collective public institutions – such as unions, publicly funded health and education systems – was unhelpfully Bolshevik.'[4]

In 1980, at the start of Thatcher's premiership, the *Sun* ran a double-page report on Tilbury with the headline 'Aggro Britain'.[5] 'This is Tilbury,' it began, 'a grey, desolate place with an evil stench of violence, where local skinheads roam the docklands like cropped rats.' Everyone who was around at the time remembers the story, partly because it was full of blatant exaggerations and untruths and partly because, in retrospect, it seemed to mark the end of one era and the beginning of another. To those buoyed by an exciting dawn of unfettered finance, places like Tilbury started to feel like an embarrassment. The port was useful, yes, but most of the people who once built, staffed and established their lives around it were now little more than an aberration. By the turn of the millennium, Britain's political class, including both major parties and the media establishment that articulated their interests, seemed to prefer that the residents of Tilbury scatter into the ether. Money is rootless, was the message, and you should be too.

In the decades that followed the notorious *Sun* feature, Tilbury's residents became accustomed to being ignored. On the rare occasions they impinged on the national consciousness, they were presented as outliers, a sneered-at 'other' whose flaws and failings provided a useful reminder to the rest of us of just how far we'd come. Tilbury regularly features on lists of Britain's 'crap towns'. When Thurrock, Tilbury's council area, finished last in a national government survey of well-being in 2012, the *Guardian* labelled it the UK's 'capital of misery' and headlined the story with the quote: 'It's one big cesspit here.'[6]

'People with power always need someone to look down on, and in this area, it's Tilbury,' observed June Brown, the retired civil servant. 'It makes people here feel rubbish, really.' She recounted a conversation with someone from English Heritage about how to market Tilbury's history more effectively to tourists: 'It's a shame that Tilbury Fort is in Tilbury,' she was told. In 2013, the comedian Sacha Baron Cohen began work on a mocking film about Grimsby, the fishing town on England's north-eastern coast. Once production was under way, it was decided that Grimsby wasn't grim enough for the cameras, so the movie was shot in Tilbury instead. Staged scenes included drunks urinating from windows and mothers handing their children beer cans in garbage-strewn streets.

The docks here have often been used by film crews – they stood in for Venice in *Indiana Jones and the Last Crusade* – and although that brings financial benefit to the port, there is some irony in the fact that whenever Tilbury comes to the attention of the wider world it is nearly always through someone else's lens, with the voices of its actual inhabitants missing from the soundtrack. 'I'll give you a nice write-up boys, make you look like working-class heroes,' the *Sun* journalist promised local youths, according to one who was quoted in the article. 'I think the reason they got involved,' observed a former teacher of several of the people featured in the *Sun* story, 'was that they're all unemployed. The situation locally is very bleak, and frankly I don't think they saw any other way of making a name for themselves.' For Charlie, all this – the *Sun*, the crushing of the unions, the marketisation of social housing (he refused to cash in by selling his, which he has now lived in for almost fifty years; 'My old man would have turned in his grave if I'd done that,' he told me) – was part of the same intentional corrosion. 'It was about destroying our unity,' he said, 'breaking us up with shame and greed.'

In August 2014, thirty-four years after the *Sun*'s 'Aggro Britain' report, *The Economist* published a short profile of Tilbury by the anonymous columnist Bagehot.[7] By this point, the financial crisis – powered by speculators headquartered in the skyscrapers just upriver – had shredded New Labour's early economic gains, and Tilbury, like Oldham 200 miles to the north, was being eviscerated by the austerity programme. School, police and library budgets were among the first to be slashed; by the mid-2010s, pressure on social care services was forcing Thurrock council to burn through up to two-thirds of its emergency reserves in a year.[8] The columnist introduced Tilbury's population as 'a polyp of hard-up,

mostly white, grumpy people' with a 'deep and justified sense
of inferiority'. The piece continued: 'What they need to get
aboard the train to Britain's future, even more than a fare,
is self-confidence ... The answers to Tilbury's and Britain's
white left-behinds are not obvious. Yet they surely lie within
their own hearts. State aid, of which they have had plenty,
cannot fix a cultural failing.'

Bagehot's profile was illustrated with a mocked-up image
of a train at Tilbury station, with a destination on the front
that read 'NOWHERE'. In the comments, someone pointed
out that 'polyp' is a medical term, referring to an abnormal
growth on the body.

*

Pastor Abraham's office features a set of rococo-style chairs
slathered in gold leaf, a book called *Beware of the Devil* and
a desk calendar advertising 'The Power of Love'. The thing he
really wants to show me when we meet, however, is the egg
splattered on the window. It's been there for over a year on
the other side of the cracked pane, its smashed contents having
congealed against the warmth of the church building. 'I've left
this one,' the pastor explained, 'because every time we replace
the windows, it just happens again, and the insurance goes up.'

Abraham Bamgbose was born in Oyo State, Nigeria, where he
used to lecture in electrical engineering. In 2003, he came to the
UK to join his wife, an advanced nurse practitioner, and settled
in south London. A year later, eager to buy a home but unable
to afford the capital's soaring property prices, they moved east
to Tilbury with their daughter. The family wasn't alone on this
journey: between 2001 and 2011, according to census data,
Thurrock's black population grew more than sevenfold. Most
of the increase was driven by internal migration from London's
African communities, particularly its Nigerian population, and
that trend has continued in recent years. 'Ambitious, upwardly-
mobile Nigerians are ... crossing London's borders into Essex,'

reported national black newspaper the *Voice* in 2013, 'in search of affordable housing, better educational prospects or simply a break from city life.'[9]

Still, Abraham said that back then, when he first arrived in Tilbury, 'you could count the number of black people around on one hand'. He initially spent many hours commuting back and forth to the city, where he led services at the Redeemed Christian Church of God, the London branch of an evangelical megachurch whose headquarters are in Lagos. One day a colleague suggested that he give up on the traffic jams and plant a new church in Tilbury instead. Abraham eventually found an unused room in the old fire station, and 'RCCG Fruitful Land' was born. 'We started with three people,' recalls the fifty-one-year-old, 'me, my wife and our daughter. But then before we knew it, the congregation started expanding. And that's when I noticed something: that there is a lot of racism around here.'

Tilbury's reputation for racial tension stretches back to the late 1960s, when many dockers came out on strike to support Enoch Powell, the Tory Cabinet minister who was sacked following an infamous public speech in which he objected to immigration and invoked the ancient priestess Sibyl prophesying rivers of blood. In the 1970s and 80s, a skinhead movement known as the Trojan Skins was active in the town and often identified by the media as being responsible for racial violence (many Tilbury residents, both black and white, deny that was the case). In 2007, soon after Fruitful Land was founded, a spate of racially motivated assaults gripped the town, prompting a major police response.[10] Gangs of youths harassed and attacked some of Tilbury's black residents; Abraham's church was targeted with a series of burglaries and fake calls to the emergency services that disrupted his preaching. 'My understanding of Tilbury's history is that this is an abandoned place, and that creates resentment,' Abraham told me. 'The racism is not just about black people here. I think the moment people find out you don't come from Tilbury, they don't like you. They don't want to see you.'

Incidents continued sporadically over the following years – many parishioners had their cars broken into, were pelted with stones and suffered attacks on their homes. The church, which has since moved into the premises formerly occupied by the Anchor Inn – the last pub in the town centre, which was closed on police orders in 2010 after numerous disturbances – is now the most secure site in the area. Ground-floor doors and windows are covered with thick boards and grills, and fifteen video cameras protect the site inside and out. 'You can see the hostility. You can feel the "we hate you". But we have to show love to them,' said Abraham, his usually calm and lyrical voice rising with emotion. 'We are for the community. The problem is education; some of the children who do the vandalising, if you talk to them, you realise that their mindset comes from the parents, from the home. But things are changing. When you used to walk, they would be throwing eggs at you, spitting at you, it was as bad as that. They don't do that any more.'

Many of Tilbury's residents have worked hard to overcome the town's history of prejudice. Today, an array of religious and secular organisations, some managed by the local authority and others operating more informally, aim to bring citizens from different ethnic backgrounds together and integrate minority groups into municipal decision-making. All the community leaders I spoke with in Tilbury were understandably eager to play down the past and emphasise cohesion as the new norm. But while Abraham's church has gone from strength to strength – today it boasts a congregation of more than 300 people and runs a programme of activities that are open to all, from homework help to marriage counselling and knitting clubs – it continues to face bureaucratic obstructions. When Fruitful Land applied to host a street party to celebrate the queen's Diamond Jubilee in 2012, for example, objections from local residents prevented it from going ahead. And although many in the town's black community insist they rarely encounter explicit discrimination any more, that doesn't mean people of colour in Tilbury can blithely put the old divisions behind them. 'It's safer now, but it didn't use to feel safe at all,' said Ese Odeje, an eighteen-year-old church attendee. 'When we first came, it was horrible. My dad's car and my mum's car used to get smashed almost weekly. Now I'd say it's better, but we still get the odd racist remark from little boys or people in shops.'

Every white resident I interviewed in Tilbury denied racial prejudice. Some went out of their way to recount personal friendships with people from different ethnic backgrounds, and many expressed frustration at what they saw as a particular line of questioning from 'London media types' – like me – that was rooted in metropolitan political correctness and snobbery, and designed to give Tilbury a bad name. 'You say the wrong thing, and people trip you up and accuse you of stuff,' one person complained. 'Like speaking to you – I don't know what words I'm allowed to use ... Tilbury's not a racist town any more, that's all I want to get across.' But when asked to characterise the town today, several white people I spoke with insisted there was a cultural divide between white and black locals and spoke negatively about the latter's influence on Tilbury. False rumours and easily debunked myths abounded: 'foreign' gangs going on rampages, and shops and services displaying 'no whites' signs in their windows. 'It used to be that everybody here knew everybody, but it's all gone downhill in the last ten years,' said one man, repeating a popular sentiment. 'All the pubs have closed, all the shops, the greengrocers, the butchers, and they've all ...' He trailed off, and gestured around him. 'We've got a greengrocers now, but it's an Asian greengrocer's – it actually advertises itself like that. And the butcher's is for African meat. They don't give you the feeling that you're welcome in there.'

A number of different residents told me that black people arriving in Tilbury were bumped straight to the top of the waiting list for social housing, or that they were given £50,000 by the local authority to help them buy a home. Neither of these claims is correct. What is true is that London's ongoing housing crisis has had a dramatic effect on Tilbury. Lower-income buyers are driven eastward from the capital; at the same time, London's overburdened council authorities find the cost of housing vulnerable residents in their own boroughs increasingly unaffordable. As one of the few stretches of London's hinterlands that hasn't yet seen a spike in prices comparable to that of the capital itself, Tilbury provides those councils with a convenient solution. According to Steve Liddiard, one of Tilbury's councillors, up to 70% of privately rented accommodation in the town is now being leased by local authorities in London in order to provide homes for their own residents. That demand pushes up local property prices – over the past two decades the market value of Tilbury's housing stock has soared by almost 350%, compared to inflation of 72% and growth in the FTSE 100 of just 41% over the same period[11] – and has made affordable housing ever-harder for Tilbury's population to secure, especially given the aggressive diminishment of the local social housing stock since the 1980s. It also means that many of those resettled in Tilbury – often Londoners who have suffered from homelessness or substance abuse, or are deemed at risk of domestic or gang-related violence – have no prior connection to the town and little motivation to develop one; their stay on the riverside will almost certainly be temporary, and their lives remain grounded in the city.

But few of the Tilbury residents I spoke with had any knowledge of the process behind this estrangement. To many, it simply looked as if new, usually non-white people kept turning up in town, provided with free or subsidised accommodation from the authorities, while they or their friends and family struggled to afford a home. To make matters worse, the newcomers seemed to show little interest in integrating with Tilbury's communal institutions, or what's left of them. In the gap between perception and reality, little shoots of resentment have sprouted and become entwined with other grievances – anger over unemployment, pub closures, a generation of elite cultural mockery – to produce a hazy and often racialised sense of injustice, one that is compounded by the feeling that our society lacks a shared language in which to interrogate it. 'It's all political correctness now,' one person I talked to said abruptly as we discussed the challenges faced by young families in Tilbury. 'I know that I'm not racist, and I know the way I talk makes you think I'm racist, and so I don't know what to say.'

Tilbury's affordable-housing shortage has nothing to do with non-white or 'foreign' settlement here – it is largely the product of four decades of systemic marketisation that has created a savage imbalance between London's economy and Tilbury's. That imbalance has marginalised Tilbury's residents twice over: first by leeching wealth and social status from the town and thus impoverishing it, and then by exploiting that impoverishment in order to provide a sticking plaster – in the form of cheap temporary accommodation leased by London councils for their most vulnerable residents – over some of the wounds inflicted inside the capital itself by London's lopsided property boom. As with the growth here in job precariousness and casualisation, it's a complex tale about the structural defects of our economic system and the uneven allocation of power and resources that follow. But that tale has not been explained convincingly, certainly not by a Labour Party that has, for most of this period, been mainly on board with the policy decisions that have driven it forward.

And so, for many of Tilbury's white residents, another tale has taken hold instead, one that seizes upon popular vexation at economic liberalism and conjoins it with a vaguely articulated critique of social liberalism. It bundles together the disappearance of things like job security with the partial erosion of privileges previously enjoyed by white citizens, especially men, back in a time when racial and gendered social hierarchies were more blatant. It identifies the betrayal of 'traditional values' as the problem, and resurgent nationalism as the solution. In the past, those telling this tale have been fascist groups like the National Front (NF), which called for the compulsory deportation of Britain's non-white population. The NF was active in

Tilbury throughout the 1970s, and Charlie remembers attending some of their meetings, although he insists he has never been into 'that sort of thing'. More recently, as Tilbury's residents gradually turned their backs on Labour – over the course of the party's reign between 1997 and 2010, Labour's vote in Thurrock almost halved – it is UKIP that has taken up the electoral slack. Cannily positioning itself as a sort of old-Labour redux, the Eurosceptic party's support here in parliamentary elections grew eighteenfold in the two decades leading up to Britain's 2016 EU referendum; the votes it garnered from Labour in places like Tilbury handed the overall constituency to the Conservatives twice in succession, and left Labour reeling in one of its own heartlands.

'The Labour Party grew out of communities like Tilbury, and now it's led by people who want to pat places like Tilbury on the head,' said Jackie Doyle-Price, a Tory MP for Thurrock. 'They've taken Tilbury for granted and neglected it … and in the past ten years, Tilbury has started kicking back.' Charlie still considers himself a Labour man, but he is one of many people I met in Tilbury who switched allegiance to UKIP and hold Labour accountable for the breach. 'As far as I could tell, New Labour was the Old Tory,' Charlie said. 'At the last election, it hurt me to put my cross in front of UKIP. I didn't want to. But then I remembered that UKIP is basically Labour now.'

The financial crash, alongside New Labour's accommodation of neoliberalism, offered UKIP and its fellow travellers on the right the space to develop a powerful narrative to pitch at voters – one that, in contrast to Third Way centrism and its fealty to global markets, offered both an account of why many people's lives in Tilbury had got harder and a purported path to reclaiming what was lost. Crucially, it wasn't afraid of using the language of class – so unfashionable in Blair's and Leadbeater's circles – to draw lines in the sand, pitting an ethnically delineated working class against an amorphous ruling elite whose power was exercised not only through economic channels but also social and cultural ones: the technocrats who run state quangos, the pious intellectuals writing in the pages of the *Guardian*, the social justice warriors who care more about the plight of Syrian migrants than they do about ordinary people living on their own doorstep. To those more familiar with UKIP as a stockbroker-belt and shire golf-club phenomenon, its campaign messages in Tilbury will come as a surprise: party officials have spoken out against the closure of Tilbury's power station and criticised a new property development by the council for not including enough affordable housing. Tim Aker, a former UKIP MEP who is sharp-suited, media-savvy and has done more than anyone to build the party's electoral base in this corner of the country, tweets enthusiastically about localist economic agendas of the type being trialled up in Preston, and is happy to condemn multinational corporations.[12] But this defence of local homes and jobs, as far as it goes, is carefully integrated into a cultural revanchism, underscored by a crusading opposition to leftist shibboleths such as political correctness, identity politics, feminism and multiculturalism.

Aker, who has now quit the party following its prolonged period of internal strife and tilt towards the far right, fiercely rejects the charges of racism that are often levelled against UKIP. 'Don't listen to the rubbish other parties put out,' he told me, prior to his resignation. 'I say to every single voter, every single person: you're as part of the community as all of us.' But Aker made his name here by fighting cleverly engineered and highly publicised battles with Thurrock council over his right to fly the British flag; one of his first moves upon winning office was to hire Robert Ray, a former local-council candidate for the National Front, as part of his political team.[13] He may have drawn the line at representing a party that welcomed English Defence League founder Tommy Robinson as a member, but he was content to serve under the leadership of Paul Nuttall, an outspoken opponent of LGBTQ+ rights who called for a ban on anyone who is HIV-positive from entering the UK and defended a senior party figure who described Islam as a 'death cult'.[14] Nor did he speak out during the Brexit referendum campaign when then UKIP leader Nigel Farage unveiled a poster depicting a group of Syrian refugees next to the words 'BREAKING POINT', which echoed imagery used in Nazi propaganda against Jews.

'What we talk about is controlling immigration, putting this country first,' Aker insisted. 'That includes first generation, second generation and however many generations you want to go back. We've all got the same problems, we all use the same public services, we all want weekly bin collections.' And yet it's hard to reconcile this studiously inclusive rhetoric with the 'BREAKING POINT' poster and the rest of UKIP's messaging – particularly for those who, like Pastor Abraham, have migrated to Britain from another country or were born here to parents who did. Aker represents a growing strand of organised political opinion that views foreigners as an existential threat to Britain as long as they are outside the country's borders trying to get in. Is the Fruitful Land congregation supposed to believe that in his eyes those same foreigners become welcome members of the community the moment they reach the other side?

Tilbury and Thurrock remain UKIP's top constituency target nationwide. Winning the EU referendum and then becoming embroiled in scandal may have diminished the party as an electoral force, but its ideas and arguments have not faded with it; on the contrary, they run through the lifeblood of Britain's mainstream politics more strongly than ever, evident both in the Conservative Party's sharp turn to the right since the Brexit vote and the emergence of the Brexit Party, which has swept up much of UKIP's support. A divide between defenders of 'double liberalism' (economic and social) accused of carelessly dismantling settled communities on the one hand, and those who set themselves up – however disingenuously – as nationalist insurgents against an omnipresent globalism on the other, is one of the central fissures of our time, and Britain is not the only country in which it has radically redrawn the political spectrum. Since 2008, political parties and politicians on the nationalist right have made huge electoral gains in Denmark, Finland, Switzerland, Germany, the Netherlands and many other European states; in Austria, Poland, Hungary, Italy, Brazil and the United States, they have seized power. After Trump's presidential victory in 2016, Gérard Araud, the French ambassador to the US, declared on Twitter, 'It is the end of an era ... A world is collapsing before our eyes.' Florian Philippot, then vice president of France's far-right Front National and strategic director of Marine Le Pen's almost-successful presidential campaign, responded, 'Their world is collapsing, ours is being built.'

From within the maelstrom, a certain genre of political commentary aimed at explaining how we got here has garnered widespread attention, exemplified by the argument of British author David Goodhart, who believes that old distinctions of class and economic interest have been 'overlaid' by a larger fault line between 'Anywheres' – those citizens who place a high value on autonomy, mobility and novelty – and 'Somewheres', who care more about group identity, tradition and place.[15] Goodhart argues that the failure of mainstream politicians to recognise that white 'racial self-interest' is a legitimate political concern, distinguishable from racism, has been helping to fuel the rise of populist nationalism. 'Since the turn of the century, Western politics has had to make room for a range of voices preoccupied with national borders and pace of change, appealing to people who feel displaced by a more open, ethnically fluid, graduate-favouring economy and society, designed by and for the new elites,' Goodhart wrote. 'The Anywheres have counted for too much in the past twenty-five years – their sense of political entitlement startlingly revealed by their reaction to the Brexit and Trump votes – and populism, in its many shapes and sizes, has arisen as a counterbalance to their dominance throughout the developed world.'

This sort of analysis is regularly deployed in relation to so-called 'left behind' social groups of the global north. Undoubtedly, the political shudders that have shaken Tilbury and many other places besides in recent years owe much to the insecurities, both real and imagined, of what Polish sociologist Zygmunt Bauman calls the 'emergent precariat': poorer white citizens who live in fear of seeing their economic and social capital diminishing any further and who are targeted by right-wing populists using racially coded language to promise an illusory 'return' to ancestral lands. But too often the arguments that develop from this are premised on the notion that 'left behind' communities do not just perceive themselves to have been monolithically white, timeless and static – single, cohesive social entities that were subsequently disrupted by immigration – but actually were so. Tilbury, though exceptional in some ways, shows how careful we must be about assuming this is true.

Migrant communities have been at the core of Tilbury's existence since the modern town was born. The docks were built by Irish and other European navvies in the late nineteenth century, and since then, Tilbury has been home at various times to large communities of Punjabis, Kenyans, Zimbabweans, Vietnamese and immigrants from the Caribbean. One of the most arresting sights on Tilbury's riverside is the magnificent Sikh Gurdwara temple that rises from the opposite bank in Gravesend. Today, more than one in five of Tilbury's residents are classified as 'black and minority ethnic', some of whom are British and some of whom are not – a figure significantly higher than the national average. Far from being a drag on welfare services, members of this group are statistically more likely than their white neighbours to be employed, and their typical education levels are better too. Many of Tilbury's white residents are second-generation internal migrants themselves, with parents who hailed from London's old East End and relocated out to Essex in the post-war period – just as many in Pastor Abraham's congregation have done more recently. Despite the mentality of some in the town, there is no immutable 'them' and 'us' in Tilbury, because the backgrounds of those who call it home have always been changing, complicated and contingent.

Nor do Tilbury's white residents have a monopoly on the physical 'Somewhere' of this town. Bukky Okunade, a fifty-two-year-old Nigerian–British woman who serves as a Labour councillor for Tilbury, knew about the cruise terminal here long before she saw it with her own eyes. She remembers seeing grainy photos of the *Empire Windrush* landing during celebrations of Black History Month when she was living in London. 'Tilbury mattered to me because it was part of my heritage, even though I'd never been there – this was where black people came to Britain and went on to different places in this country, and when we thought about that history we'd always talk about Tilbury,' she told me. 'When I finally moved to this part of the world in 2002 and I saw the docks, it felt symbolic and emotional.'

Okunade is one of the few black councillors in Thurrock's history. She has represented Tilbury since 2006 and, at almost every election she has contested, a white ethno-supremacist group – usually the British National Party – has run candidates against her. She has seen them all off, although in 2008 an election for the other seat in her ward resulted in a BNP victory, and Okunade was forced to spend two uncomfortable years working alongside a fascist. 'This is a small town, close-knit, where everyone knows each other,' she said. 'Yes, there have been issues. Yes, I face hostility sometimes on the doorstep. And yes, there are myths that need to be burst. But I think that bursting is happening. I've been here, in office, for more than ten years, and I've seen a lot of changes.' Her lips crept into a smile. 'And look,' she concluded, 'I'm still here.' Okunade's story is a reminder that although place matters far more than the high priests of globalism have reckoned for in recent years, attempts to rescue the notion of 'community' from political purgatory need not depend on the construction of imaginary white idylls, as many nationalists would have us believe.

Of course, Tilbury's better days rested upon the contribution of black and Asian working classes not just within the town but far beyond; as a port, its wealth has always been derived from the labour of men and women across the planet, especially in the global south. Similar economic processes that have devastated Tilbury more recently have produced victims in other places too, some of whom arrive folded into almost airless hiding spaces among the goods lifted by Tilbury's cranes on to British shores. In 2014, staff at the port heard screaming from inside a shipping container; upon opening it, they found thirty-four Afghan refugees, alongside the body of one who didn't survive the journey.[16] The question posed by Tilbury is not about how liberal democracies can respond to the racial self-interest of a non-existent monocultural majority. It is about whether those left behind by privatisation, financialisation and globalisation will be united by their shared economic interests, or divided by a racialised insecurity capable of taking root even in a place with such a cosmopolitan past.

'We tell people that this place belongs to everybody,' Pastor Abraham said with the oratorical flourish of a practised preacher when I asked him what message he was trying to spread to Tilbury residents outside his congregation. 'We explain that we need to work together, because none of us can achieve what we want to achieve by ourselves alone.'

*

On a bright and chilly afternoon in January, with time to kill before a Dockers match, I went for a drive with John Heath, a sixty-year-old fan who used to work at Tilbury's Riverside railway station, along with his friend and colleague Mick. 'It's our town, and it's our club,' John said when I asked him about his relationship with the football team. 'It ain't nothing really, but it's ours.'

We turned out of the parking lot and down past the spot where the carnival man stores his fairground rides in a jumble of gaudy pink, and then out on to the main road. In John's and Mick's company, Tilbury's streets became a map of densely woven social connections and micro-histories that spanned decades, populated by aunts and uncles, scandals and surprises, as well as the many different sites where the pair of them had once earned a living. 'Find an old photo of the docks off Google Images,' John told me, 'then go inside and stand there and compare it. You know what's missing from the picture today? People. When you go into the docks now it doesn't smell of fish, or coal, or graft. Just machines.'

I would later take John's advice and visit the port, watching as ships the size of clifftops heaved into view through the rain. Tilbury has been described as a northern mining town transplanted to the banks of the Thames, but the reality is that unlike old pit towns in Northumberland, Yorkshire or Lancashire, the industry behind this formerly industrial community continues to boom: in an age where the financial flows that structure our lives have never felt more abstract, this is the rare spot where you can actually touch the network – rub up against metal and concrete, run your fingers across its edges, and occasionally get caught on a snag. Despite a sharp reduction in its workforce over the past half-century, Tilbury handles 16 million tons of cargo each year and is home to 120 different companies. There are still some people here, and they are friendly, skilful and highly trained. Some control the high-tech clamps that hold huge reels of imported paper on the front of forklift trucks; others operate the elongated straddle-carriers gathering up shipping containers off the ground like giant yellow arachnids sweeping prey into their innards before whizzing them off in a blizzard of beeps. The port was a busy economic hub when Charlie, John and Mick were young men, and it's an even busier economic hub now; the difference is that it no longer offers jobs to them, or to their children, and there is a cruel irony in the fact that a place which perhaps more than any other asserts globalisation's physical form is also a place which perhaps more than any other has been locked out of that system's successes. The port's owners believe they are doing what they can to maintain a link with the town that sprung up beside it – the football club, for example, is sponsored by the Port of Tilbury, and a major expansion is currently under way that will extend the docks over to the other side of old Tilbury Fort; it's not their fault that technology has mechanised many of the processes that were once carried out by human hands. But as June Brown, who once helped her grandmother scrub the loos here, puts it, 'It does annoy me, with how much wealth the port has brought into the country, how little of it has trickled down into the town.' June is right, and so is John: the docks don't smell of coal or fish any more.

Just beyond the cruise terminal, John showed us the railway station he helped run for a quarter-century – or at least, he showed us the empty space where the station used to be. We could see where the platforms once stood and the shuttered entrance to the building that housed the ticket office. Tilbury Riverside, a relic from the time when the area around the docks still hummed with humanity, closed in 1992. John locked up on that final day. He searched out some old graffiti he'd doodled about the cricketer Ian Botham and slipped into a reverie as he recalled the long-lost cafeteria and the dance hall and the night the storm blew out glass from the roof. He told us where the weathervane that once crowned the station's dome can be found today – underneath someone's clothesline in nearby Chadwell St Mary, it turns out. For Tilbury's famous 1978 cup match with Stoke, the club organised a special train from Riverside station to make sure as many townspeople as possible could make the journey north for the match. It was John who coupled the carriages to the engine before hopping aboard to join the knees-up. 'So much stuff went when the station closed,' he said, shaking his head and pulling his jacket tighter. 'Nice chairs that were worth money, things that had been there for a hundred years, just chucked on to the skip.' We turned and walked along the old passenger ramp that leads down toward the river. 'They threw out people's lifetime's work, and I guess the work of future people too,' he continued. 'I don't mind admitting I shed a tear when I switched all the lights off that last time, and turned the key.'

Like almost everybody over the age of thirty I met in Tilbury, John voted for Brexit; in the 2016 referendum, Thurrock delivered the fourth-highest 'leave' vote in the entire UK. When asked for the reasons behind their decision, most people I interviewed mentioned democratic sovereignty and what they saw as an unhealthy degree of influence exercised by unelected foreign bureaucrats over British law. Many also cited uncontrolled migration from EU countries under the bloc's freedom-of-movement guarantee – with emphasis on the 'uncontrolled', rather than the 'migration'. When pressed for details on how EU migrants were impacting the town, however, the answers were often contradictory. Charlie does some part-time work as an instructor of forklift truck drivers and has trained many Poles and Bulgarians. Free movement through the EU has benefited him financially, and he spoke approvingly of the new arrivals: 'They want to learn, and they want to work, much more than our young lads.' I asked him why, in that case, EU migration was a negative. He paused, then eventually responded: 'Well, it used to be "I know your lass, you know my lass" around here. You knew people then and could trust them. You left the house key inside the letter box. My house is lit up with security cameras now. I want to go back.'

A certain caricature of the Brexit voter has become commonplace in the British media: the defensively insular, working-class man with authoritarian instincts and a desperate pining for days of yore. As in the US, where the post-industrial Rust Belt Trump supporter is often credited as being the main factor behind his triumph – despite the fact that most of Trump's votes came from the traditional and more prosperous Republican support base – the actual demographics of the EU 'leave' camp are more complicated.[17] They include some ethnic-minority communities in major cities, as well as large numbers of traditional middle-class conservatives living in the suburbs or counties that surround London.[18] But focus on a misplaced 'nostalgia' as being one of the main factors behind the referendum result remains widespread and has provoked many meditations on the topic. 'We recognise that with time every human being will cease being, will only have been,' wrote the novelist Mohsin Hamid in a compelling essay on the subject. 'And so we seek to resist time. We rebel against it. We are drawn like lovers to the unreachable past, to imagined memories, to nostalgia ... The kind of futures we would like to inhabit seem unlikely to occur. The futures that we suspect are likely to occur, meanwhile, fill us with anxiety. And so we are left stranded: unstable in the present, being dragged from the past, resistant to the future. We become profoundly angry, vulnerable to the dangerous calls of charlatans and bigots and xenophobes. We become depressed. And in our depression, we become more dangerous too.'[19]

We are all losing the past, all the time, but the losses involved have not been distributed equitably, and our ability to absorb them is dependent on how confident we are in our ability to shape the future to our liking. Without thinking about who has more reason to be nostalgic, and what it is those people are nostalgic for, accusations of nostalgia risk becoming little more than a 'mute' button on those who have lost the most. Alongside jobs and social capital, one of the most abject losses experienced by the residents of Tilbury has been the erosion of a sense of influence over their lives, just as those lives have grown harder – not a theoretical loss, but a concrete and institutionalised one that has accompanied a generation-long, top-down dismantling of municipal governance, long pre-dating post-2008 austerity. The state as we know it and the protections it provides have been shrunk; Thurrock is in the bottom five for funding per citizen of all unitary councils in Britain and has the third small-est budget overall. At the same time, lines of local democratic accountability have been scrambled – with less money and less power, elected councillors have fewer tools at their disposal to change anything, and dissatisfied citizens find it harder to know who it is they should be registering their dissatisfaction with. In 2005, for example, Thurrock council outsourced its office services to the private contractor Serco; the deal proved to be such a disaster that even the local Conservative-controlled administration had to admit it was unsustainable, and in 2015 it proceeded to buy out Serco's contract five years early at a cost of almost £10 million.[20] Tilbury's residents may have got off relatively lightly; three years later, the collapse of Serco's rival outsourcing giant Carillion cost the British taxpayer at least £148 million nationwide.[21]

Many Britons have suffered from what the writer Tom Crewe called 'the strange death of municipal England'.[22] In that respect, Tilbury is hardly unique. But those whose economic and social networks are especially concentrated geographically have experienced that suffering with a special intensity. Research by the think tank Demos has revealed that one of the key predictors of a person's likelihood to support Brexit is the degree to which they have friends outside their home town and travel to other parts of the UK and abroad.[23] High-mobility citizens were more inclined to vote 'remain', lower-mobility citizens to vote 'leave'. 'I moved away from Tilbury once,' Mick told me. 'It was only six or seven miles, but it felt like forever away to me.' Later, in the clubhouse at the football ground, regulars showed off their local patois – which they insisted that residents of Grays, less than two miles west, could not understand. 'We're all enclaves here,' said Vincent Offord, the local Labour Party activist. 'There are Tilbury-ites and Grays-ites and so on, and people feel that those things are very different.'

Nostalgia is unmistakeably present in Tilbury's political cadences, but the term on its own does nothing to capture the forces behind it: that slow-burn stripping of the identity, agency and security that form the building blocks of a decent life. When it came to campaigning in the EU referendum, the overwhelming message from the pro-remain establishment – largely the same political and financial leaders that had long told the residents of Tilbury that on a macro level their town's downturn was in everyone's best interests – was hollow: the argument that Britain's economy would be recklessly imperilled by Brexit is predicated on the assumption that there is a single, unified thing called the 'economy', and that it affects everybody equally. But late capitalism hasn't affected everybody equally: it has created winners, and it has designated losers, and it has told those losers that they only have themselves to blame. The political economist and sociologist Will Davies has called Brexit 'the revenge of politics on economics'; to understand it, we must acknowledge Britain's socio-economic pathologies, which include not just the hoarding of opportunities and wealth by certain industries, locales and individuals, but also the psychological implications of how this hoarding has been represented and justified over the past four decades, and the message that gave about the underlying moral worth of different communities.[24] 'We've got our personal pride, and Brexit made all those MPs sit up and listen,' said Peter Hewitt, a retired police officer in Tilbury who founded the Tilbury Riverside Project and has been recognised with an MBE for his community service. 'The prime minister – all that lot – they got a right kick in the teeth, didn't they?'

Much like London's waste, which arrives by barge at the Tilbury docks for processing, unpopular decisions have flowed east down the Thames for many years. To many, a vote on EU membership was a chance to send something back in the opposite direction. 'Take back control' was the Brexit campaign's slogan, and here it was crushingly effective. It encouraged voters in Tilbury and many other places like it to use the referendum to answer questions that were not the one written on the ballot paper. 'I think it's woken people up,' said Charlie of the outcome. 'Everyone's waking up, and that's got to be good.'

*

Over the next two decades, between 10 million and 15 million more British jobs are expected to be replaced by automation.[25] In December 2016, an investigation by the Institute for Public Policy Research warned that this trend risked entrenching a new era of economic feudalism, with a tiny minority who own the robots reaping the rewards and the rest, especially at the lower-skilled end of the labour market, struggling as humans become less and less important to the production process.[26] 'These changes have the potential to create an era of widespread abundance, or a second machine age that radically concentrates economic power,' wrote the report's author, Mathew Lawrence. 'Which path we take – a future between *Star Trek* and *The Matrix* – will depend on the type of politics and institutions we build.'[27] Far from being 'left behind', it is in places like Tilbury that these politics and institutions will be brought to life. The town was dismissed by *The Economist* as a polyp, but in many ways it is a window on to an economic fate that, for better or worse, may soon belong to us all.

Which path will Tilbury take in the decades to come? On a stretch of dying grassland between the football stadium and the main roundabout, one part of the answer has already risen from the ground: a mammoth Amazon fulfilment centre, the company's newest to date and its thirteenth in the UK. The company claims the plant will eventually provide more than 1,500 jobs, alongside 'the most advanced Amazon Robotics technology'.[28] Local officials have hailed Amazon's investment as a sign that Tilbury's fortunes are about to change – this time for real. But if the pattern of Amazon's existing distribution hubs is replicated, much of the work done here will involve hard, low-wage labour on insecure contracts, and the productivity gains obtained from increased automation are not likely to be captured by the local community or even the national Treasury (in 2017 Amazon paid £7.4 million in corporation tax on a UK turnover of £1.46 billion).[29] Instead, they will be funnelled elsewhere – maybe into tax havens, or into the private Blue Origin firm run by Amazon founder Jeff Bezos, who is currently engaged in a twenty-first-century space race with several other of the world's richest men in an effort to be the first to send a manned rocket to Mars. Meanwhile investigations by the media have exposed allegations that Amazon's warehouse workers are penalised for taking sick days, and some are so impoverished that they are forced to camp in tents nearby to save money on commuting costs.[30] Trade unions have accused the Internet giant of making staff 'physically and mentally ill'; Amazon has responded by launching an all-out war on union organising on the shop floor.[31] 'Having a union could make it hard to stay competitive,' explains one character in a training video provided for Amazon-employed managers at Whole Foods. 'They don't share our same values.'[32]

Mick, whose twenty-year-old daughter juggles three cleaning jobs, all on zero-hours contracts, remains sceptical. 'That kind of "work",' he said, grimacing. 'She gets called in three days a week sometimes, and then she'll have two days' work across the whole month. There's no control.' He harked back to the days when he used to manage a small team inside Tilbury's (then-nationalised) power station. 'You looked after the guys, and they looked after you. It's not like that any more with these companies – there's no bonding. They don't pay their taxes. It's not about the community now. It's about how much money they can make.' Whether Mick's fears about Amazon's employment practices prove correct or not, there is no doubt that in terms of its relationship to Tilbury, the new fulfilment centre will have a very different look and feel from the power station or docks of his past. The building is drab and almost windowless, just another node in a global web. It's the sort of thing, as the writer James Meek put it, that marks the land but isn't a landmark.

Is an alternate path possible for Tilbury, and other post-industrial communities like it? Despite everything, Tilbury is home to many institutions that have clung on amid the free market's atomising storms, and from which a grass-roots vision of something more collective might yet be forged: the football club, Fruitful Land, the dance academy that sits opposite the church on Civic Square, the martial-arts school that is home to local kickboxing hero Dave 'The Grenade' Gould, and the famed Tilbury brass band, which can trace its history back almost a hundred years. No single group can lay claim to these vital shared spaces, and younger residents of Tilbury – while remaining as fiercely proud of their town as their parents are – appear to be less concerned than older generations with the matter of cultural borders. 'Not everyone in Tilbury gets on with everyone, obviously,' noted Abigail Collins, a sixteen-year-old student at the dance academy. 'There's a mixture ... but as time goes by, everyone is going to become used to it, because more people are born, and that's what they're going to live with.' Olamide Olufemi, a nineteen-year-old member of Pastor Abraham's congregation, said that contrary to what those unfamiliar with the place might think, Tilbury has plenty of self-esteem. 'I've experienced it; people from the outside might see it as an area you wouldn't want to be in, but I don't want to put anything down. You have to embrace where you come from. If you don't put some positivity into your town, then who will?' And yet the losses – of shared spaces, of future hopes, of control – continue; in 2018, the council earmarked the martial-arts school for closure, and the World's End pub went up in flames. Across Britain, eighteen pubs shut down a week; the number of nightclubs has almost halved in a decade, the number of youth centres has fallen by 600 in the space of six years, and 127 libraries closed in 2018 alone.[33]

On my last trip to Tilbury, I went to another Dockers' football match and took up a place in the stadium's only elevated stand, where a row of fold-down plastic chairs faced west into the setting sun. From where I sat, with the pitch below me, I could see a small band of Tilbury diehards – Charlie, John, Mick and Mavis among them – clustered in the far-left corner, singing with gleeful abandon. In the days ahead, John and Mick would clock into their temporary gigs at the old power-station site, where – in what seems like a lifetime ago – they both used to have steady jobs. Their current gig is helping to prepare the building for demolition. It's the second time in his career John has been tasked with shutting down a place that once employed him. 'You start with the soft strip,' he told me. 'Wood, fittings, anything that can be removed by hand. Then you take the interior metal out, and then you explode the walls.' Mavis would be at the hospital bed of a friend she'd known all her life and who, she told me with a tremble, was nearing the end. Charlie would be heading off to a pigeon meeting in Blackpool. He raises homing pigeons – famed for their ability to return home, to the place they know best – just like his grandfather did; the old man was so good at it, runs the local legend, that the authorities commandeered his birds during the Second World War.

But that winter evening, with the grey prefab walls of Amazon's new warehouse looming large against the sky behind them and the cranes of the docks glinting in the light beyond, the football fans were bouncing up and down as the game unfurled before us. At that moment, Haringey, Tilbury's opponents, scored a goal. It didn't matter. Standing at the edge of the field with their team down 1–0, wrapped up against the January chill, the Dockers kept on singing.

3

Work

Westminster, London

... trouble is inevitable and the task, how best to make it, what best way to be in it

—Judith Butler

As a teenager, Fatima Djalo dreamed of being a doctor. When she was twelve years old, her mother – a single parent who was left to bring up the family alone after Fatima's father was killed in a bicycle accident – sold her rickety camp bed, gave the money to Fatima's older sister, and instructed her to take Fatima to the city. 'She wanted me to study, and she ended up sleeping on the floor to make that possible,' remembers Fatima. 'To this day, I'm the only one of my siblings who can read or write.'

The journey west from Sonaco, a small town in the grassy interior of Guinea-Bissau, was 120 miles long and a bus ran once a week. This was the mid-1970s, and the early, febrile days of a brand-new nation on Africa's Atlantic coastline that had just fought a bitter war of independence against the Portuguese; the roads were hard, and sometimes dangerous. But Fatima wasn't scared, not really – the fear inside her got crowded out by the thrill. She had grown up in a place where life was often difficult, and food, healthcare and education scarce. Her father had been an informal tradesman, purchasing bits and bobs where he could and selling them on to anyone who would take them; her mother cooked for locals in a kitchen. Her sisters would soon be married off, and one would go on to have fourteen children. For Fatima, the ticket to Bissau, Guinea-Bissau's bustling port capital, was a doorway to a future that was foggy, but different.

At first, things went well – Fatima enjoyed her lessons, and adjusted to a world far removed from her old home. But when it came to choosing specialist courses and preparing for an adult career, that wasn't enough. Becoming a doctor meant studying medicine, and studying medicine meant lots of extra school fees that Fatima and her family didn't have. Instead she became a secretary, typing by day and living frugally by night, saving and saving until one day, at the age of seventeen, she had enough money to buy another ticket to a different future, this time consisting of a plane to Lisbon. 'I didn't know anyone in Portugal,' she tells me. 'My plan was to finally get the chance to study further, but it didn't work out.' She ended up doing low-paid work to survive on this unfamiliar continent, eventually starting a family of her own. Still, the lure of an alternative existence – somewhere else just over the horizon, one more door away – endured. In 2008, in the thick of the global financial crisis, Fatima folded up her life again and made her way to London. She knew it would be tough – like Lisbon was, and Bissau before it, and Sonaco before that – because ultimately everywhere is tough, even if the shape and texture of that toughness varies from place to place and the strain feels differently against your skin. 'But I thought things would be better,' she says. 'I wanted to become a bus driver.' Bus drivers have secure jobs and get to explore vast portions of the city; they are a highly visible part of the urban infrastructure, and everyone can see how much they're needed. 'I had lots of hopes when I arrived here,' smiles Fatima. 'But that's life: nothing works out as you planned.'

For the past decade, far from exploring vast portions of the city, Fatima has run on rails. She wakes up in the early hours of the morning to be in with a chance of being able to use the bathroom at her small house in Stratford, which she shares with nine strangers – some are Italian, she thinks, and some might be Eastern European, but nobody socialises with one another as they're all too busy working, so she can't really be sure. Almost every possession Fatima owns remains permanently packed in two large suitcases, because she knows what the landlord is capable of: he demands payments in cash, and retains a personal key to every room. 'I have my creams and my hair products out on the side table, and that's it,' she explains. 'When he throws me out on to the street, I'll be ready.' By 6.30 a.m. she's on the tube and heading to the Ministry of Justice headquarters near St James's Park for the first of two jobs. Over the next nine hours she will walk up and down sixteen floors of UK government office space, cleaning each of the male and female toilets on every floor five times per working day. She will walk for miles and miles, until 5 p.m., when she will gather her things, walk down the road for half a mile more, and begin another set of cleaning rounds – this time at the Supreme Court. For all this, she will be paid £7.83 per hour, the legal minimum wage for her age.[1] By the time she gets home, it will be past 9 p.m., and she will be exhausted. She spends her weekends at home, queuing up to use the house's single washing machine, and catching up on sleep. And then on Monday, she will start all over again. 'It isn't any kind of life,' she says.

But today is a different kind of life. Today, she is spinning in the middle of a Westminster pavement as rain pours from the sky, with glitter on her face and strips of ticker tape in her hair. She is blowing on a horn and dancing deliriously, flanked by a line of security guards on one side and a line of police officers on the other. The air is fat with music and shouting and flare-smoke and promise, and Fatima, now fifty-four, is at the heart of it all, walking through yet another doorway into the unknown.

Work structures our world, outside and in. We use it to define ourselves, to weigh our own worth and that of others, to mark the passage from childhood to maturity, and most importantly to survive. Our politicians, economists and media commentators rely on work to measure how well we are doing as a nation; its vital statistics are common shorthand for the health of our society. Yet in modern Britain, work is in crisis. Following the financial crash, real wages in Britain have fallen by a percentage point every year; by the mid-2010s the typical worker was earning 10% less than they were before 2008 and some had lost over a third of their earnings – compared to average wage *rises* over that period of 11% in France, 14% in Germany, and 23% in Poland.[2] Seven in ten workers in the UK are now 'chronically broke', according to a major study by the Royal Society of Arts (RSA),[3] and the level of 'wage theft' from workers by unscrupulous employers is conservatively estimated at £4.5 billion per year.[4] 'Work is the best route out of poverty,' Theresa May declared on several occasions, wrongly.[5] In fact, 7 million people in Britain living below the bread line – that's two-thirds of all those in poverty – have jobs, but jobs that simply do not pay enough.[6] 'There's no justice for workers here and it doesn't seem like there's much justice for workers anywhere in this country,' Fatima once said to me as we stood outside the Ministry of Justice entrance doors, and the statistics bear her out. The Bank of England's chief economist Andy Haldane has described the ten years following the crash as a 'lost decade' for workers in Britain; economic insecurity for workers, according to the RSA, is now the 'new normal'.[7]

The story of what has happened to workers – of how that insecurity got normalised – is part of a wider tale about the ways in which processes of economic production have been altered under the twin influences of globalisation and financialisation. Gone are the days of mammoth, vertically integrated industries stockpiling everything one needs to build a car, run a communications network or retail groceries to consumers; now goods zip back and forth across borders via 'just in time' supply chains, spending as few moments as possible on a ware-house shelf. They are ferried along by a workforce subjected to fewer benefits, greater outsourcing, and more temporary contracts that ebb and flow in accordance with the needs of capital than at any other time since the end of the Second World War. As all aspects of production become computerised, the companies best placed to flourish are increasingly the ones able to collect, interpret and exploit the vast reams of data generated by economic activity, fuelling the rise of competing 'platforms', specialised in everything from aircraft engines to website infrastructure, whose aim is to control the ground upon which everyone else does business.[8] Some of those same technologies and business models have fuelled a cornucopia of more consumer-facing, on-demand services – from food delivery to DIY and driving – providing plentiful but casual work for millions at the bottom end of the labour market; between 2016 and 2019 the number of people working for digital platforms in the UK doubled to 4.7 million, almost one in ten of the entire workforce.[9] Meanwhile younger workers in traditional professions are being 'proletarianised' as their wages fail to keep pace with the rising cost of living: early-career lawyers, lecturers, accountants or architects face lower pay, less stable jobs, poorer working conditions and higher levels of freelancing than their older colleagues ever experienced, and even junior judges are operating under zero-hours contract conditions.[10] Up to 10 million people in Britain are now estimated to be in some form of precarious work, a trend that stretches well beyond the newfangled 'gig economy' and into occupations that have existed for centuries, like teaching, caring and hospital-ity.[11] Across all these sectors, talk of workplace 'flexibility' is increasingly entwined with new forms of intensive manage-ment – often, in many industries, now conducted by algorithms rather than human bosses – and the growing surveillance of workers that goes with it.

These tendencies have atomised and fragmented workers, especially because they have been accompanied by a relentless political assault on trade unions. Organised labour, runs the prevailing narrative, has never been weaker when set against the growing power of capital. Official trade union membership figures support this: whereas half of all workers carried a union card in the 1970s, only a fifth do so today. Among young people in the private sector, where most economic growth is concentrated, that figure falls to 6%. In 2017 the number of strikes in the UK was the lowest since records began and the number of total strike days lost numbered just 170,000 – compared to 29.5 million in 1979, year of the so-called 'Winter of Discontent'.[12] 'The strike is dead. Or near as dead as makes no difference,' claimed Sean O'Grady, a senior editor at the *Independent* newspaper, in response to those figures.[13] O'Grady went on to marshal a familiar argument as to why union activism was apparently withering. 'The reasons for this historic level of UK industrial calm are well known,' he explained. 'Unions are nowhere near as powerful as once they were. That, in turn, is down to structural changes in the workforce, such as casualisation – how does a freelance journalist, for example, go on strike? The gig economy and the rise of self-employment have also destroyed the very concept of a strike, because you can't go on strike against yourself, or work to rule when it's you making the rules, can you?'

All of which makes sense – if the only kind of labour militancy you're familiar with looks like the battles of the past, with old-school, beer-swilling union bosses on one side of a table hammering it out with buttoned-up corporate executives on the other. But it doesn't account for how, in the places where workers are seemingly most marginalised and vulnerable, an unlikely movement is currently under way to rewire the economy from within. O'Grady's argument has nothing to say about the maintenance cupboards where agency staff are busy plotting wildcat walkouts, nor about the takeaway couriers using their bikes and motorcycles to bring major roads to a standstill, nor about the glitzy London gallery openings that are being overrun by protesting workers, nor about the warehouse operatives organising clandestinely through WhatsApp, nor about the pub pint-pullers and the film ushers and the security guards and the video-game coders who are watching all this, learning, and following suit. It has nothing to say about Fatima, and her defiant, dizzying dancing in the rain, because it has failed to notice how the changing economy has fuelled new and dramatic forms of workers' resistance, and exposed new frailties for capital. The reality is that labour militancy hasn't died at all. It is simply playing out on fresh terrain, and fizzing with life as it does so.

*

In the early hours of 1 May 2018, I drove to a provincial roundabout on the outskirts of Cambridge to see what that fresh terrain looks like. It was a bright, cloudless morning, and on the edge of a McDonald's car park, rising above the dawn traffic on Newmarket Road, a twenty-four-year-old named Tom Holliday was bellowing into a megaphone. 'I!' he shouted, throwing his whole upper body into the cry. 'I!' echoed a crowd of onlookers. 'Believe!' Tom continued. 'Believe!' the group responded. 'That we!' he roared, 'Will win!' Those around Tom bobbed up and down to the chant, and a thickset man with a shaved head and long overcoat who was standing further off by the restaurant doors quietly took a notebook out of his pocket and scribbled something down. I wandered over to chat, but he wouldn't tell me his name or job title. 'Direct all your questions to the McDonald's national press office,' he said curtly, staring past me.

The man's irritation, and that of the McDonald's management team he represented, was understandable. This was the workforce that supposedly could not be unionised, the company whose virtually limitless financial power and global reach meant that in any battle with its low-pay, insecure employees, the latter would always be crushed. But now instead of standing behind the counter and serving up Egg McMuffins for the

morning rush, Tom was out here by the roundabout, demanding a living wage of £10 an hour and sending rhythmic jolts
through potential customers with yells of 'If we don't get it,
shut it down!' He was joined by his colleague Annalise Peters,
a twenty-year-old student studying French and economics who
looked part proud, part awestruck to be the focus of so much
attention. Later, as we travelled fifty miles south to join up with
other striking McDonald's staff in Watford, the home town
of company CEO Steve Easterbrook (who in 2017 was paid
£8,200 per hour, 113,000% more than his striking staff), we
were also joined by twenty-six-year-old local Richard Shattock,
by twenty-three-year-old Ali Waqar from Manchester, by his
co-worker Lauren McCourt, by Shen Batmaz and Lewis Baker
from Crayford, and by many, many others: all young, pissed off
and fearless, all pumped with that unique tincture of exaspera-
tion and elation that comes when you're at the end of your
tether but have resolved to do something about it.[14] 'It's hard
because everyone is spread out, everyone is on different shift
patterns,' explained Annalise, who had been trying to organise
her fellow staff at the Cambridge branch for nearly a year. 'It
was kind of scary because McDonald's just hasn't seen this
sort of thing in the UK before; they put a lot of messaging out
there which is anti-union, anti-rights, and there was a lot of
push-back from management. To be honest with you, I think
the managers were scared as well. They didn't know what they
were dealing with.'

What management were dealing with was a slow spread
of whispers – from shift to shift, restaurant to restaurant –
announcing that things didn't have to be this way, and that
some people were organising to change them. 'You hear the
stories all the time at work: how everyone is struggling to pay
their bills, what an awful experience they have if they get ill,
if they fall out with a manager who can then mess with their
hours,' Ali told me. 'They don't see us as humans, or workers.'
Lauren, who was earning £7.25 an hour at McDonald's – which
equates to £290 for a forty-hour working week – agreed. 'We're

worker-bots to them,' she said. She often relied on the single free meal she received at work to see her through the day, and was in constant fear of being made homeless. Ali, who like two-thirds of single Britons in their twenties was still living with his parents, described the choice he faced between working enough shifts to keep his head above water, or spending any time with family or friends.[15] 'Human beings are social animals, we're supposed to be able to connect with one another,' he said. 'People are sick of having to deal with that shit. The problem is how to translate those feelings into organising; there's a lot of obstacles in the way, a lot of misinformation. The biggest issue is that there's a systematic lack of knowledge about workers' struggle that has been building for decades, and most people our age just don't know what a union is.'

The solution, according to Shen – who helped organise the very first 'McStrike' in the UK back in 2017 – was to simply start up conversations in the workplace about the lived experience of colleagues. 'I know it sounds really small and stupid, but no one normally comes up to you and just asks, "How are you doing? Is your money situation OK, is your living situation OK, are you getting by, what's happening?"' she explained. 'People will talk to you for hours if you ask them that, and if you show them that you really care. And then the next stage is to say, "OK, what are you going to do about it? Are you going to live on low pay, are you going to be bullied by this manager every day, are you going to live like this for as long as they make you live like this, or are you going to stand up?"' Shen said she often asked her colleagues whether they agreed with the American civil rights movement, or the suffragettes, to which the answer would invariably be yes. 'And I'm like, "Well if you were there at that time, would you have joined those movements and done something?" And people would say yes, of course, because we all like to think we would fight back if we were in the shit, if those around us were in the shit. And so I'd say, "Well we're in the shit now, so let's do something now." You can pass out as many leaflets as you want, you can put up as many posters as you want, but unless you're actually in the workplace, having these conversations, then nothing is going to happen.'

The organisation that Shen started having those conversations with, and for which she now works, was the Bakers, Food and Allied Workers' Union (BFAWU) – a movement that is more than 170 years old, but displays a keen understanding of the specific problems faced by workers in the twenty-first century, particularly the children of the financial crisis like Annalise, Ali and Lauren. 'Young people today are angry,' says Sarah Woolley, a thirty-one-year-old who started work aged sixteen at the bakery chain now known as Greggs, and went on to become a full-time BFAWU official. She knows of McDonald's employees who sofa-surf because they cannot afford rent, employees who spend the night in their cars, employees who sleep on an inflatable mattress with a slow puncture that requires them to get up every few hours to blow it up again. 'They're angry because the lives their parents had are beyond them. I'll be lucky to retire when I'm seventy; there are young people today who feel like they'll be lucky to retire at all. You talk to young people about holidays and they look at you like "what do you mean, holidays?" Young people are so poor they're not reproducing, they're postponing having children because they simply can't afford to. All of the things they were promised growing up are not there for them when they do.'

Crucially, argues Sarah, the very casualisation and insecurity that Sean O'Grady believes is destroying worker militancy is actually fuelling it, because with so many precarious minimum-wage jobs available offering equally crap conditions, there is nothing much to risk by fighting back. 'Young people today are generally not burdened by mortgages,' she says. 'Thatcher's dream was to load workers with debt, frighten them into not taking strike action for fear of losing their home, and often it worked. But most young workers don't own homes now, they're more likely to be sharing rent with five or six people. So workers in the fast-food and hospitality sectors are not

afraid of losing their jobs in the same way as older generations were, because they know that if they get sacked at KFC
they can walk across the road to a Wetherspoons and get a
similar job, on similar poor terms and conditions, and similar
rubbish pay. This generation is not filled with the same fear
of loss as the last generation because they've got nothing left
to lose. That's why young workers are more likely to take
action, and that's why young workers can win.' Shen, with a
wry smile, pointed out that she is the perfect example of this.
'I'm twenty-three, and I have none of the opportunities that
my parents had,' she told me. 'My dad was an immigrant to
this country, and so that's saying something – the fact that he
had so many opportunities and my mum had so many opportunities, compared to me. I won't ever own a house, at least
it seems like that at the moment. I'm in twenty grand worth
of debt as I stand, and I don't have any hope of paying it off.
So again, that question – are you going to live like this for as
long as they make you live like this, or are you going to stand
up? Once someone asks you it explicitly, when you're forced
into that moment where you have to think about it and answer
one way or another ...' She trailed off, and shrugged. 'You're
already in the shit, so why not do something?'

In Cambridge, at the start of the day, just after an initially murderous-looking drive-thru customer was persuaded
to respect the picket line and turn back around without his
milkshake – 'I explained what the protest was about, and also
pointed out that he wasn't wearing a seat belt which is a bad
look for the cameras, and lo and behold he decided to support
us,' grinned Martin Harding, a member of the Fire Brigades
Union who had turned up in solidarity with the McStrikers – a
young Hungarian woman came up to me and asked what was
going on. After telling her about the strike, she snapped some
pictures on her phone excitedly and sent them to a WhatsApp
group of her colleagues. It turns out she worked at a Starbucks
branch in town on a zero-hours contract. She didn't want me
to publish her name, and nor did she want to chat to the union

organisers – for now, she said, she just wanted to watch. She did just that for what seemed like ages, brushing her hair out of her eyes as the wind swirled around us and nodding softly at Tom's chants. 'We should do this,' she concluded, thoughtfully. 'We should be doing this now.' Later, outside the McDonald's store in Watford, I mentioned this encounter to Richard, one of the workers there who had walked out to join the strike. A few moments beforehand he had been up on a soapbox, addressing his managers – who were watching on through the restaurant windows – with such candour and vehemence that it almost hurt to watch: 'You cannot belittle me, you cannot belittle my friends and comrades in our union and in our workplace,' he belted into a microphone, as if daring them to come out and contradict him. Now he was back down on the pavement, wiping the sweat off his brow and swigging from a bottle of water. He'd be back at work tomorrow, and given the speech he'd just made things 'might be a little awkward', he remarked cheerfully, in what struck me as a drastic under-statement. But Richard was more interested in the Starbucks woman, and her brief exposure to the McStrike movement, than he was in discussing the potential personal consequences. 'I believe 100% that we are inspiring other precarious workers, people like her,' he said, breathlessly. 'Because this is not really about McDonalds alone, it is about momentum building up, confidence spreading, and a ball rolling up and down the high street, up and down the country.'

A ball is rolling. Five months later, McDonald's workers walked out again, this time accompanied by striking workers from Wetherspoons, TGI Fridays, Deliveroo and Uber Eats, all demanding a living wage. As well as the McDonald's branches that had taken part in the May Day action, strikes or protests were also recorded in that single October morning at fast-food or pub outlets in London, Bristol, Brighton, Newcastle, Plymouth, Southampton, Milton Keynes, Glasgow and Cardiff. In the past two years, the struggle for a living wage has been taken up by low-paid workers at Sports Direct, Addison Lee, the Picturehouse cinema chain, City Sprint couriers, the catering giant Compass, the pathology service-provider TDL, the University of London, the Royal College of Music, the Royal Opera House and the National Gallery, to name but a few. There is no area of the economy untouched by this wave of protest: no product you have bought, or service you have used, or cultural event you have enjoyed that does not, if you unspool and follow the threads which lie behind it, have a recent workers' confrontation knotted deep within its ecosystem. Some of these mobilisations, such as the McStrike movement, are being led by large, traditional unions like the BFAWU; others, like most of the Deliveroo actions, are not formally organised at all, arising instead out of loose and sometimes spontaneous networks of colleagues. In between those two poles, though, lies something else: a new generation of small, radical, insurgent trade unions that, beyond the radar of most mainstream media outlets, are racking up improbable victories and bringing giant corporations to heel. They're doing it by rethinking what worker militancy looks like, by ignoring all the old rules of union organising, and by putting their faith in people like Fatima – the invisible woman at the heart of Westminster, who decided to make herself seen.

*

In room L67, deep within the bowels of SOAS University's Russell Square campus in central London, a poet, a politician and a sex worker are making polite conversation. United Voices of the World (UVW) don't really do ground level, except when they're marching through streets and blockading entrance doors. Renting ground-level spaces costs money, and UVW has very little of that; instead their meetings tend to take place either below the earth or high above it, looking up or down at the land they plan to storm. Merrily, chaotically, people stream in and find chairs. Then the introductions begin. Everyone in the room takes a turn saying hello; three different languages are spoken, and each word is patiently, painstakingly interpreted for the benefit of everyone else – Nick handling Spanish, and Molly responsible for Portuguese. 'For many in this room,' declares Petros – a lumbering, friendly bear of a man who co-founded UVW in 2014 and remains a key organiser – 'the action next week will be their first strike, and that's a big deal. The stakes are high for the workers involved, and they're high beyond that: these strikes are important politically, socially and culturally. We can set an example here, and leave other unions with no excuse not to follow in our footsteps.' A murmur of approval seeps through the room, triple-staggered as the translations are completed. All the while Petros is speaking, there are fresh arrivals: waving latecomers, groaning buggies, and piles of snacks being repeatedly manoeuvred into position. What started out as a small circle gradually widens and fills to such an extent that it becomes impossible to say where the focal point of the meeting is, or even if there is supposed to be a focal point at all.

There are other trade unionists present, alongside Class War anarchists, earnest students and veterans of UVW's previous campaigns: outsourced cleaners like Susana, for example, who was fired from her job at Topshop for union organising and won an epic legal fight, or Beverley, who helped force the London School of Economics to bring the employment of her and her colleagues in-house. Everyone, without exception, is clapped by everyone else when they have finished saying their hellos, not least because these introductions – which take well over an hour – are not mere formalities or an adjunct to the main proceedings, but the very point of why we're here: they make the breadth of solidarity tangible and visible, large enough and bright enough that you can pick it out with your eyes. The heartiest cheers are reserved for the last group to rise to their feet and address the room: outsourced cleaners from the Royal Borough of Kensington and Chelsea and from the Ministry of Justice, who will be walking out of their workplaces as part of UVW's first ever co-ordinated multi-employer strike in three days' time. 'I've never been in a struggle like this, but I can see now that there's a lot of people fighting like us,' says Marianna Crespo, a tall, refined woman with dark red hair tied back, in a ponytail, who sweeps the floors at the town hall of Britain's richest council. Her colleague Suzete, clad in a stunning print dress and wearing a waterfall of earrings, tells us about the health problems she has suffered in her job and how the outsourcing company which controls her work, Amey – part of the multinational contractor giant Ferrovial, which recorded a net profit of €454 million in 2017 – had washed their hands of responsibility.[16] 'No one is made of steel,' she concludes, prompting a flurry of nods. Carlos, a soft-spoken Brazilian with a thin, kind face who cleans the Ministry of Justice building, talks of how difficult life is when your earnings keep you anchored below the poverty line. 'This is not just for us,' he says. 'We want to change our own history, but also the history of London.' And then finally Fatima, beginning with a long silence and a deep breath to steady her nerves, stands to speak. 'I've worked at the ministry for nine years,' she begins. 'In that time, we have been cleaning the same toilets for almost the same money, but we have been passed between lots of different companies, each of which mistreats us in different ways.' There are managers who bully, she explains, and others who intimidate; as a cleaner, you can be accused of something small and impossible to verify, like bumping into someone with an equipment trolley, and then be placed on disciplinary measures that lead ultimately to dismissal. Fatima is not a natural public performer, like some in the room, but nor is she paralysed with anxiety, like others; she talks slowly, and compellingly, using the breaks for translation as a chance to steady herself and go again. 'In all that time, my pay has gone up by one pound an hour,' she continues. 'But just as bad is the lack of respect. They want people like us to hide away and make do with it.'

The tale of how Fatima, who speaks little English and has never previously been a member of a trade union ('I didn't know they existed,' she told me), found UVW is, in her own words, a *história complicada* – as complicated, perhaps, as the story of UVW itself.[17] When she ran into trouble with her bosses at both the Supreme Court and the Ministry of Justice on the same day a few years ago, Fatima's colleague Eduardo at the latter told her about an organisation he had discovered that could represent workers like her and stand up to managers on their behalf. Without recognition agreements with employers or any advertising budget to speak of (in its last accounts, UVW recorded spending of £3,358 on office communications; the equivalent spend by Unite, Britain's largest union, was just under £3.5 million[18]) the union relies almost entirely on word of mouth to reach new workers, and lives or dies on its reputation among members. With each campaign, that reputation has spread through networks of largely Latin American migrant communities: from the lowest-paid 'facilities management' staff at Sotheby's auction house to the Barbican arts centre, from waiters and kitchen staff at Harrods to recycling-sorters at the dust-sodden Orion Waste plant in east London's Canning Town, and cleaners at the gleaming towers of the Bank of New York Mellon at Canary Wharf up the road. 'We met Petros at first,' remembers Fatima, 'but we couldn't understand each other because he only spoke Spanish, not Portuguese. Then we spoke to Molly, and she explained everything to us and we felt the pride that would come with belonging to a union – *our* union.'

For Petros, that feeling of ownership on the part of members is what makes UVW different from the big, legacy unions of the past, and what is driving the organisation's current record of success. 'Being members-led is about internal democracy and decision-making processes, of course,' he told me. 'But it's also about everything we do being in the interests of our members: every event, every activity, every strike. We could tell people, "join this union and we'll send you emails for the next six months and get some MPs to talk about your campaign" and sure, those things might be useful components of a labour struggle. But they are not going to help build a movement and a community which empowers workers and puts workers at the forefront. We're a fighting, members-led union because through us our members are struggling to be active agents in their workplace, to redefine their relationship not just with their bosses but also with the city they live in, the communities around them.' At UVW, a trade union is not merely a service provider or lobbying organisation for its members, but rather something alive and antagonistic, something that percolates up from the shop floor and bleeds beyond the edges of the workplace.

That vision is born in part out of Petros's early frustrations upon having returned to Britain from Venezuela, where he had spent a few years in the late 2000s. Like Ed and Jacob, founders of the Demand the Impossible radical education workshop that Layla, Kyle and Hannah ended up joining in Manchester, Petros found those years following the financial crash to be a disturbing wasteland of non-disturbance: everything had changed, and yet everything appeared to stay the same. He threw himself into Latin American solidarity activities in London, but found their limitations dispiriting, particularly when he came across migrants who had employment problems. At the Latin American Workers Association, where Petros volunteered most Saturdays to help with English classes, the best they could do was refer people to the gargantuan public-sector union UNISON. 'I was looking for some way, any way, to directly support workers in their struggles,' he remembers. 'I wanted to offer whatever help I could, even though I didn't know what that help was yet.' In 2012, he saw references on Facebook to a picket line organised by the UK cleaners' branch of the International Workers of the World (IWW), the venerable labour movement better known as the 'Wobblies' (the origin of the nickname is unknown, but theories range from it being an accidental mispronunciation of the organisation's initials by non-native-English-speakers to it being a code word for industrial sabotage).[19] He and his then partner, Vera Weghmann, decided to check it out, but ended up going to the wrong meeting place and only came across the striking workers by chance on their way home. It was a *Sliding Doors* moment;

from then on, the pair threw themselves head-first into union organising. 'I was so eager to get involved that at first they thought I was an undercover cop,' Petros grinned.

When a family friend who knew Petros's mother from the local church got in touch to say that she and her largely Brazilian and Colombian colleagues were being made redundant from their cleaning jobs at the medical school St George's, University of London, Petros and Vera agreed to help represent them. In retrospect, it's clear that the dynamics of that dispute would go on to shape the DNA of the yet-to-be-created United Voices of the World; at the time, however, they felt like they were making it up as they went along. 'I googled some employment law and went into a meeting with the management,' Petros said. 'I didn't know what I was talking about, but I put a load of questions to them and when they couldn't answer I told them that what they were doing was illegal. We followed that up with a protest against the redundancies and thought, while we're at it, fuck it, let's demand the living wage as well.' This fly-by-the-seat-of-your-pants approach was a million miles away from the glacial, bureaucratic machinations of traditional trade union decision-making, including that of the local UNISON branch which had a formal recognition agreement at the time with St George's and quickly distanced themselves from the cleaners' militancy. 'We are dealing with this diplomatically,' insisted UNISON's branch secretary, in a letter sent to those supporting the cleaners' campaign. It went on to describe solidarity with the cleaners' actions as 'not appropriate' and 'unhelpful'.[20] 'I would ask you not to interfere in our branch affairs,' the letter concluded. Petros and Vera pressed on: messages were sent to every member of staff at St George's, petitions circulated, and friends and family mobilised to make some noise. Within a few days the redundancies were cancelled and the cleaners were granted a 30% pay rise. 'We pulled this off with a handful of people, a few emails and flyers, the workers at the forefront, and we didn't have to kidnap anybody,' recalled Petros. UNISON, meanwhile, put out a press release taking credit for the victory and saying that they were delighted to see the cleaners finally obtain the living wage.[21] 'They didn't know the name of a single cleaner there, let alone represent them or support our campaign in any way,' spat Petros, still visibly angry all these years later. 'We didn't have a big organisation behind us, or any resources, but we got something out of nothing. My feeling was that we had won with so little, imagine what we could do with much more.'

UVW was founded in 2014, and that feeling – of winning with so little, and pushing at the limits of possibility to achieve even more – continues to permeate everything it does. 'What we tried to do is create a trade unionism which fits the working environment of the twenty-first century,' Vera told me. 'And so we had to be creative, because that environment is different now.' All members have an equal say in campaigns; UVW does not generally seek official recognition agreements with employers, has not affiliated with the national federation of trade unions, the TUC, and remains the only trade union in Britain not to have a general secretary. 'We're not interested in providing a doctor–patient relationship, where workers come along for a quick consultation and an expert diagnoses their problem and solves it for them,' says Petros. 'We are building a movement.' At one of the union's monthly gatherings, held in a dilapidated office space high above the Elephant and Castle shopping centre, I watched about seventy members work through employment law case studies below a huge UVW banner, creased and war-specked, which was affixed with pink fluorescent tape to a Blu Tack-stained wall. Around us lay the flotsam of countless autonomous struggles in the precarious economy: leaflets put out by the striking Ritzy cinema workers calling for a boycott of the Picturehouse chain; press cuttings about recent actions taken by UVW's sister union, the Independent Workers of Great Britain (IWGB); notes from the English Collective of Prostitutes, who were in ongoing talks with UVW about joining forces. 'When are you entitled to a written contract and can you ask for it to be in

Spanish?' queried one young woman. 'What if the boss tells you he prefers hiring Ecuadorians over Colombians?' asked her friend. An older man in a smart hat, pink polka-dot shirt unbuttoned to the mid-chest and a silver cross swinging from his neck demanded to know whether it was legal for a manager to reduce your wages after you'd already started working for them. 'It's only legal for a manager to do this if he informs you of it and you don't say no,' replied Petros, the cranes and towers of south London's skyline shimmering in the summer haze behind him. 'It's only possible if you don't speak up, don't join a union, don't resist.'

On the last weekend before Fatima and her colleagues at the Ministry of Justice were set to walk out, alongside their counterparts at the Royal Borough of Kensington and Chelsea, UVW held a fundraising party for the strike in a ramshackle old industrial unit in Hackney Wick. Excitement was building, and so were nerves. After half a decade as the most prominent face of UVW, Petros was stepping back for a while to make space for a new, all-female generation of organisers to take the lead, and it was a transitional moment for other reasons too. UVW had taken on some huge names in the past during its campaigns, but never, directly, the government itself; nor had it attempted to combine strikes by multiple workforces in multiple workplaces in a single action. Press interest was growing, and big, TUC-affiliated trade unions like the Public and Commercial Services Union were making noises about working with UVW to support the cleaners' campaign. Always the underdog, always the outsider, it suddenly felt like UVW's successes, achieved stubbornly and spectacularly on its own terms, had propelled it to the cusp of something bigger, although nobody knew quite what. 'Next week is huge for us,' Petros confided, fighting to raise his voice above the music. 'I just hope ...' He trailed off, and gave me that apologetic smile you give when you can't make yourself heard at a party. The venue, consisting of an outdoor corridor, an oversized living room, and a single loo ('No drugs in toilet / PS anywhere else is good' read a handwritten sign on the door) was furnished with a broken bathtub, a sheet of MDF serving as a makeshift bar, and a mishmash of sofas spilling their stuffing into the gloom. A small round stage had been erected at the back of the room, and on it a succession of pole dancers – the night had been co-organised by the East London Strippers Collective – whirled into light. Old wooden beams above our heads shook with the bass, and the space was heaving with people. Petros surveyed the scene with what seemed like an almost nostalgic satisfaction, then leaned his head towards me and tried again. 'I just hope we do ourselves proud,' he shouted.

*

In 1906, author Upton Sinclair published his novel *The Jungle*, which journeyed into the dark underbelly of the American food industry and revealed the indignities and abuses imposed upon its workers. At the heart of these abuses stood the factory assembly line, a relatively new innovation in mass production that was relentlessly and unapologetically engineered to 'use everything about the hog except the squeal'.[22] 'It was pork-making by machinery, pork-making by applied mathematics,' observed Sinclair, who had spent weeks labouring undercover in the Chicago meat-packing district to gather material. And it wasn't only the pigs which he saw as being disembowelled by this technological leap forward; like many who were concerned about the future of working-class organisation throughout the early part of the twentieth century, Sinclair feared that the assembly line could destroy the power and militancy of those who manned it too. 'They were beaten,' he wrote of his two main protagonists, Lithuanian immigrants struggling to cling on to their humanity and survive on the edges of a brutal economy. 'They had lost the game, they were swept aside.'[23]

But the assembly line, which offered such advantages to capital in the form of increased efficiency and profit and initially threatened to homogenise and deskill industrial work, handing technical control of production to managers and making it easier to draft in reserve armies of casual labour – severely weakening the collective bargaining power of workers in the process – did not result in the collapse of labour militancy.[24] In fact, the opposite occurred: by the mid-1930s, when a huge strike wave roiled America's auto industry, it was clear that this technology also provided workers with new pressure points to exploit, new opportunities to disrupt. After the great sit-in at the General Motors plant in Flint, Michigan in late 1936 and early 1937, which lasted for forty-four days and saw workers using hinges and bolts to fend off armed police who were trying to seize the factory, it became apparent that even a small number of labour activists in a single plant were capable of bringing the whole assembly line to a halt, and that gumming up production in one location had a knock-on effect across a company's entire corporate empire.[25] As at every stage of capitalism's evolution, new modes of economic production had simultaneously created new forms of exploitation *and* new forms of resistance – both of them drawing on the same tools.

If Sinclair were writing a novel about dehumanising work in the post-crash economy today, it might be Amazon warehouses in towns like Tilbury that he would seek out: the meat-packing assembly lines of our own age, where technological advances meld with capital's need to extract every last ounce of efficiency from its workforce. Like the McStrike protesters, Amazon employees complain of being seen as robots by their bosses, who electronically track the speed of their work, subject them to impossibly ambitious performance targets, and force them to toil through sickness and late-stage pregnancy. A union has also reported being told of a women who claims to have suffered a miscarriage on the job ('We don't recognise these allegations as an accurate portrayal of activities in our buildings,' responded Amazon in a statement).[26] In the US, Amazon has been granted patents for ultrasonic wristbands which, when attached to workers, are capable of tracking their every hand movement and providing 'haptic feedback' (i.e. vibrations) if it detects that a worker is carrying out their tasks suboptimally.[27] As far as monitoring of workers goes, such wristbands may already be outdated. In 2017, a vending-machines company in Wisconsin made global headlines by microchipping dozens of its workers; when paired with a GPS app, anyone with the appropriate authorisations can track the wearer's location twenty-four hours a day. 'We decided to put it in employees as a form of convenience for them,' explained CEO Todd Westby.[28] 'We do not plan on taking it out.' Some Chinese firms have reportedly implanted sensors in hats and helmets which scan workers' brainwaves to detect feelings of fatigue, stress and anger.[29]

Brain-scanning helmets and their ilk fascinate us because they appear to be quirky outliers, portending some vaguely dystopian future. But an entire sub-industry of employer surveillance tools has evolved in recent years to enable bosses to follow their workers' web activity, the strokes of their keyboard, and even the tone of their voice.[30] And for many tens of thousands of workers in Britain's gig economy, core elements of that dystopian future are here now, already mundane. The work of most Deliveroo riders and Uber drivers, for example, is governed almost entirely by the companies' smartphone apps; their only physical contact with the firms comes when they initially sign up, and even then it is likely to involve nothing more than a meeting with another precarious worker brought in to staff the recruitment centres.[31] Sinclair described a world of work in which figures of authority were ever-present on the assembly line, 'ranged in ranks and grades like an army … managers and superintendents and foremen, each one driving the man next below him and trying to squeeze out of him as much work as possible'.[32] Over a hundred years later that process of management has, for many of us, been entirely automated: it is the app itself that assigns jobs, records and ranks performance, and delivers feedback in the form of both incentives and discipline. Jamie Woodcock, a sociologist of work at Oxford University, calls this 'management by algorithmic panopticon', in reference to the philosopher Jeremy Bentham's vision of a prison and surveillance system in which inmates are motivated into submission by the knowledge that they are potentially being watched at any time. 'Deliveroo workers have detailed how "there isn't that person telling you what to do, it's the algorithm" and that "the algorithm is the boss",' says Woodcock.[33] 'The management function comes mainly in the form of emails that rate performance – although these don't tell workers the actual targets, only whether they were meeting them or not. This introduces that demand to self-regulate found with the panopticon, inculcating the feeling of being constantly tracked and watched, despite the lack of a physical boss or supervisor.' As James Farrar, an Uber driver and chair of the United Private Hire Drivers branch of the IWGB – UVW's sister union – points out, algorithmic management disempowers workers in relation to capital not only through the imposition of constant surveillance, but also through an imbalance in access to the data generated by it. 'They do collect an awful lot of information,' he says.[34] 'One of the things they will report to you on a daily basis is how good your acceleration and braking has been. You get a rating. The question is: why are they collecting that information? My concern with it is, this information is being fed into a dispatch algorithm [the automated app-based process deciding which drivers are assigned journeys requested by customers]. We should have access to the data, and understand how it's being used.'

With this level of technological surveillance by bosses, and the asymmetries of power created by their one-way control over the information gathered, what hope remains for workers' attempts to challenge their decisions – especially when that technology is embedded within an employment system that classifies Deliveroo riders and Uber drivers as self-employed contractors, shorn of many basic labour rights? The answer is: plenty. As Woodcock puts it, the digital outsourcing model upon which Uber and Deliveroo are built throws up a double precariousness: one for workers, who enjoy little protection if they are injured on the job or find their earnings dipping below the minimum wage, and another for bosses – who, with virtually no human managers overseeing their workforce, have few tools at their disposal to deal with organised resistance.[35] And organised resistance by digitally outsourced workers has erupted repeatedly on the streets of major cities in recent years, usually beginning in the back-alley spots where delivery riders are encouraged by their apps to congregate and then fanning out rapidly through WhatsApp networks, word of mouth, and some technological trickery. In 2016, for example, an announcement by Deliveroo that it would soon be unilaterally altering its rider payment structure prompted a six-day 'strike' in which riders acted en masse to make themselves unavailable for orders.[36] Colleagues from Deliveroo's rivals, Uber Eats, swiftly followed suit, and began taking advantage of a promotional offer within the app which granted new customers £5 off their first order. By repeatedly creating new accounts and ordering low-value meals to be delivered to the picket line, the strikers amassed both a mountain of free food at Uber's expense and a steady stream of fellow riders, who would turn up with the order only to be met by a sea of radicalised peers cheering their arrival and chanting 'Log out, log out!' In the words of one Deliveroo rider, the very technology that was designed to control workers was now being turned against their managers, allowing riders to 'occupy the system in a way'.[37] Not unlike the assembly line of the last century, and the auto strikes in Flint that subverted it, a tool engineered for capital was being hacked by the labour force. 'If it's a wildcat strike,' the Deliveroo rider told Woodcock, 'it's like a sit-in.'

That sort of hacking can be found throughout the contemporary economy. New apps abound which allow workers to log abuse by managers, read up on their rights, organise their workplace and compare pay rates both with those in similar jobs in their industry and with their own company's financial results – a powerful weapon for agitating colleagues and rejecting management explanations for low wages.[38] The information asymmetry at the core of digital platforms like

Uber that union rep James Farrar referred to is being gradually undermined by a vibrant network of driver forums with hundreds of thousands of members sharing stories, advice, communications from Uber received through the app and payment details – including screenshots of receipts and monthly income tallies – enabling drivers to collectively gain an understanding of how the app's secretive ratings systems and dispatch algorithms actually operate.[39] Among other things, this sort of crowdsourced information provides drivers with the opportunity to game the system, for example by agreeing to log off from the app simultaneously, thereby tricking Uber's algorithms into thinking there is a shortage of drivers and implementing surge pricing to tempt them back.[40] Supermarket pickers – the staff who gather items from store shelves to fulfil online orders for home delivery – have developed an array of techniques to push back against the anxiety and humiliation that comes with missing impossible performance goals. Because targets for each worker are set by algorithms based on the speed with which they picked orders the previous week, as logged by handheld electronic devices carried by each member of staff, some pickers deliberately leave the handsets on during their lunch break so as to drive down their average speed and generate lower targets for the following week; others intentionally store their devices incorrectly in the charging station at the end of a shift, ensuring that the handset will run out of battery during work hours the next day and give them an extra unplanned break while a replacement is sorted.[41] 'These acts are just two examples of latent resistance with which workers are constantly experimenting to make their jobs easier,' says Adam Barr, who worked as a picker at a large Sainsbury's store in north London.[42] He argues that these technologies are a platform upon which the workers' struggles of the future will be fought.

Worker subversion of new management and surveillance technologies is merely one among many clandestine vulnerabilities inside the current economic system. Another can be found within those long, just-in-time supply chains that may appear to whip car parts and chicken meat and consumer electronics effortlessly across dozens of national borders but which are, in reality, almost entirely reliant on dense physical infrastructure. That network includes factories, warehouses and lorry depots, and the airports, stations, hotels, hospitals and schools that go with them: all firmly embedded in their geographical surroundings, and all highly susceptible to strike actions by those who maintain, guard and – like Fatima – clean them.[43] In Britain, the cleaning sector alone employs 700,000 people.[44] And, as the McStrike movement indicates, the very precariousness of those workers is itself a fuel for labour militancy; the more that low pay and casualisation becomes the norm, the more that those on the wrong end of it have nothing to lose by striking back. Previously, those with financial support from their family or the privilege of a higher education were generally able to avoid this kind of insecurity. Today, as the trade unionist and former Deliveroo rider Callum Cant argues, the middle is being hollowed out: there are a lucky few on a path towards permanent insulation from money worries, and the rest who are on a downward trajectory in terms of real-term income and work/life satisfaction.[45] Half of all young people now attend university, where many will learn about times when things worked differently; after they graduate, the majority will join Britain's fastest-growing social class, the 'lumpen-bourgeoisie' – a stratum occupied by people whose background would traditionally have guaranteed a relatively secure and professionalised working life, but who instead find themselves struggling to make ends meet. Here, the gap between life expectations and outcomes yawns wide, and there is fertile soil from which shoots of resistance can grow taller.[46]

That is not to suggest that there are no gradations and contradictions within the large body of people increasingly disempowered by today's economy. Those with salaried jobs, even under fast-degrading working conditions, still enjoy more security than their freelance or gig-economy counterparts. The working life of a self-employed creative professional, however stressful, is qualitatively different from that of somebody on a minimum-wage, zero-hours contract. It shouldn't be forgotten that precarious employment has been the norm for centuries, and that for many around the world – especially in the global south – that fact of life has continued uninterrupted into the present day.[47] 'The young mother who now waits on call for a day's work is the direct descendant of the nineteenth-century prole, hanging around the waterfront for a sliver of waged labour,' the labour academic Steven Parfitt has observed.[48] But what binds the lived experiences of many different social groups in the UK today is the sense that work in all its many guises is not working for them, and that there are tools within reach that might change that. In 2019, UVW reached another milestone with the opening of its Legal Sector Workers United division, bringing together paralegals, solicitors, barristers, receptionists, interns, personal assistants, administrative staff and cleaners. 'We don't ask who you are,' explained Vera, arguing that the idea of trade union branches determined by a single job title is outdated. 'What matters is that you want to achieve workers' justice, and are happy to see workers in that struggle at the forefront.'

That struggle is global. It is not a coincidence that participants in the McStrike protests used chants adapted from the US 'Fight for $15' movement against low pay, nor that organisers from the SEIU – an American trade union representing precarious workers – joined the rally in Watford. The wildcat strikes by Deliveroo riders in British cities have been inspired and replicated by colleagues in Belgium, Holland, France, Germany, Australia and Hong Kong, to name but a few.[49] On the WhatsApp thread shared by UVW's organisers, barely a day goes by without a message from a similar union or workers' collective abroad being forwarded on to the group – hotel chambermaids in Paris, textile operatives in Mexico, migrant workers in Uzbekistan, Ukraine and Moldova – requesting help, sharing advice, or offering solidarity. Historian Eric Hobsbawm once described surges in labour militancy as 'accumulations of inflammable materials which only ignite periodically, as it were under compressions'.[50] Throughout the post-crash world, such compressions are piling up at pace upon workers.[51]

*

Like all great rebellions, things didn't really get started until the loudspeaker turned up. It was balanced perilously on a dodgy sack truck, big, dented and moth-eaten at the corners, packing a punch firm enough to shake walls. Up to that point, the picket line was solid, but dutiful: Molly, crouched in the Ministry of Justice doorway, shaking a bucket; Suzete handing out leaflets to tired-looking civil servants arriving early at their desks; Carlos and Fatima standing sentinel at each end of the giant UVW banner, stretching it out across the windows of government so that its fierce yellow canvas obscured the dark-tinted glass behind. Fatima had a plastic bag tied around her wrist that she had carefully filled with snacks and bottled water, and which she clung to tightly throughout the day. After the immense risks she and her colleagues had taken, all the frenzied anticipation and strained positivity that had been necessary to get to this point, I thought that she might feel deflated at the sight of so many of her desk-job colleagues ignoring the strike action and barging into the entrance foyer regardless; judging by how few of them stopped to engage with the cleaners on their way in, it appeared that hardly any of them looked upon Fatima as a colleague at all. But Fatima was beaming, her head held high in the early-morning sun, her smile cracking wider with each sup-portive car horn, each clink marking a donation to the strike fund, each original protest chant that Molly bellowed into the megaphone with a primal roar. 'This is beautiful,' she told me, surveying the scene. 'I love it.' Two days previously, an arti-cle about the forthcoming walkout had been published in the *Observer*, accompanied by a photo of Fatima. 'You know, there was a particular woman here,' Fatima divulged, chuckling with disbelief, 'who came into one of the bathrooms recently while I was cleaning it and ordered me to move aside. I explained I had to be there to clean it, but she pushed me out of the way and walked in anyway. Well, yesterday that same woman came up to me because she saw my photo in the newspaper, and she said, "I'm sorry that I spoke to you really badly."' Fatima paused and looked up at the brutalist shell of 102 Petty France, the giant office complex which houses the ministry. 'I couldn't sleep last night thinking about that, and thinking about the strike today. She treated me like a human being. Now anyone who wants to mistreat us has to think twice.' There was a screech, and then a crackle; earlier, someone had been sent off to the shops around Victoria to track down a working aux cord, and now someone else was trying to jam that cord experimentally into different connection points on the back of the speaker. After a further blast of unhappy static there was a click, and suddenly our little corner of Westminster convulsed with sound. The music was Spanish punk band Ska-P and their rollicking anthem 'El Vals del Obrero' ('The Waltz of the Worker'). '¡*Sí, señor! ¡Sí, señor! Somos la revolución, tu enemigo es el patron* ...' the speaker blared, as passers-by cheered and Molly and Maria twirled manically around the pavement, clapping and hollering and chest-bumping with glee. 'Yes, sir! Yes, sir! We are the revolution, your enemy is the master ...'

Over the next three days, UVW's most ambitious strike to date unfolded with a wild plasticity: if you tried to prod or push or contain it within one corner, it simply flowed around you and reformed somewhere else. Decisions were made on the hoof via text message, or impromptu huddles in the pub, or shouted questions and nodded answers flung over the noise of sirens. Everywhere was a fiesta, so much so that by the end it felt hard to imagine that any trade union protest could ever take place without being drenched in dancing, salsa and song. When the time came for the first movement of the flying picket line, necessitating a three-mile journey west from St James's Park to Kensington and Chelsea town hall, we packed up and traipsed through the winding backstreets and major thoroughfares of

Belgravia – Molly at the helm with a microphone, an inexhaustible font of choral dynamism, while Ministry of Justice striker Osvaldo and UVW's unofficial photographer Gordon took turns to drag the speaker behind her, sweating hard and attempting gamely to keep it within Bluetooth range. I was under the impression that we were looking for the bus, the one UVW must have hired for the day to transport everyone between the different strike locations; it was only after fifteen minutes of haphazard marching that I realised we were looking for *a* bus, any bus, that happened to be travelling in the right direction. 'I'm going to be a mother today and advise you to preserve your energy,' Shiri – one of UVW's key organisers – said quietly to Molly, as we rolled our mobile carnival through the doors of the No. 52. Onboard, someone began buttering dozens of sandwiches; someone else whipped out a laptop and began tapping out a press release on the fly. I looked around. No one was in charge, and although each person was doing all they could for everyone around them, nobody was doing anything on someone else's behalf. There weren't any passive victims or noble saviours to be found here, just a bunch of people crammed on to the top deck of a bus to Willesden Garage, fighting to take control of their future by organising collectively for themselves.

That evening, Kensington and Chelsea council held a planning meeting at the town hall. Concealed, to some degree, within a steady stream of genteel locals, UVW supporters filtered in to the conference room under the direction of scouts who had been sent ahead. Inside, the councillors were seated around a large table, flanked on one side by rows of chairs that were quickly filled by public attendees: neat lines of pastel shirts and floral dresses, interrupted occasionally by a green Mohican or a red UVW T-shirt reading '*No más invisibles*' ('Invisible No More'). The committee chair, Quentin Marshall – a Conservative councillor who is also director of Weatherbys, a private bank (he previously oversaw £30 billion of assets at Coutts) – opened proceedings with a somewhat nervous cough, and was swiftly interrupted by a yell from the back of the room demanding to know what the council was going to do about their cleaners' campaign for a living wage.[52] Marshall couldn't see exactly where the question had come from, but he flashed a pained smile in its general direction. 'Erm, thank you,' he said, 'but I'm afraid that's not one of the areas we'll be discussing today.' There was a rumble of dissent, and Petros clambered to his feet. 'Excuse me, but I don't accept that answer,' he responded. Petros has the kind of voice that is set by default to thunder; it gives him a tremendous ability to fill a room with words, without ever sounding like he is breaking into a shout. 'Everyone sitting around that table has the power to influence the outcome of a dispute that the cleaners are engaged in with the council. The cleaners have been impoverished by this council over the past ten, twenty, thirty years. They have been cruelly kept on the lowest possible legally minimum wages. They have been over-worked, they have been disregarded, mistreated, disrespected, and they've been forced for the first time to take strike action today. All they're asking for is £10.20 an hour, to be paid in a year what some of you guys claim in annual expenses.'

The councillors sat frozen; no one dared move or interrupt for fear of becoming the focal point of Petros's fury. Two security guards stood braced by the door, waiting for instructions, but none materialised. It was as if all the power bound up in the minutes and schedules and paperwork on one side of the room had suddenly been angled on a slant; no one knew whether it would hold on, or tumble to the floor. 'The contempt that you as councillors have held for the cleaners over the years is nauseating,' continued Petros. 'No matter how many hours your cleaners work they will live below the poverty line, and to be paid a wage which pushes you below the poverty line in this city, within a council that has so many millions in its coffers and so many rich councillors, is unforgivable. You are playing with these cleaners like they're your bloody servants.' Marshall glanced around the table in search of an escape route among his colleagues, but all their eyes avoided his. He pulled his shoulders back, swallowed and turned to face Petros. 'Thank you very much for that contribution,' he ventured, optimistically, 'but as I mentioned this is a meeting to discuss planning and is not the right forum ...' Petros's volume dial leapt up a notch; now he really was shouting. 'The cleaners have been trying to have meetings with the council for the past three months!' he boomed, and I saw Marshall wince at the force of it. 'They have sent ten invitations to meet with the council's leadership team, but no one has even had the common decency to provide an official response to the cleaners' demands! So with all due respect this *is* the right forum, because you haven't given them any other!' Amid general uproar, Marshall rose and announced that he was adjourning the meeting; most of the other councillors joined him as he gathered his papers and made rapidly for a door that led to an inner chamber which was barred to the general public. That might have been that, except for the fact that the UVW supporters stayed where they were, singing and chanting and waving their banners until the last of the sunlight had gone and darkness was creeping through the windows. Eventually a councillor named Catherine Faulks, who sat on the council's leadership team, addressed the occupation and suggested that senior council members could meet with the trade union in exchange for an end to the ongoing disorder. 'Nine o'clock tomorrow morning, on the picket line,' insisted Petros after conferring with those around him. You could tell from Faulks's face that this wasn't what she'd had in mind at all, but of course UVW rarely does what others have in mind, which is precisely how it had got as far as this. 'OK,' replied Faulks, looking weary. 'We'll come to the picket line in the morning, and we'll talk about this.'

She was true to her word. Faulks was there at nine o'clock sharp, accompanied by three of her colleagues: Barry Quirk, the council's chief executive; Sarah Addenbrooke, another member of the council's leadership team; and Ian Wason, a newly elected councillor with a background in South African debt management.[53] They stood at the bottom of the town hall steps, at the centre of a surreal tableau, with Petros and Maria on one side, a small group of police officers standing watchfully on the other, and a ring of people who for years had tidied the quartet's desks, swept their floors and scrubbed their toilets surrounding them: Suzete and Mirna, Rafael and Marianna, Nestor, Alba, Alexandra and many more – some holding children in their arms, others clasping vuvuzelas, or maracas, or pots and pans in one hand and spoons with which to bang them in the other. The inhabitants of two realms of work that had long existed alongside one another, while remaining a universe apart, were now colliding, and it was obvious to anyone present who was drawing strength from that collision, and who was leaking it. 'We're not going to have this meeting out here, we'll have to move it indoors,' muttered Faulks to Quirk under her breath, but it was too late; Petros was already introducing everyone over the loudspeaker, and handing the microphone over to Faulks so that she could get things under way. She looked at it as if it were a hand grenade, then rallied. 'Hello, hello, good morning,' she began brightly, and then leapt out of her skin as Maria chimed in on a second microphone to translate her words for non-English speakers. Quirk, clad in a blue-check blazer and red tie, tried to nod supportively. Wason kept his hands crossed solemnly in front of him and alternated between staring down at the floor or up at the clouds, as if he were observing a minute's silence, or about to launch into the national anthem. One by one they listened wordlessly, awkwardly, as the striking cleaners took turns to describe the impossibilities of their working lives, the challenge of surviving without a living wage, and the humiliation, as Nestor put it, of functioning 'not as human beings, but machines'. After more than half an hour of this, Quirk apologised and explained he had another meeting to get to. 'It's been thirty-five minutes, and some of these cleaners have been waiting eight years for this opportunity,' replied Petros, without skipping a beat. 'I think a few more minutes are in order.'

At the end of it all, Quirk took a deep breath, asked for the microphone, and announced that the council would accept the implementation of a London Living Wage in principle, promising to set up a meeting between UVW and the overall leader of Kensington and Chelsea council, Elizabeth Campbell, to discuss the details. I was expecting a volley of cheers, but Petros didn't flinch. He demanded that a date for the meeting was set there and then, and refused to draw anything to a close until that happened. Incredulously, Quirk and Faulks fished out their diaries and began flicking through pages in the breeze, as we all watched on without a sound: the cleaners, Petros and Maria, the rest of UVW's supporters, the council administrators who were leaning out of their windows to catch a glimpse of what was happening, and the police, whose walkie-talkies occasionally hissed and spluttered across the silence. After some minutes, a day and a time were confirmed; the council representatives shook hands with each of the cleaners and took their leave. In the open air, a few feet below their offices but a million miles away from their comfort zone, they had been forced to fight a battle with low-pay Britain on unfamiliar terrain; they had been made to negotiate, made to supplicate, and they had lost. On the way back to the Ministry of Justice – we took the tube this time – the trusty speaker pumped out 'Despacito', and our carriage pulsed with joy. UVW rarely simply travel along the public transport network; they seem to ripple and reverberate through it, leaving inquisitive glances and involuntary grins in their wake, and that was never more true than now. Petros stood propped against a door, gasping hoarsely. Molly swung from a pole. Suzete was in tears. When we finally arrived back at 102 Petty France, there was little discussion needed. Nobody gave an order or made a signal, but everyone knew. A flare was released, a cry went up, and we surged past the security barriers to begin an occupation of the ministry.

It would be easy to dismiss Kensington and Chelsea council, and the Ministry of Justice, and McDonald's, Uber and Deliveroo as the chief enemy in all this: cartoon villains that might be persuaded to do the right thing if only enough pressure could be applied to them. But the problem that those at the forefront of the movement against low pay and precariousness are confronting is not really unethical employers, nor uncaring managers, nor the flaws of new technology. What is pinning them down is the conviction that our current political economy is the only one available; that insecurity is an inevitable by-product of our yearning to escape the bad old days of Fordist drudgery, of our desire to be flexible and free. The choice so often presented to us is one between our current trajectory – with its haptic-feedback wristbands and the scrubbing of sixteen floors of toilets, five times each per day – and a retrograde return to the past; between the something workers have now and a nothing inside the space where an alternative should be. 'As long as we accept disempowerment of workers in the name of greater efficiency, as long as we prioritise the rights of individual corporations to gain market share over our collective rights as people, then the underlying conditions will stay the same, and the exploitation epitomised by the gig economy will not go away,' argues Wendy Liu, a former Silicon Valley software developer and start-up founder who now writes about labour, technology and political change.[54] 'We don't necessarily need to return to the initial starting conditions. We can be much more ambitious than that: we can imagine an entirely different world, one that requires a fundamental rethinking of the current economic system.' By exposing and jabbing at the limits of the way things are, Annalise, Richard, Shen, Tom and the other McStrikers, alongside Fatima and her many colleagues in UVW and its sister unions, are all on the front line of a battle to reimagine the way things could be. Their numbers are still small, and their actions seemingly amount to the merest flicker of change, easily missed amid the daily clamour of the cities which surround them. But the workforces they represent are what the workforces of tomorrow are increasingly going to look like, and the fights they are fighting now are the ones that will help define the future of work in this country for everyone. In the most recent set of figures, union membership, after a long period of decline, was shown to be on the up once again, particularly among the young.[55] On one estimate, a quarter of the overall growth has come from the IWGB alone.[56]

UVW's occupation of the Ministry of Justice entrance foyer did not last long. Within minutes of us storming the doors the police had arrived, security guards had been scrambled, and low-level managers were dispatched to identify strike leaders, set up meetings, and draw this immediate disruption to a close. In such a highly surveilled government building, ongoing protest inside the walls is virtually impossible, and besides, many of the cleaners couldn't stay – they had second jobs to get to, or long commutes home to catch up on sleep before tomorrow's shifts. But before the strike came officially to an end, one last rally was held in the street that runs alongside the front of the ministry, just as the sweltry weather turned and great sheets of rain began lashing down upon the flagstones. Someone produced a giant pink *piñata* – a papier-mâché pig stuffed with sweets and suspended from a stick – and the striking cleaners took turns battering it with a drumstick as we all danced around, singing and cheering and sliding in the torrent. When it came to Fatima's go, she ignored the drumstick and grabbed a large umbrella. She was wearing jeans and a blue T-shirt with no jacket, and had tied a sheet of clear plastic around her hair that had once formed part of a bin bag. She barely seemed to notice the deluge that poured off its creases and ran down her arms and legs. There would be many more strikes to come for the Ministry of Justice cleaners, and many more leaps into the unknown for UVW; within a few months Petros, Molly, Shiri, Susana and the rest would be organising new groups of workers – at strip clubs, at a city farm, at London's *Lion King* musical and at luxury brands like Louis Vuitton and Chanel – and winning victories for underpaid staff in the most unlikely of quarters, including the offices of the *Daily Mail*. Boxing classes would be put on for female members, plans for a new office in Birmingham initiated, and new collaborations with major trade unions forged. In May 2019, the prime minister was even asked in Parliament about whether or not she would support UVW's campaigns.

But at that moment, all Fatima was concentrating on was the *piñata*, and all of the might and muscle which had been necessary for her to take so many leaps into the unknown appeared just then to be coursing through her body. 'This has changed my whole life, because for my whole life no one listened to me, and now they do,' she had told me earlier. She brought the umbrella down with a crash upon the *piñata* again and again and again, until it burst open and a flood of brightly wrapped lollipops and ticker tape and glitter spilled forth and mingled brilliantly with the rain. Amid the celebrations, one of the ministry's outsourced security guards who had been ordered to watch and contain us sidled up to a UVW organiser and asked for their contact details. He and his colleagues were fed up with their pay and working conditions, he explained quietly, and they wanted to join the union.

4

Borders

Dungavel, South Lanarkshire

> Like all walls it was ambiguous, two-faced. What was inside it
> and what was outside it depended upon which side of it you
> were on.
>
> —Ursula K. Le Guin, *The Dispossessed*

Theo is a pillar of the community, and he'll tell you so
himself.[1] 'Everybody knows me here,' he grins. 'I'm a landmark!' Theo is in his late fifties; he has a square face and a
stocky frame, and the words 'Cheap Shot' tattooed on to his
arm. It's his son's nickname, a reference to when he was a
young boy and receiving boxing lessons from his father. 'He'd
put a punch in when I wasn't looking,' says Theo, beaming
even brighter. 'You know, the kind of jab you're not expecting. The kind that's unfair.'

There are pictures of Theo's son and daughter on the wall
of his small terraced house in western Glasgow, on a long
street sandwiched between the Forth and Clyde Canal and
Garscadden Burn. His grandchildren are on the wall too, looking down on a parade of dog statuettes arranged around the
fireplace, and on Mia, a real Cavalier King Charles Spaniel,
who frisks about the sofa and worries at a bone. Theo loves

dogs, beer and family; he hates aeroplanes, and goodbyes. 'You can ask my wife, I don't say goodbye to anyone. It's too emotional,' he explains. That's why the job offer, when it came, was a mixed blessing.

Theo is, or was, a carer for people with learning difficulties; he worked the night shift at a local charitable institution, but in 2014 a similar role opened up at the council, and that meant better pay and a decent pension. He'd heard nothing for three months after he applied and forgot all about it, but eventually a letter landed on the doormat announcing that the position was his. It would be hard to leave the people he'd been working with for eight years now, but you can't stand still forever in life, you'll seize up and fossilise and forget how to move, and this council job was a big step forward. So, despite his misgivings, Theo and his wife Shirley danced up and down the living room when they got the news. 'That's how it all came out,' he says.

Theo tends to punctuate his words with forward lunges and jabs of the air, and you can gauge the state of his emotions by how frenetic his movements are. They were small and metronomic before; now, as he runs through exactly what it was that came out, they grow in intensity, and his body becomes a freewheeling, fast-rocking blur. 'I've been working and paying my taxes and National Insurance for thirty-six years,' he tells me, tearfully. 'I've done jury service six times. I've never missed a vote.' He counts each of these facts out on his fingers, an unsolicited ledger that puts his legitimacy in the black, and makes what happens next, in his eyes, so violent, so egregious. His new employer asked to see his passport. It was a routine request, part of a policy regime that had just been put in place by the then home secretary Theresa May, aimed at creating a 'hostile environment' for 'illegal migrants' in the country. Theo didn't have a passport, he hadn't been abroad in more than half a century. His siblings and everyone else in the family did though, so there was no reason to think the application would be any trouble. But then the woman from the Belfast passport office called him on the phone, and what she said scrumpled Theo's life in an instant. 'I'm sorry,' the woman told him, 'we can't give you a passport, because you're not British.'

In the space of a few weeks, Theo lost his new job, he lost his old job, he lost free access to the NHS, he lost his state benefits, he lost his legal right to live in Glasgow, Scotland or anywhere in Britain, he lost his self-worth, his confidence, and his famously good cheer. It was an avalanche of loss, so gargantuan and unexpected that, in Theo's words, it ripped the soul right out of him. 'I used to be the life of the party,' he says, quietly. 'We built our lives, we paid our mortgage, we worked hard, we weren't well off but we were comfortable. I was happy as Larry. Then they stripped me of every dignity, one by one, and now I'm on twenty-two tablets a day and don't go outside.' During the months following the phone call, Theo and Shirley provided the Home Office with fifty-one separate categories of documentary evidence to help establish his immigration status: these included his parents' passports, his children's birth certificates, three polling cards, fifty-seven bank statements, a photo of Theo as a schoolboy in Slough, and accounts from those closest to him outlining why they thought he should be allowed to remain in the UK. 'My dad gave me life and without my dad, my life would not be worth living,' wrote his daughter. 'I honestly cannot comprehend why I am writing this letter.' Not long afterwards, Theo received an official response from the government, recommending that he leave the country.[2]

*

Political crises, by their very nature, pose questions about who we are as a community – where the fault lines in our society lie at the present moment, and where, instead, they should be. In Britain, those questions have habitually been answered, both by those in power and those who seek it, using the language of nationalism, which requires us to decide not just what the country is, but also, inextricably, what or who it isn't. It happened in the early seventeenth century, when England experienced crippling food shortages and Queen Elizabeth I wrote to city mayors complaining of the growing number of 'blackamores' in the realm, before demanding that 'those kind of people be sent forth of the land'.[3] It was true of the mid and late nineteenth century, when huge political upheavals forced successive expansions of the franchise, and social struggles ensued over what a proper, worthy citizen looked like. In the periods following both the world wars, collective demands for a different kind of political system exposed uncertainty over what exactly the collective was. 'This is not a crisis of race,' wrote cultural theorist Stuart Hall in the late 1970s, just as Thatcherism began to take shape and its leader was speaking publicly about her fears of Britain being 'rather swamped' by people with a different culture. 'But race punctuates and periodises the crisis. Race is the lens through which people come to perceive that a crisis is developing. It is the framework through which the crisis is experienced. It is the means by which the crisis is to be resolved.'

Time and again, the resolution of national crises has involved the imposition of new borders or a reactivation of old ones, and it is across the bodies of the most vulnerable that these borders are inevitably laid. At this time, when our own crisis is fuelled in part by a backlash against the outsized strength of global capital, and when expressions of the nation – from calls for economic protectionism to suspicion of supranational entities like the EU – have become a mainstay of our public discourse, the imposition of borders has become particularly fierce.[4] At this time, our own time, it is people like Theo that have been forced to bear the weight of them.

Theo was born in Kenya in 1960, when it was still a part of the British empire, to parents who originally came from the Indian subcontinent, when it was another part of the British empire. They both held British passports designating them as a 'British subject: Citizen of the UK & Colonies', and when Theo was eight years old, as the Kenyan government carried out an 'Africanisation' programme that targeted foreigners – especially those of Asian heritage – for discrimination, it was to Britain that they came. Theo's father announced abruptly one day that they were leaving Nairobi, and told Theo to say goodbye to his best friend. 'I didn't want to say cheerio, not to him or to his wee puppy,' Theo remembers. 'I started crying, and just said, "My mum and dad are taking me away." They had to drag me to the plane, and I was petrified. I was sobbing through the whole flight.' He has never stepped foot on an aircraft since.

The family wound up in Berkshire, scattered among distant relatives. Theo worked from a young age, helping his mother make Christmas crackers and his father sell cheap clothing from a market stall. He was sixteen when his older brothers invited him along for a trip to Blackpool. There would be a disco, they told him, along with drinking, dancing and women. 'I was a recluse, I'd never seen a disco before in my life and my dad would never have allowed anything like that,' said Theo. 'But I went with them and as soon as I saw all those lights and the music blaring I thought, my God, what is this?' It was 1976, and John Miles was thumping from the speakers; the delighted older brothers dived right in. One of them made eye contact with a Scottish woman, and ordered Theo to look after her friend. 'He said, "We're going to chat this lassie up, so keep her mate occupied." I said, "What do you mean?" I was so shy, I barely knew what girls looked like. We went over and before long my brother and this lassie are smooching away like hell, and I'm just standing there like this!' Theo stood up and mimed being completely rigid, with a look of sheer terror plastered across his face. 'At one point my brother came over to me and asked me how I was getting on. I said, "I'm not getting on with anything! I don't like her, can we please get out of here?" My brother laughed and said not yet, he was doing alright. I begged him to at least promise we wouldn't see these girls again, and he said, "Don't worry, we'll get rid of them." And at the end of the evening he just turned to the pair of them and asked, "What are yous doing tomorrow?"' Theo didn't say a word to the eighteen-year-old standing next to him: not that night, not the next morning, and not throughout the next two days they all spent hanging out together on the seafront. 'I thought he couldn't speak English,' says Shirley. 'He was sweet though, and innocent.' Theo winked. 'I was good-looking too,' he assured me. At the end of the holiday, the pair kissed. They've now been married for more than forty years.

While we were talking, Shirley handed me a copy of their wedding photo: she in a wavy sky-blue dress, he in a navy suit with huge lapels, a flamboyant ruffle-front shirt with matching bow tie, and hair the size of Scotland. They moved up to Glasgow together a few years later, and Theo marvelled at the tenement buildings that seemed to stretch out forever in a cascade of sandstone, at the accents and idioms that he'd never heard in Slough. They made their little place in the world, out of jobs and homes and friends and children, and they have pieces of paper to prove it: letters from doctors, P60 tax records, yellowed payslips, insurance cards and council-tax bills. It's all gathered in boxes in Theo's and Shirley's living room, exhumed from dusty attic corners and distant archives. At one point the couple paid Abbey National to do a special trawl of its historical records to find mentions of Theo's name; another time they were forced into a desperate correspondence regarding his parents' marriage declaration with the Municipal Corporation of Lahore. 'No matter what you give them, it's not enough,' observed Theo. 'They told me to produce class reports from the primary school I attended in the late 1960s, which was closed down in 1983. They take, and take, and take, they take everything from you until there's nothing left that you can give.' All the milestones in Theo's and Shirley's shared lives – the memories and complexities, the big and little stories we all fall back upon to tell ourselves who we are – have been recast as something cold and factual, marbled with suspicion. We gazed at the wedding photo a little while longer, laughing fondly at its 1970s sepia. 'We had to send this to the Home Office too,' said Shirley suddenly, matter-of-factly, snatching it from my hands and placing it back in a folder. 'That's why we dug it out. We had to send it over.'

We think of borders as lines on a map, marking the outer limits of a territory. But borders are processes rather than objects, verbs instead of nouns. Their visibility, indeed their very reality, waxes and wanes in accordance with personal and political circumstances, and they can run in any direction that those with the power to draw them see fit. In late-capitalist Britain, they have been drawn more extensively, and drawn inwards.

The accession of ten new member states to the European Union in 2004, largely from Central and Eastern Europe, led to an increase in incoming migrant numbers to the UK that was far higher than the government at the time antici-pated. Alongside new citizens of the bloc who exercised their freedom-of-movement rights to come and work temporarily or settle in Britain, sections of the media ramped up reports on the arrival of irregular migrants – those who in some way or another were not in full compliance with official immigration requirements.* Reliable statistics on irregular migration are obviously hard to come by, but the most recent academic study on the subject put the total number of irregular migrants in the UK at any one time as being 618,000, or 1% of the country's total population.[5] It should be noted that, since 2004, there has also been an average *emigration* from Britain of more than 350,000 people every year. To put all these figures into context, it's worth bearing in mind that the vast majority of the world's refugees – the category of migrant that is perhaps the most fre-quent subject of doom-mongering by tabloid newspapers – live not in wealthy countries but the global south; some individual

---

* Although widely used, the term 'illegal immigrant' is deeply misleading: it is often wrongly applied to asylum seekers, despite the right to claim asylum being enshrined in the UN's Universal Declaration of Human Rights, and many other undocumented migrants have broken administrative rules rather than criminal law.

states such as Turkey and Pakistan host more refugees than all of Europe combined.[6] The UK is home to a microscopic fraction of the worldwide refugee population, and yet nearly half of Britons believe that one in ten people residing here are refugees (in fact the proportion is 0.4%).[7]

Still, politicians and public sentiment, or at least dominant representations of public sentiment, became locked in a vicious circle of 'concern' at levels of immigration, and with few policy tools available to restrict EU arrivals, successive governments, including New Labour, the coalition and the Conservatives, vowed to crack down on irregular migrants instead. 'What we don't want is a situation where people think that they can come here and overstay because they're able to access everything they need,' Theresa May told the *Daily Telegraph* in 2012.[8] 'The aim is to create here in Britain a really hostile environment for illegal migration.'

What that hostile environment meant in practice was the construction of new borders: through homes, hospitals, banks, offices and schools. The government doesn't have enough staff to patrol all these new borders, so to ensure they are effective it needs everybody to become a border guard. Under plans either publicly announced or secretly leaked in recent years, officials have demanded that teachers conduct immigration checks on pupils and 'deprioritise' the children of irregular migrants for education; that doctors carry out passport inspections on their patients; that landlords establish the citizenship status of their tenants before agreeing to offer them accommodation.[9] The Home Office has used records of child maintenance payments, often the thin line between survival and destitution for single-parent families, to target suspected irregular migrants for arrest and deportation; it has brokered data-sharing agreements for the purpose of immigration enforcement with driving-licence authorities, state-benefit providers, and organisations whose job it is to walk the streets and help rough sleepers.[10] Members of Parliament, to whom everyone is encouraged to turn for help when they are in difficulty, have used an immigration enforcement hotline to report their constituents on hundreds of occasions.[11] In 2017, a woman who informed police officers that she was the victim of kidnapping and rape was then arrested for suspected immigration crimes inside a sexual assault centre, where she had gone to receive care.[12] The government has deployed advertising vans emblazoned with the words 'Go Home Or Face Arrest' around urban areas with a high concentration of migrant communities and ethnic minorities. Members of the Civil Service told ministers that elements of the hostile environment programme were 'almost reminiscent of Nazi Germany', but went on to implement it anyway.[13]

Just as Stuart Hall observed in the 1970s, during the last great displacement of Britain's political tectonic plates, a national crisis – in our case, the post-2008 economic crisis – is being reframed along very different lines: lines concerned primarily with ethnocultural identity. The hostile environment has been about giving those lines a concrete form; the *Windrush* scandal – in which individuals like Theo who arrived in the UK legally and had spent the majority of their lives here suddenly found themselves harassed, impoverished, and in some cases forcibly removed by the state – was an inevitable consequence of it. As of 2018 more than 5,000 potential *Windrush* cases had been reported to the Home Office, but it is estimated that a great many more people may have been impacted.[14] Central to the hostile environment's rationale was the establishment of a public target limiting overall net migration to the country, as well as private internal targets for the enforced removals that would help achieve it, and those targets incentivised the authorities to cast their dragnet ever wider. 'They did see enemies everywhere,' one senior Whitehall official said of the Home Office at the time, and Theo – who, despite not being born in the Caribbean, is a member of the '*Windrush* generation' that arrived in Britain from the Commonwealth before the early 1970s when immigration laws changed – was one of the enemies they saw.[15] For almost all his life he has known only one state: without warning, it spun borders around him like a spider's web, and told him that he was standing on the wrong side of them. 'What country is this? What country do I know?' he asked me.

The denial of Theo's citizenship, and hence his right to stay in the UK, not only cost him the opportunity to work but also any eligibility for welfare. After a battle lasting four years, which included the couple hiring a QC, spending thousands on legal fees, and getting their MP to ask about the case in Parliament at Prime Minister's Questions, the Home Office finally backed down and recognised Theo's British nationality in 2018. The entire episode has broken him, though; he has gout, which his doctors believe has been induced by stress, and depression, and together these conditions have made finding work again almost impossible. To make matters worse, due to the gap in his National Insurance contributions record from when he was forbidden to work, the government claims he is not eligible for unemployment allowance, nor many of the other benefits that are normally afforded to those on low incomes.[16] When we met, he and Shirley wore their Sunday best, but after we had got to know each other better, he showed me with wet eyes and wounded pride what their dinner that night consisted of: tinned mince and tinned pies, collected from the local food bank. Their children have been supporting them financially for half a decade. Money is so tight that when Shirley got a bad toothache over Christmas she avoided going to the dentist for fear of the cost; instead, she took painkillers – too many of them – and ended up in hospital. The government's *Windrush* compensation scheme, established after media investigations exposed the extent of the scandal, has considered Theo's case and concluded that it is 'compelling'. At the time of writing, they have offered him a grand total of £364.

All this has filled Theo with a rage that now lashes out in all directions: towards the government that built the hostile environment, to its many agents that implemented it, to the friends who he feels failed to support him when their support was needed, and, perhaps most jarringly, to others who – like him – have become the target of the state's mistrust. 'I've become the biggest racist on the planet,' he told me. 'I hate Africans, I hate the EU people. They get everything under the sun, they've come in here somehow and they're walking around in designer clothes!' He was shouting now. 'Their kids have everything too, and here's my kids who I've had to rely on for money, and my grandkids who I can't give a thing!' Theo doesn't leave the house now, apart from the occasional trip to the pub across the way. 'I'm scared I'll knock somebody out,' he admitted. 'Honest to God, I'm scared.'

Britain's political terrain is steeped in the stories of people like Theo; understanding them is key to understanding the divergent visions of the future competing for our support. One of the most critical questions we face is whether this will be a country that resists the logic of the hostile environment, or one that extends that logic further. What lends that question such power, and peril, is that what happened to Theo did not arise merely out of one particular set of policy decisions made by one particular administration: the things that harmed him were fashioned out of raw materials that can be found, mined and mobilised in all of us. The hostile environment comprises not just laws but social attitudes that, like all social attitudes, have been shaped by centuries of myth-making – in this case, myths concerning national identity and empire.[17] As Theo knows, these attitudes reveal themselves not just in institutional acts of aggression or omission, but in individual ones too – in the stereotypes we reach for when we want to assert our own rights, to confront our own exclusions at the expense of others. To be British is to be exposed to and exist within these attitudes, and Theo's experiences have rendered him both victim and perpetrator of their cruelty.

In 2014, YouGov polled Britons on the statement 'The government should encourage immigrants and their families to leave Britain (including family members who were born in Britain)'. Forty-three per cent of respondents disagreed; the majority were either in favour of the idea or weren't sure.[18] My conversation with Theo left me with the impression that, depending on mood, his own answer to the question could go either way.

*

I once read a disturbing detail about the effects on the human body of scurvy, the disease which spreads when we are deprived of sufficient vitamin C. Normally, in response to an injury, we repair our skin with collagen, a kind of protein that is the major constituent of all our connective tissue, and this binding is replaced continually, invisibly, throughout our lives. But in cases of advanced scurvy collagen can no longer be produced, and so past injuries that we thought long-cured can magically reappear.[19] 'Given the right – or, as it were, exactly wrong – nutritional circumstances, even a person's oldest injuries never really go away,' explains the writer Geoff Manaugh. 'In a sense, there is no such thing as healing. From paper cuts to surgical scars, our bodies are mere catalogues of wounds: imperfectly locked doors quietly waiting, sooner or later, to spring back open.'[20]

Britain's historical injuries are legion – both the abuses it has inflicted on other parts of the world, and the unresolved traumas that empire formed within – and Loudoun Hill, which stands about thirty miles south of central Glasgow on a stretch of undulating moorland marking the dividing line between Lanarkshire and Ayrshire, is an excellent vantage point from which to view them. Two great battles have been fought here, one real – Robert the Bruce's victory against English forces in 1307 – and the other fictional, a supposed triumph by William Wallace a few years earlier in the Wars of Scottish Independence. 'To Lowdoun Hill past in the gray dawyng,' wrote Scottish minstrel Blind Harry in his epic (and historically inaccurate) poem of Wallace's life, which went on to become one of the most popular texts ever published in Scotland.[21] From the summit, you can see for miles. There are wind farms on the horizon, and the ground below, scored by brooks that glimmer when they catch the sun, looks like felt stretched over bumps and knolls; these mounds are named after the graves of soldiers from across the border, the ones who never made it home. Through a clump of trees to the east, the outlines of a large beige building are visible, with miniature steeples on its corners and high perimeter fences. This is Dungavel House, an immigration detention centre run privately by an American prisons company on behalf of the British Home Office, and it stains the landscape like a bruise.

Dungavel is one of ten immigration detention centres scattered across the UK. They can be found tacked on to the edges of airports, shoved into defunct military bases, and shrouded in banality at provincial business parks alongside pet crematoriums and indoor skydiving facilities. Together they hold up to 3,500 people at any one moment, and although in theory detainees are placed in these centres pending forced removal from the country, in reality the government can incarcerate them in perpetuity and the vast majority – despite not necessarily having committed any crime – have no idea how long their detention will last.[22] Britain is the only country in Europe not to set a statutory time limit on this sort of imprisonment, and in some cases individuals have remained locked up for several years. More than half of those detained are formally classified as vulnerable adults due to their health status or prior experience of torture, and every single day on average, somebody, somewhere, on what authorities call the 'immigration detention estate', requires medical treatment for self-harm.[23] At Dungavel, which initially held children and infants before supposedly reverting to an adult-only facility in 2010, one in fourteen detainees is on suicide watch at any time.[24] 'Because of detention, I am a nervous wreck,' read one of the contributions made by ex-detainees to a 'Life After Detention' project run by Scottish Detainee Visitors, which facilitates support visits to those locked up at Dungavel.[25] 'Because of detention, I have lost my way forever,' stated another. 'The anxiety that comes with having experienced detention is like an octopus inside you,' Shirley Gillan, who co-ordinates the Life After Detention group, said to me. 'The limbo and the fear are pervasive.'

Yusra knows the octopus, and she knows the disruption that can be fashioned from it too.[26] She was seventeen years old when she arrived in Britain to study, leaving her parents behind in Qatar where she was born and raised. Within a year, she received word that her father – a Sudanese activist who opposed the dictatorship in Khartoum – had been arrested by the Qatari security forces. Qatar is politically aligned with the Sudanese government, and soon afterwards her mother disappeared too. At the time, Yusra was staying with cousins in London, but the living situation was tense and her relatives offered little sympathy. 'I remember waking up at 5 a.m. feeling like I couldn't tolerate my own skin, and just running out the front door,' she told me. 'I ended up knocking on the door of a friend in the middle of the night and saying, "I'm really sorry, I've lost contact with my family, I don't know where home is, I don't know what to do."' A few days later, Yusra applied for asylum in the UK on the grounds that were she to return to Qatar, she would be in danger. From the moment her application was submitted, she was barred from working or having recourse to most public funds. She was sent to a hostel on the outskirts of London where she ended up sleeping on a floor, and then to a different hostel in Birmingham where dirt was caked on to the walls and she feared the corridors at night, and then to shared accommodation for asylum seekers in Nottingham run by G4S, where she was housed with a woman who ran around brandishing a knife during psychotic episodes. 'We complained to G4S, we said this woman needs help and it's not safe to place her with other people like this, but they just said they didn't have anywhere else to put her,' Yusra recalled. 'So we'd lock ourselves in a room until the sun came up and she calmed down. You get used to being scared, in the end. You learn to accept it.' Yusra's head was all over the place: she had to check in at regular intervals to a Home Office reporting centre, calculate how to survive on the £37.75

weekly cash allowance she was granted as an asylum seeker, and navigate a series of legal prohibitions on where she could be and what she could do while her claim was considered. 'I walked in Sherwood Forest for hours on my own, just walking,' she said. 'I reminded myself that just because the Home Office makes it so hard for you to exist, hard for you just to be, it doesn't mean you're not a person. Just because they make you an asylum seeker everywhere, it doesn't have to define you. In your head, you can still be you.' It was July 2016, the sun shone bright, and Britain had just elected to leave the European Union.

The referendum was about many things, and Yusra, through no choice of her own, was one of them. She could not vote herself, of course, and asylum applications like hers from non-EU countries would not be directly affected by the outcome. But still, the referendum was in part about her because many of the leaders and media cheerleaders on one side of the campaign decided to use her, or at least a fuzzy outline of her, to make their case. Migration – all migration, not just the European Union's freedom-of-movement rights – was the animating factor behind public debate in the run-up to the referendum. Ninety-nine front pages on the subject appeared before the election, more than any other topic, and four-fifths of them were published in leave-supporting newspapers.[27] 'REVEALED: Shock £29bn migrants bill for Britain's crammed schools', 'HALF of all rape and murder suspects in some parts of Britain are foreigners', and 'MIGRANTS PAY JUST £100 TO INVADE BRITAIN' are examples of just three *Daily Express* headlines in the month running up to the vote.[28] In the week immediately preceding polling day, over a thousand articles focused on migration across the UK media.[29] Within this generalised onslaught of migration-anxiety, adverts circulated by pro-Brexit campaign groups drew special attention to Muslim and Middle Eastern communities coming to Britain. Material produced by the official Vote Leave campaign declared that 'TURKEY (population 76 million) IS JOINING THE EU', alongside an image depicting the British passport as an open door through which a long line of footprints were marching. Nigel Farage's infamous 'BREAKING POINT' poster, released by Leave.EU, featured Syrian refugees crossing the Croatia–Slovenia border next to the words 'The EU has failed us all'; he later suggested it was this image that won the referendum for 'leave'.[30] In reality, migrants make a huge net contribution to public finances, the violent crime rate for foreign nationals almost exactly matches that of those born in the UK, and Turkey is not about to join the EU, but none of that was relevant. The news stories and posters weren't designed to communicate facts, they were about excavating and stimulating concerns regarding a hazy 'other' in our midst, and the distance between what that 'other' represented now and Britain as it used to be. Yusra – who came to Britain to study, as two-thirds of non-European immigrants now do, and was then forced to seek refuge from persecution, as an unfortunate 8% of non-European immigrants must do – is what this 'other' looks like once the haze is cleared away.[31] 'We want our country back,' Nigel Farage insisted at the previous year's UKIP conference. But what country is it that we want back, and who are 'we'?

Brexit has brought these questions into sharp relief. British nationalism as articulated by the leaders of Brexit – and in particular the form it takes in England, the nation where the 'leave' vote was strongest – is rooted in both imperial nostalgia and anti-imperial insurgency; it demands the resurrection of Empire 2.0 (the official term used by government to describe post-Brexit trade links with the Commonwealth), and a revolutionary liberation from the yoke of foreign interference. 'There is a pattern consistent throughout history of oppressed people turning on their oppressors,' declared Brexit Party MEP Ann Widdecombe in 2019, 'slaves against their owners, the peasantry against the feudal barons, colonies against empires, and that is why Britain is leaving.'[32] It's a domineering nationalism but simultaneously a defensive one: we long for the days when the sun never set on Britain's colonial dominion, at least in part because under the rule of transnational finance and faceless bureaucrats in Brussels, Britain has itself become a colony stripped of its sovereignty and self-respect.

In the service of this sentiment, Brexit's figureheads activate imperial imagery, drawing all the while on a collective amnesia about what empire was, and how it lives among us today. 'Above all, we can find our voice in the world again,' proclaimed Boris Johnson the day after the referendum – that last word, 'again', freighted with a meaning that dare not explicitly speak its name.[33] The *Windrush* scandal was a textbook example of this concurrent remembering and forgetting. The mistreatment of people who, as Theresa May put it, were 'part of us', was met with public outrage, yet there was little consideration of why this 'part of us' is British and the challenge it represents to Brexiteer narratives of a culturally homogeneous yesteryear now shattered by migration.[34] 'THE EUROPEAN UNION WANTS TO KILL OUR CUPPA', read one of the Facebook ads released by pro-leave campaigners in the run-up to the vote. But the leaves in 'our' cuppa come from India, China and Africa; its sweetness from the Caribbean, from where the *Windrush* itself set sail for Tilbury. 'I am the sugar at the bottom of the English cup of tea,' declared Jamaica-born Stuart Hall. 'That is the outside history that is inside the history of the English.' Or, as Sri Lankan novelist and one of Britain's foremost public intellectuals Ambalavaner Sivanandan once noted, 'We are here because you were there.'

The referendum result and its aftermath have shown just how fallacious any unified narrative of Britain and British identity really is. We are a country all out of collagen: fragmented by nation, region, education and class, divided between urban and rural areas, young and old, rich and poor. And while delusions of imperial grandeur weren't the main reason for the Brexit win – narratives of empire featured far more heavily in the language of the campaign's political leaders than they did among most of its supporters – the use of that language still matters a great deal. It enabled politicians on the right to gloss over those fragmentations in favour of casting Brexit as a singular national project – the threatened English cuppa, the society at breaking point due to an influx of outsiders, the Brexit that would win our (singular) country back and find our (singular) voice in the world again – and they did so highly effectively, especially when set against a remain campaign whose equivalent unifying 'project' was saving the existing economy from harm, an existing economy that many people were not particularly keen to save at all. That disconnect reveals much about the ways in which those on the hard right hope to remake Britain in the years to come, and the selective stories of years gone by that they will be relying upon to do so. After all, Brexit's rallying cries referenced a past that belongs to Yusra and Theo just as much as it does to Farage and Johnson. Yusra's family come from Sudan, a country that was part of the British empire from the late nineteenth century until the early 1950s; Theo was born 4,500 miles from Glasgow, but as a British citizen. Yet as Brexit unfolded each of them found themselves encased in the hostile environment, and muted.

In early 2017, Yusra was informed that her asylum claim had been refused. At her Home Office interview, she was asked detailed questions about Sudan and her family's history there, even though Yusra herself has never set foot inside its borders. Unbeknownst to her, the Home Office compared her answers to those given by her father on an old UK visa application from many years ago, and the discrepancies were deemed sufficient to rule against her. 'It's fine to be upset and it's fine to cry – for five minutes,' said Yusra. 'Then you flip the page and carry on.' She failed in her appeal, but her lawyer encouraged her to push the case to judicial review, which would involve judges assessing the legality of the Home Office's decision-making process. Meanwhile, Yusra was told to keep appearing at a Home Office reporting centre at regular intervals. When she got a letter asking her to come and sign in the following week, outside of the normal reporting schedule, it set alarm bells ringing, although she also allowed herself a glimmer of hope that it might mean she was about to be granted asylum after all. 'I thought maybe, just maybe, they've looked at my case and thought: "she's nineteen, she's studying, she wants to work, we could benefit from her",' Yusra remembers. 'I was wrong.'

At the reporting centre in Loughborough, a nondescript brick building located between a student housing block and a board-gaming shop just south of the town centre, everything initially seemed normal: Yusra was searched, took a ticket, and waited with many others to be called to a window. When she got there though, rather than just having her ID checked, she was instructed to proceed to a back room. There, an officer announced that she was being detained ahead of enforced removal to Sudan and ordered her, as a security precaution, to remove her shoes. 'There were things I wanted to say, that I wanted to explain, but I was crying like a baby and I couldn't speak,' Yusra told me. She can remember the scene with devastating clarity, right down to the moment the officer complimented her on her novelty dinosaur socks. 'I'd been given them as a present,' Yusra said. 'The officer smiled and asked me where I'd got them from, and I could only answer through snivels and sobs.' After seven hours of waiting, Yusra was handcuffed and placed in the back of a van. She had no idea where she was being taken to; there were no windows in her part of the vehicle, just bright lights and a CCTV camera. 'The driver and his colleague in the front were playing loud music and singing,' she remembers. 'I thought, really? Is this like water to you? Is this your normal?' Ever since she was a young child Yusra had always sought out the sky when distressed: gazing at it calmed her down and restored her equilibrium. 'If something upset me at home I would just run into the garden and sit for hours looking upwards,' she said. 'And that's what pissed me off more than anything in that van. I couldn't see anything. I couldn't see the sky.'

When she first arrived at Yarls Wood – Britain's most notorious immigration detention centre, located on an industrial estate in Bedfordshire – Yusra saw posters advertising the in-house gym and regular arts and crafts sessions. She took comfort from that, convinced herself that maybe her stay there wouldn't be so bad. 'It's all a mistake, I told myself. I'll be out tomorrow. But then we were taken to our sleeping quarters, and on the way I saw rooms filled with personal belongings: clothes stacked high, photos of people's families covering the walls,' she said. 'They were the rooms of people who had been here for years, rooms that had become people's homes. And then I noticed the guards walking around with keys, I heard the first roll call – we had one every night before bedtime, and every morning after we woke up – and I saw the whole place for what it was. It was an artificial world. It was a prison.' Soon afterwards, she began to scream.

For Yusra, the worst part of her time in Yarls Wood wasn't the boredom, the drudgery, or the claustrophobia of confinement. It was the particular dread that came with having been placed in a 'removal window', an official three-month period in which the Home Office is legally entitled to force somebody on to a plane out of the UK with only seventy-two hours' notice. 'I got panic attacks whenever I heard footsteps,' she remembers. 'Whenever there was a lockdown, whenever an officer passed my room. Especially early in the morning, because that's when they would often take people, while everyone else is asleep.' When a removal was under way, staff would shut the open areas around the person they were targeting to stop others from seeing what was happening. But everyone could hear the shouts and bangs echoing down the long corridors, the muffled yells and distant clanking of doors. On one occasion, Yusra and another female detainee were in the Yarls Wood mosque, and through a crack in the curtains around its window they were able to watch a removal being enforced. 'We heard a sound, and I saw her through the glass,' said Yusra. 'She was in her sixties, and not mentally stable. I'd spoken to her a few times. It was four big men, security escorts, pulling her by her hair and pushing her on to the floor. Another man was filming it. The woman was terrified, what could she do?' Her companion in the mosque couldn't bear to look, but Yusra's eyes remained glued on the window. 'I thought, is this really the UK, is this really what I'm seeing?' said Yusra. 'You know, before that I'd never shivered before in my life, from shock, or being scared, or anything like that. But now I was shivering.' Yusra remembers the lengths people went to in an effort to thwart being dragged to the airport – one woman stripped naked and covered herself in baby oil to make it harder for the guards to grab hold of her – as well as the toll all this took on those left behind to wait indefinitely for their turn. 'There were so many attempted suicides,' she said. 'One time I went to get coffee in the morning and I saw a stream of blood running from inside one of the rooms into the corridor. She had thrown a glass mug on to the floor to smash it and then used a piece to slash her wrists.' Yusra doesn't know what happened to the woman involved; officers arrived and pushed everyone else back, and that was the last time Yusra ever saw her. 'I didn't blame her. I thought about it every single day. The mug method, the plastic bag method, finding a way to hang myself. My belief in God is the only reason I stopped myself. But at times it felt like it would be so much easier than carrying on with the uncertainty, the anticipation: will they come for me today, will it be tomorrow, will it be in a year.'

Yusra remained in Yarls Wood for four months in the end. When she was eventually handed a plane ticket – Heathrow to Khartoum – there was a twisted irony in the fact that it was for a flight with Qatar Airways. The country she'd grown up in, and which had since revoked her residency permit, was now going to facilitate her removal from the place she'd sought asylum, Britain, to a country she had never seen before, Sudan, where she faced potential retribution from the security services for her father's political activities. Her last hope was the judicial review; if the courts accepted it in principle, her removal would have to be postponed to allow a full hearing to take place. 'Three officers came, and said it was time,' recalls Yusra. 'They began to escort me.' That was the moment her lawyer called. 'She said don't let them touch you, the review's just been accepted and I'm faxing the documents right now – tell them to check the fax machine, don't let them take you to the airport!' Three days later, Yusra was officially released. 'Where are you going to?' she was asked, as if that were a simple question for someone who had no contact with her family any more, who was no longer entitled to housing provision for asylum seekers, who remained under legal order to leave the country and who still didn't know where home was, or where it could ever be. But there was one place she knew of, where her old friend from London was now studying at university and which was about as far away from both the capital and Yarls Wood as it was possible to be. 'Glasgow,' she replied. Staff at the immigration centre gave her a train ticket and, for the first time in a long while, Yusra began a journey of her own choosing.

*

Those first few weeks were ghastly: no sleep, no appetite, a worry so taut and dense that Yusra would jump if she heard a pin drop. 'It was me, but not me,' she said. Her boyfriend, whom she'd first met back in Nottingham, was looking for something that would give Yusra a reason to get out of the house, something that might break her out of the depressive loop. He searched online for volunteering opportunities, and came across the Unity Centre, a small organisation south of the river near Ibrox stadium. 'The system pushes your head to the ground,' Yusra explained. 'Unity let me look up again.'

Unity fills a double shopfront in Cessnock, next to an iron-monger and just around the corner from the Home Office's formal outpost in the city, a low-rise trio of office blocks with security guards on every door. By contrast, Unity's door is almost always open, jammed ajar to the elements below a sign proclaiming the centre's name: big white letters on a painted-black fascia, with an empty space where the 't' should be.

People wander in and out, sometimes for something specific, often just to seek out company or make a call. Chairs, sofas, bikes and snacks are scattered about; useful phone numbers, guides to legal rights, and messages in different languages are pinned chaotically to the wall. '*Kolina ma'a ba'd*,' reads one, in Arabic. 'All of us together.'

The centre was born in the mid-2000s, an unintended by-product of New Labour's own complex record on immigration and the often paradoxical language used by senior members of the party to support it. As well as the rise in EU workers coming to Britain from 2004 onwards, which the government opted not to place any transitional controls on, Blair's administration also relaxed the criteria for non-European work permits, and doubled the number of international students.[35] This wasn't the result of a particular policy goal, but rather the outcome of various Third Way impulses: the embrace of neoliberal economic principles, for example, which included liberalisation of the labour market, but also a more intangible cosmopolitanism that celebrated the 'saris, samosas and steel bands' of modern Britain. Yet this stylistic makeover of the country's national identity was accompanied by a raft of anti-migrant legislation and political sentiment too, particularly regarding the fate of those who had their asylum claims rejected. It was under Home Secretary Jack Straw that the practice of immigration detention was formalised and expanded; Straw's successor David Blunkett insisted that, when it came to the issue of migration, the party had no choice but to accommodate the views not just of the mainstream conservatism advocated in tabloids like the *Sun* but also those of far-right 'ultras' too.[36]

What this meant in practice was a raft of asylum-seeker dispersal and containment policies which aimed to concentrate refugees in locations outside of London and the south-east. Glasgow was the first city to sign up to the scheme, and soon thousands of asylum seekers were being corralled into the vast, post-war housing estates that rear over each of the city's four corners. It was here that new forms of migrant activism took root, including community vigils which sprang up to help resist the terror of dawn raids by immigration officials. Led by asylum seekers themselves, with support from their neighbours, the vigils assembled at Kingsway in the west, at Cardonald to the south, and at the iconic Red Road tower blocks in the city's north-east. Unity was established in 2005 as an asylum seekers' union that could forge a more durable movement out of these sporadic mobilisations. Its base was chanced upon during a protest outside the Home Office building, when someone noticed a 'To Let' hoarding above a nearby dilapidated retail unit. The Home Office facility doubles up as one of the reporting centres where those like Yusra who are claiming asylum must regularly 'check in'. Today, Unity encourages them to stop by on their way over and share their details; if they don't reappear by the end of the day, volunteers know that the individual has probably been detained and can start marshalling resources.

What struck Yusra on her first visit to the centre was not just the wealth of support it provides to those navigating the Home Office's immigration bureaucracy – directing people towards avenues of financial and legal help, for example, or liaising with lawyers, doctors and politicians on detainees' behalf when needed – but also its philosophy: explicitly politicised, and ranged against the state. 'The Unity Centre is a collective of friendly volunteers, who provide practical support and solidarity for anyone affected by the UK government's racist and oppressive system of immigration controls,' reads the first line on Unity's website. After training and a few days of volunteering, anyone can join the collective and help run the centre. Decisions are made by consensus, using hand signals where appropriate, and care has been taken to identify the ways in which the hierarchies of social power – class, gender, sexuality and race as well as cultural capital, language ability and immigration status – can amplify some voices and muffle others, and to try to mitigate against them. 'Unity is ... an egalitarian organisation working for a world which is free from prejudice,' the centre insists. 'We are determined to not be passive in these aims.' After spending so long being disciplined by hierarchies, Yusra found the atmosphere and energy here exhilarating. 'No one is superior, but everybody cares for one another,' she told me. 'We still haven't found the best way to run meetings, to settle on choices, but we're trying to work it out as equals. All of Unity's imperfections make it perfect.' The centre will try to respond to immigration raids and forced removals by scrambling volunteers or lobbying airlines involved in deportation flights, for example, but like UVW its core principles are based on self-organisation and empowerment rather than reactive operations or top-down consultation. 'Talk to people around you,' Unity advises detainees who are trapped in removal centres like Dungavel or Yarls Wood. 'You will be amazed at how others can help you deal with your case, and in turn how you can then pass this knowledge on to others facing similar problems in the asylum detention process.'

Yusra and Unity are on the front line of a battle, not only with the current state and its dehumanising immigration policies, but also over that state's future. Her refusal – legal, logistical and psychological – to be outcast by the Home Office and its hostile environment is the foundation of a completely different vision of politics from the one propagated by leading Brexit nationalists. This one is likewise constructed around a mass struggle against an unjust establishment, but unlike the right-wing version it does not render Yusra politically inert, and conceptualises that establishment differently. One of its enemies is the tale that has been told in recent years about traditional 'left behind' communities like Tilbury and the 'white working class' who live there. According to this tale, Britain's current chaos is grounded in class conflict, with a ruling class – not necessarily those who have benefited materially from capital, markets and financialisation, but rather a cultural assemblage of liberal technocrats, intellectuals, media personalities and professional politicians – conspiring to degrade the living standards of authentic working-class Britons, in alliance with foreigners beyond our borders and those who lurk within them. This 'authentic' working class doesn't just exclude Yusra but exists in explicit opposition to her: the tale treats diversity, migration and multiculturalism as elite code words for the systematic appropriation of prosperity from true, ordinary citizens, and borders as the means by which this larceny will be reversed, the country heroically renewed.

It's a tale that has been told time and again through British history, with different inflections and a variety of 'outsider' groups cast in the role of the usurping other against which 'real' working-class identities should be measured. Not all of these outsider groups are non-white, but they have all persistently been racialised – presented as something distinct from white, Christian, Anglo-Saxon norms – and that racialisation has often been driven by labour movements, the political representatives of the working class, themselves.[37] Irish Catholics, described as members of an inferior Celtic race with a distinct and unappealing physiognomy, fulfilled that function in the mid-nineteenth century, and West African and Chinese sailors did the same in the aftermath of the First World War. In 1919, trade union leaders in Glasgow incited merchant-navy sailors to attack their foreign colleagues for supposedly undercutting their wages, part of an attempt to build support for a general strike which was scheduled in the city a few days later. A group of seamen from Sierra Leone ended up besieged in their lodgings on Broomielaw on the north bank of the Clyde; several were later charged by police on rioting offences, while no action was taken against those assaulting them.

Sandwiched between these two periods was the 1905 Aliens Act: the first modern border controls in Britain, specifically targeted against working-class Jews. My own family were migrants twice over to the UK: first as Russian Jews leaving Eastern Europe as part of a great wave of migration fuelled by anti-Semitic violence and discrimination, ending up in the textile sweatshops of Leeds; then, after my great-grandfather Charlie fought for Britain in the First World War and accepted free passage to South Africa in recognition of his service, all over again half a century later, when my dad arrived in Ealing, west London, and consigned himself to a lifetime of despondency supporting Queens Park Rangers, his local football team. The Aliens Act was designed to stop people like us ever making it here, or as the *Manchester Evening Chronicle* editorial expressed it, to ensure that 'the dirty, destitute, diseased, verminous and criminal foreigner who dumps himself on our soil and rates [i.e. taxes] simultaneously, shall be forbidden to land'.[38] Its legislation was officially passed by a Conservative government, but the impetus for the act came from the left as much as it did the right, and then as now the running themes in public discussion were pressure on jobs, leeching of benefits, and the potential erosion of working-class bargaining power if too many foreigners slipped in. According to socialist publication the *Clarion*, Jewish immigrants were 'a poison injected into the national veins'. Beatrice Webb, a founder of the leftist Fabian Society, observed that 'the love of profit distinct from other forms of money earning [is] the strongest impelling motive of the Jewish race' and that Jews 'have neither the desire nor the capacity for labour combination', while a representative from the Navvies Union told a TUC conference in 1900 that most Jews 'had no patriotism, and no country'.[39]

Unity taps into an alternative history of working-class organisation, one that resists attempts to border economic struggles and has repeatedly been galvanised by members of 'outsider' groups themselves. Irish Catholics ended up playing a key role in the new unionism of the late nineteenth century, which transformed the labour movement from a collection of older craft unions into the mass-membership entities that we are more familiar with today. Despite the bigotry they faced, Jewish workers were at the forefront of popular agitation against immigration controls and played a leading role in early twentieth-century union activities. 'If the English worker has reason to be dissatisfied with his lot, let him not blame his foreign fellow working man; let him rather study the social and labour question – he will then find out where the shoe

pinches,' wrote Jewish textile workers in a pamphlet entitled
'A Voice From the Aliens', even as some Jewish MPs – who
were longer-established in Britain and economically prosperous – actively campaigned in favour of the Aliens Act. After
the Second World War, black and Asian communities launched
seminal struggles like the 1963 Bristol omnibus boycott, and
the epic 1970s strikes at Leicester's Imperial Typewriters factory
and the Grunwick film-processing plant in north London; they
also organised a chain of street mobilisations against fascists
and police violence that stretched from Southall to Sheffield.
And in bringing that history to bear on the course of our
present crisis, Unity is not alone.

In early 2018, I joined a week-long training programme run
by the New Economy Organisers Network – a nationwide
web of people involved in campaigns for social and economic
justice – on the ground floor of a former school on the edge of
Glasgow's Kelvingrove Park, which serves as the headquarters
of the Scottish Trades Union Congress and doubles up as a
comedy club in the evening. The workshop brought together
activists from across the city to share their stories and discuss
tactics. Exercises included mapping the ecology of political
movements – who works within the system, who organises
outside of it, what respective audiences are they trying to reach?
– and crafting the story of an organisation's struggle using the
tropes of a fairy tale; the rivalry between affiliates of different
1990s boy bands was used to explore the intelligent harness-
ing of public polarisation in campaigns. Beyond the windows,
snowstorms battered the city; from the ridge at Drumchapel,
the high-rise housing columns that speckle the city seemed to
dissolve into cloud, and the Clyde was smudged away.

Inside, members of the Unity Centre sat down to discuss
the dilemmas they faced alongside other migrant solidarity
organisations operating in Scotland – the Oficina Precaria, for
example, which assists Spanish-speaking migrants in Edinburgh,
as well as groups involved in refugee community kitchens, the
sharing of language skills among migrant communities, and

support for migrants who have survived sexual violence. How do you sustain a campaign when so many of your resources are sapped by a sense of enduring emergency, when on average every forty-nine minutes someone, somewhere is being forcibly removed from the UK?[40] What are the dangers associated with pushing the most 'sympathetic' victims of Home Office mistreatment, such as pregnant women locked up in immigration detention centres, to the forefront of media coverage, at the expense of those with less straightforward stories – like young men previously convicted of a crime – who are also being violently marginalised by the hostile-environment regime? Is it ever acceptable to co-operate with government entities in order to gain access to migrants in detention centres who need help? And how might a mass mobilisation of undocumented migrants, analogous to the 'Dreamers' movement in the US, ever coalesce in Britain? There are no easy answers. But across the country there are more and more people, not least those like Yusra who have felt the sharp end of the hostile environment for themselves, asking similar questions, and coming up with innovative ways to disrupt the Home Office's systems in response. Flights chartered by the government for migrant removals have been targeted by the End Deportations Collective. Immigration enforcement vehicles have been physically obstructed by campaigners who share information through the Anti-Raids Network, which also helps spread information in different languages about how to assert one's legal rights during a Home Office raid. On Valentine's Day in 2019, people browsing Tinder at major British airports found themselves matched with campaigners from 'Lesbians and Gays Support the Migrants', who then provided information about enforced removals and encouraged their new 'dates' to take action against them.

The post-2008 disintegration of late capitalism's erstwhile promise for the future has left mainstream Conservatism with no story of its own to tell. For younger generations, Margaret Thatcher was able to paint a picture of aspiration – home ownership, private-sector jobs, the dynamism of free enterprise – that proved, for all its desperate flaws, highly persuasive to many, winning her three general elections in a row. But at the close of the political era she helped usher in, her successors lack any equivalent intellectual project to rally around: home-ownership is collapsing, job security vanishing, each future generation on course to be poorer than before. And so many of those within her party, having little else to offer, are now tacking to the hard right – drawing on narratives of ethnocultural identity that have festered throughout Britain's political history, rehabilitating them in an effort to cling on to power through the tempest and convince us that they rather than anyone else should be the ones to rebuild from the debris. The compatibility of such narratives with neoliberal economic principles should not surprise us. Enoch Powell, for example, was one of the first mainstream British politicians to advocate for neoliberalism, paving the way for Thatcher's rise to power a decade later.[41] Powell's unshakable faith in the 'doctrine of the market' and simultaneous claim that only a willingness to loudly assert 'plain truth and common sense' would ensure 'victory over those who hate Britain and wish to destroy it', could well have been lifted from the newspaper columns of many prominent political figures today; in recent years the *Daily Mail* and *Daily Telegraph* have run front pages and news reports on the Brexit imbroglio decrying MPs and judges as 'Enemies of the People', 'Traitors' and 'Mutineers', alongside photos of the accused.[42] The 'BREAKING POINT' poster unveiled by Nigel Farage, who has repeatedly praised Powell in public, was a visual embodiment of Powell's infamous 'Rivers of Blood' speech.[43] In April 2018, on the fiftieth anniversary of the speech, the BBC replayed Powell's words in full on national radio as part of a 'rigorous journalistic analysis' of their significance.[44] The day of the broadcast, I travelled to Sevenoaks in Kent and watched activists from 'Generation Identity', a pan-European proto-fascist movement that campaigns to 'stop the Islamisation of Europe', attempt to march openly through the streets after gathering for their first conference in Britain; anti-racist counter-protesters broke up the meeting and clashes raged until the police arrived. '"Rivers of Blood" should not be memorialised like an artefact,' wrote journalist and political lecturer Ash Sarkar in response to the BBC's decision.[45] 'Its rhetoric is a living tradition which shapes Britain to this very day.'

Not all proponents of the free market are aligned with the hostile environment and everything it represents, but as the old paradigm caves in it is those entwining these two forces in a neoliberal nativism – such as Farage, Jacob Rees-Mogg, and Donald Trump in the US – that have the most political momentum behind them. But increasingly, the casualties of both systems are aligned too. When the private outsourcing company Serco, run by Winston Churchill's grandson, announced in 2018 that it would be evicting hundreds of asylum seekers in Glasgow who had received Home Office rulings against them, rendering them no longer eligible for free housing, Glasgow council warned that doing so could spark a humanitarian crisis. 'Living Rent' – a union of largely young, precarious private renters – quickly joined forces with the Unity Centre to help organise a huge mobilisation against the evictions; IWGB, the migrants-led, anti-outsourcing sister union of UVW, has now also opened a branch office in the city.[46] As some market liberals find common cause with the hard right in search of one conception of the future, so migrants, tenants, the generationally excluded and the economically insecure are drawing closer as they work together on another. 'The situation we are facing in Glasgow today must be seen as a turning point, or else we must turn it into one,' declared Living Rent in a statement ahead of the Serco protests.[47] 'This must be only the beginning.' None of this on its own will rectify the injustices inflicted upon Theo, nor does it end Yusra's ongoing immigration nightmare. 'There's no rest,' she admitted. 'I've never laid down and just thought, aaah, everything's OK.' But being part of this movement is enough to put a different perspective on that stress; to lend it, at the very least, some sort of propulsion and meaning.

'When I knocked on my friend's door in London in the middle of the night after losing contact with my family in Qatar, I said I didn't know where home was,' Yusra told me. 'I do now, and it's Unity.'

*

The first thing you notice on the approach road to Dungavel House is the security cameras. They droop elegantly from curved poles like hanging flower baskets; a pair of actual flower baskets, suspended from a lichen-mottled post by the entrance sign, creak in the wind and are filled with weeds. A twenty-feet-high fence topped with coils of barbed wire encircles the building, and the scene feels almost preposterous: conical turrets and elaborate weathervanes, an out-of-place Alpine postcard clad in suburban pebble-dash, then wrapped in a metal skin. Formerly a hunting lodge and later an official residence of the dukes of Hamilton, this is where Rudolf Hess, Hitler's deputy, was aiming for when he set out on his doomed solo peace mission to Britain in 1941 – although he ended up ejecting from his plane before reaching his target, and landed in a field some twelve miles to the west. Reporters are barred from immigration removal centres, but by clambering up the soft mossy banks that run parallel to the fence on two sides it's possible to peer over into the grounds and see the outlines of human shapes moving behind opaque windows. In June 2019, it emerged that children were still being locked up here, almost a decade after the practice was banned.[48] Detainees at Dungavel can work on-site doing cleaning and gardening jobs, for which they are paid just over a pound an hour, one-eighth of the minimum wage; in 2017, GEO Group, which runs the facility, made a net profit of £1 million from its contract with the Home Office.[49] The company was a major donor to Donald Trump's election campaign, and is now the largest provider of private immigration prisons – the population of which has soared under Trump's presidency – in America.[50]

Dungavel, where selected individuals have been banished in an effort to cohere the rest of us, offers a unique angle from which to take stock of Brexit, and the modes of thinking that Brexit builds on. It is the only place of its kind in Scotland – a nation that has long grappled with its own complicated questions about borders, nationalism and identity, questions that may yet unpick the UK's stitching. In 2014, a majority of voters in nearby Glasgow supported breaking away from Britain; under the strain of our political unravelling, independence is on the agenda once more. There is a neat irony to the fact that at a time when, as the Irish journalist Fintan O'Toole puts it, 'it is harder to know what to make of England because it is harder to guess what England makes of itself', a political project – leaving the European Union – that was largely made in England has repeatedly stumbled due to pieces of vestigial Britain beyond England's borders, most notably Northern Ireland: those remnants of empire again, slowly reopening their wounds. For its own part, Scotland's independence referendum in 2014 was the harbinger of a wider political dislocation to come that is still reshaping Britain: it was followed in consecutive years by the takeover of Labour by Jeremy Corbyn in 2015, the Brexit referendum in 2016, and the general election in 2017, and nothing has been the same since. Continued union with Britain eventually won the day in Scotland, but reporting from Glasgow in the run-up to the vote I saw glimpses of a divide which would soon burst into the open all over this country: a gulf between an establishment bereft of political imagination and incapable of promising anything other than fear of the unknown ('If you don't know, vote no', read one campaign slogan), and a growing population that had lost any instinctive faith in it. When Deutsche Bank, a financial institution that played a key role in the 2008 crash, warned that a vote for independence would create economic uncertainty, people I interviewed laughed openly, and angrily.[51] 'We've stopped thinking like consumers, and started thinking like citizens,' said Darren McGarvey, a Glaswegian social commentator and rapper who goes under the stage name 'Loki'. 'The books we read as we're growing up always tell us that fortune favours the brave, and optimism usually wins the day,' a twenty-one-year-old independence campaigner, Josephine Sillars, told me. 'Why did they ever think we'd be afraid of ourselves?'

Perhaps because of its own ambiguous entanglement with empire, Scotland's recent nationalist revival exhibits a degree more self-awareness than its neighbour's south of the border. In 2018, Glasgow University published the results of a year-long study into the wealth it garnered from the slave trade, which amounted to almost £200 million. On my most recent trip to the city I visited a community centre in Govanhill where some curious objects were on display: old maps, newspapers, rusted beer cans and colonial bank notes, all discovered in the attic of the former St Rollox railway stock works in Springburn by members of 'Saheliya' – a group of black, minority-ethnic and migrant women promoting mental health in Glasgow who are now based in the same building. In its heyday, the St Rollox plant manufactured train carriages for every corner of the British empire, which would go on to carry weapons, extracted resources and, in the words of Churchill, 'the letters, newspapers, sausages, jam, whisky, soda water, and cigarettes which enable the Briton to conquer the world without discomfort'. Now its secrets are being uncovered by Glaswegians who in some cases hail from the very communities those train carriages passed through many decades ago. 'It's about how we can all locate ourselves in the history of this city,' says Mia Gubbay, who is helping to curate the items for Glasgow's museums. 'It's about recognising a local history that is inherently global.' As Satnam Virdee, a professor of sociology at Glasgow University, has argued, it is those members of the working class who have been racialised as outsiders throughout Britain's history who are best placed to see through the fog of 'blood, soil and belonging', and to lead a fight over Britain's future.[52]

In the main courtyard of Dungavel House, behind the razor wire, a flag flies high bearing the GEO Group's corporate logo, tattered at the edges. At the foot of the fence there are plastic bags and empty Capri-Sun packets, as well as the occasional casing from a spent smoke flare. Detainees here have held hunger strikes and rooftop occupations in protest at their imprisonment, and they've been supported by demonstrators on the other side of the barrier sending plumes of colour into the sky and insisting that 'these walls must fall'. The graphic designer Sarah Boris recently produced an alternative version of the UK flag, with packing tape reading 'Fragile' replacing the usual white crosses, and I wondered as I stood there whether that might be a more appropriate banner to symbolise Dungavel, and the land beyond it, as we all lurch into the unknown.[53]

That evening, back in Glasgow, I took a walk along the Clyde and came across the granite piles of an old railway bridge that connected the south of the city to Broomielaw, where the seamen from Sierra Leone were forced to shelter from mob violence a hundred years before. Upon one on them, passages of text have been engraved with lines in English and Greek.[54] 'All Greatness Stands Firm in the Storm', declares the former. I assumed the Greek words must mean the same, but later, when I looked up the translation, I was surprised to find that they conveyed almost the exact opposite sentiment. 'All Great Things Are Precarious', they read.

5

Homes

Kensington, London

The ache for home lives in all of us, the safe place where we can
go as we are and not be questioned.

—Maya Angelou

The city of Leeds is offering bowls of fruit and complimentary
sweets. For North Kent, it's branded mints. 'Constellation' – a
partnership between Cheshire and Staffordshire – has baked
biscuits, thousands of them, and piled them up into hulking,
crumbly pyramids. Listburn and Castlereagh, the Northern
Irish district south of Belfast, is handing out bottles of locally
distilled potato vodka, famed for its subtle notes of vanilla and
long, clean finish. The exhibition booth where I'm given the
vodka is mocked up like a giant chessboard, with the words
'Make the Move' emblazoned on its walls. 'Last year, we had
a jigsaw theme,' explained Allan Ewart, the region's alderman
and development committee chair. He was standing on a white
square and I on a black one; a colossal queen piece, at least
twelve feet tall, loomed over us as we talked. 'This year it's
chess,' he shrugged. 'It makes us stand out.'

At MIPIM UK – one of the country's largest property fairs,
designed for 'international real-estate professionals whose

passion is to understand the UK market, and exploit its potential' – everyone is jostling to stand out. Stoke-on-Trent has a stand clad entirely in ceramic tiles, lending it the air of an outsized bathroom-store display window. Norwich and Suffolk have joined forces to build a vast curved advertising hoarding proclaiming 'The East', below which a series of thin plasma TV screens and fat pleather sofas have been installed. No metre of floor space, sheet of paper or courtesy tote bag has been left unbranded in the breathless chase by Britain's places to get noticed: Basingstoke bumps up against Plymouth; Stevenage wrestles with Surrey; Lancaster, Knowsley and Hull do battle with Bicester Garden Town. At the end of my first day at MIPIM, in need of a rest, I left the main exhibition space and walked upstairs to find a cocktail reception under way on the mezzanine. People in suits were milling around in small groups picking at gravlax, while a DJ played forgettable EDM and a table was laid with gloopy bowls of macaroni, pulled brisket and shallots. A man in a pink bowler hat ushered me to a seat and placed a bottle of Staropramen next to my food. Below it was a large flyer, printed in strong black type against a bright yellow background. 'Invest in Wigan', it implored me.

MIPIM stands for 'Le marché international des professionnels de l'immobilier' ('the international market of real-estate professionals'), and as Richard Leese – the council leader who reshaped Manchester to the tune of global capital, transforming the lives of young people like Layla and Kyle in the process – told me, 'The important word within MIPIM's acronym is *marché*. This is a marketplace, and the reason that we and other cities are here is that we are selling our wares.' The prospective buyers of those wares, who are real-estate investors from across the planet, are led quietly from stall to stall, maquette to maquette, amid a cacophony of local economic growth figures, low-tax guarantees, and aspirational slogans that sound like they've been generated by a corporate-catchphrase alliteration bot: 'Accelerated growth accelerating opportunity', 'Reimagine, Renew, Regenerate', 'Connect, Collaborate, Compete'. I watched a delegation of Chinese financiers gather around a large-scale model of north-west London's Old Oak development project – which at 1,600 acres and a value of £26 billion is currently the biggest in Britain – and stare on impassively as project leaders from the mayor of London's office danced around the glass case and pointed out highlights with laser pens. There was a pause to allow some noticeably less enthusiastic translations to reach the investors' earpieces. Then one of the group took a photo, and they all moved on, without a word. The tableau appeared so hopelessly lopsided that it bordered on the comical. Here were representatives of democratically elected bodies bowing, scraping and jesting in an attempt to win the favour of silent real-estate emperors and their entourages, and being rewarded with little more than the flash of a selfie stick in return.

If the Old Oak ambassadors wanted to up their game they could have attended one of MIPIM's many panel discussions, which featured titles like 'Liberating Land', 'Investors Summit: Risk and Reward' and 'Attracting Investors to UK Places'. One event was headlined 'Delivering Investor-Ready Regeneration Projects in the UK'. 'How easy is it to do business in your place?' Deborah McLaughlin, head of property consultancy GL Hearn – part of the outsourcing conglomerate Capita, which was sponsoring the discussion – asked the audience. 'Have you got a planning department that is pro-growth? Have you got people who understand the language of investors?' She raised her eyebrows sceptically, and unveiled a PowerPoint slide with the words 'Think Like An Investor' written in large font at the top. People sitting around me, largely delegates from local authorities, began frantically scribbling notes. Sir Edward Lister, chairman of Homes England – a government-sponsored housing body – nodded in agreement from the stage. 'I'm afraid,' he said, in the tone of a disappointed parent, 'that it's really hard to get investable propositions out of some places. They just haven't got it.' He reminded us that red tape and regulation are a turn-off for investors, and warned that councils needed to be more adaptable to the needs of developers; after all, other cities and other countries were forever out there, competing for money and attention. 'What I don't think people realise is the reputation you get for being "can-do", and how easily it's destroyed by somebody who is just really difficult and providing poor service,' he insisted. Ricardo Mai, development director for property giant Landsec, wrapped up the session. 'At the end of the day, if you want delivery, investors are looking for speed and pace, and certainty,' he concluded. 'So I think there's an issue of balance in there.' Landsec are the company behind central London's notorious 'Walkie-Talkie' skyscraper, which won planning permission despite being outside of the capital's designated area for tall buildings and was heavily criticised for failing to meet its community obligations. One newspaper described it as 'a stark reminder of forces that rule the City'.[1] After completion, Landsec swiftly sold the development on to a Hong Kong-based holding company, generating a record 167% return on their investment. Last year the company's profits rose to £42 million.[2]

Outside the Olympia exhibition centre, across the railway tracks and north up Russell Road, autumn leaves have slushed the pavements in a riot of red and bronze. It's quiet here, in the back channels between the exhibition centre and the massive Westfield shopping mall at Shepherd's Bush; distant enough from the auto-thunder on nearby Holland Road to hear snatches of conversation drifting out of windows in Arabic, English, Spanish and Romanian. Once-grand houses have been subdivided into flats and then partitioned even further, stippling opulent facades with motley doorbells. On the other side of the roundabout, a group of kids blazes up at a bus stop and an elderly man shuffles slowly into Jazz's barbershop while bellowing into a mobile phone. It's by the little parade of shops opposite St Ann's Villas, just before the Yara Students building – a new complex owned by a management firm that 'focuses on investing in the UK property market for Middle Eastern clients', and which offers rented studio accommodation for up to £19,000 a year – where the signs begin.[3] They are stuck on to lamp posts outside Nile Butchers and taped across pillars by the launderette. 'Have you suffered breathing problems following the fire?' they read. 'Call the NHS hotline now.' Still, there's nothing noticeable in the sky until you reach Sirdar Road, a bit further along, from where a black smudge becomes visible in the sky behind the trees. As you get closer, the tower begins to assume edge and form: it peeks out over rooftops and backfills chimneys and satellite dishes; it stains the space behind the climbing frame in the playground of Avondale Park school. There are more signs now, crowding fences and electricity boxes – not in official type, like the NHS ones, but in faded ink and handwritten scrawls. 'This is an atrocity' says one. 'This should not have happened' states another. At the foot of Treadgold Street, a series of identical notes have been laminated to protect against the rain. 'Please no photos,' they ask. 'This is the site of our loss'.

*

Britain's housing crisis has many roots and manifestations; its tendrils curl far and wide, around every space that anyone calls home. But there is a common stem that runs through all of it, and that stem is most visible here, along the byways and thoroughfares that link Olympia with the Lancaster West estate. The novelty chess pieces and overstuffed canapés of MIPIM feel a long way from the horrors of the Grenfell fire, but they are separated by only four months and barely a mile. Both are monuments to a particular vision of who housing is for and what it should look like: a vision of homes as commodities above all else, rather than as a necessity, or as a social good, or as places in which people's relationships to one another might be the function of shared experiences, of memory, ritual and affection instead of money and markets alone.

The first time I met Rasha Ibrahim, it was the day after she had been shown the remains of her sister and nieces in the morgue. We sat in the lobby of a west London hotel, the silences between us filled by the sounds of the frothing of the coffee machine, someone making a phone call to a taxi company, and her four-year-old son's beeping computer game. 'He has a problem with his nerves,' Rasha told me. 'It got worse when he saw Rania on the television. He went into a kind of fit, screaming and beating and breaking a lot of stuff. He hasn't been the same since.' It had taken ninety-nine days from the blaze on 14 June 2017 to the moment at which the authorities were able to formally identify what was left of the bodies of Rania Ibrahim, who died aged thirty-one, and her daughters Fethia and Hania, who were five and three respectively. 'They put her skeleton on the bed – not one piece, but different pieces,' said Rasha, urgently, making sure I understood. 'They put the different pieces together so that it looked like a skeleton, but some pieces were missing and the other parts were very burned. It was the same for the children.'

Rania and Rasha grew up in Aswan, the southernmost city of Egypt. It's where the Nile tumbles over its final cataract – a stretch of twists, turns, islets and boulders – before running straight across the desert, out towards the delta and the sea. 'We lived in one of the old houses,' remembers Rasha. There were seven siblings in all, but Rania was the one who made everybody laugh. She and Rasha worked in a pharmacy and Rania combined that with a law degree at university, but the truth was that she didn't like the course; she preferred reading her own choice of books, and larking around with her family. One of their older sisters, Sayyeda, had moved to London, and when Sayyeda was diagnosed with cancer in 2009 Rania flew out to help provide care and support. While visiting the UK, she met a young man called Hassan who worked at the al-Manar mosque in Westbourne Park, in the shadow of the Westway flyover. Rania stayed, and in 2011 she and Hassan married. In the wedding photos, you can see them sitting on glitzy thrones with an elaborate fruit-topped cake before them, he in a dark suit and her with a bright pink hijab and floral dress, each of them upright and tall. Later, there is a shot of the two of them alone, unstraightened, her head against his chest and her hand clutching at his shirt, both proud and vulnerable, both smiling. 'She was joyous,' says Rasha. 'We looked like adults, but when we saw each other we just fell back into childhood. The last time she came back to Egypt we just opened the fridge and started throwing eggs at each other. We were laughing and making a mess. It's how we lived life.'

In 2015, soon after their second daughter was born, Rania and Hassan were moved into Grenfell Tower by Kensington and Chelsea council. The views were incredible up there on the twenty-third floor, and Hassan toiled to make the flat feel like the home they had dreamed of, doing up the walls, ceiling and floor. The kids discovered the world on that floor, and revelled in it: at the Grenfell Inquiry, Hassan shared pictures of them bashing at bowls of cereal with plastic spoons, lathering themselves with shaving cream, and grinning through clouds of laundry powder that they'd tipped out of the box. 'Hania always followed her sister,' recalled Hassan. 'If Fethia wears a pink shirt, Hania wants to wear one. If Fethia drinks water, Hania wants to drink water. If Fethia wants to sleep, Hania wants to sleep. If Fethia says, "I love you Mama," Hania says, "I love you Mama."'[4] Like many of the Grenfell residents, Rania was scared about what might happen in a fire; enough to complain to the council about aspects of the tower's maintenance, and enough to demand information from Hassan about what to do if a conflagration ever broke out. Hassan spoke with the neighbours, and relayed back the official instructions: stay in your flat, and don't try to leave. 'I come back to my wife and I tell her, "Listen love, I'm going to leave the flat very nice for you and for my two kids, don't worry." She say, "Do you know, anywhere you go, where you stay, I'm going to be with you,"' said Hassan. 'I think that's the only mistake I do, when we came to Grenfell Tower.'

And so their lives unfurled: inside the new home, down through the tower block where they developed a tight-knit group of friends, out across the Lancaster West estate and beyond, where they would walk and sunbathe and picnic when the weather was fine. 'We don't have any plan,' said Hassan. 'Just we walk out, and we go as our feet will take us, and we enjoy the time.' Hassan told the inquiry that he could never have imagined harm would befall his young family here, in this place, for a reason so obvious that he repeated it three times: 'We are in London, in London, in London.' Rasha spoke with similar incredulity. 'How come this is London?' she asked me, and I didn't know what to say. To both of them, there was a disconnect between the baseline security that London promised, and the cataclysm it engendered, one that defied straightforward comprehension. Rania was forced to see the city differently. At the end of the video she live-streamed to Facebook on the night of the fire – after she opens her front door and welcomes lost neighbours into her flat out of the smoky void, after she tries to calm her panicked children, after she looks all the way down at the blue-lit pandemonium on the ground, feels the heat of the flames closing in from the flat below, and recites the Muslim declaration of faith – she finally turns her camera to the slanted skyline of the capital, dark and glittering through the haze. 'We are in London,' she says, simply. 'Where else?'

Who caused the deaths of Rania, Fethia and Hania, along with sixty-nine others in Grenfell that night? 'I want the people in charge to punish whoever was responsible,' Rasha told me. 'My message for the judge is please, from the inside of your heart, work for justice,' Hassan said at the inquiry. 'If it will take a hundred years, we want justice,' added Rania's and Hassan's family friend Munira, who also lived in the tower. 'Justice for everyone, please. Justice.' But justice is not a fixed quality; who and what it touches depends not just on where you point the lens of culpability, but how far you choose to widen it. We know now that Kensington and Chelsea council ignored warnings about fire safety from its residents at Grenfell, with whom it had developed a fractious relationship via an arms-length management organisation, and we know that when it was presented with different options for refurbishing Grenfell that the management organisation chose the cheapest one, resulting in the use of insulation and cladding components that were the main reason for the fire's devastating spread.[5] We know, too, that for many years standards of safety testing for building materials and fire risks had been falling, in part because many aspects of the regulatory regime had been privatised, fuelling competition between inspection units – a trend going back to the days of New Labour and intensifying with David Cameron's subsequent 'bonfire of red tape'.[6] But should we also consider the fact that fire services in London had been cut back in the years leading up to Grenfell, and that when then-mayor Boris Johnson was challenged on this by critics, he responded by telling them to 'get stuffed'?[7] Is it relevant that legal-aid provisions have been slashed away at by successive governments, making it harder for residents with safety concerns to ensure councils are answerable for their failings in the courts?[8] Did the construction industry's well-documented practice up until the late 2000s of blacklisting trade unionists, particularly ones who had a record of raising health and safety concerns on site, contribute to a culture of unsafe building practices, and did a cross-party effort to diminish trade union power over several decades contribute to the blacklisting?[9] The problem with accountability for the Grenfell fire is that in the intensity of its violence and the bluntness of its imagery it has come, rightly, to symbolise a collective failure in the way we organise ourselves as a country. And once you begin picking apart the tangle of a failure that broad, its filaments appear almost endless.

But there is one theme that ties together many of those filaments and leads back down the road to MIPIM: the story of what has happened to social housing in Britain over recent decades, which is itself part of that wider question about what homes themselves are for. In the late 1970s, at the start of the last great shift in this country's political tectonic plates, 42% of the population lived in council homes; today, that proportion has fallen to just 8%.[10] Margaret Thatcher's 'Right to

Buy' policy saw 2 million socially built and collectively owned housing units move into the private market – in the capital, as in Ancoats and Tilbury and everywhere else – and nearly half of them are now in the hands of landlords who let them out at rates which have grown far quicker than wages. In some London boroughs, rents have risen 42% since the financial crisis, and nationally one in seven tenants now hands over at least half their monthly income in order to keep a roof over their head. The provision of housing benefit, which offers state support for renters on low incomes and was designed in part to offset the decline of social housing, has simply resulted in a mass transfer of wealth from the public purse to the bank accounts of private landlords; it's been estimated that were every benefit claimant in London to be housed in council rather than private accommodation, local authorities would save almost £1 billion a year.[11] Meanwhile the social housing that does still exist pays for itself many times over and makes a profit for local authorities – Grenfell Tower generated more than £3.5 million in rent for Kensington and Chelsea council in the six years leading up to the fire, for example, while just over £500,000 was spent on standard maintenance and repairs during the same period[12] – but a web of central-government restrictions makes it exceptionally difficult for councils to build any more.

Although the basic economics are stacked so heavily in favour of social housing over the private rented sector, it is council housing, and council estates, that have repeatedly been associated with housing crises and stigmatised by leading politicians. Tony Blair made his first set-piece speech as prime minister at the Aylesbury estate in south London, rightly pointing out that many of its inhabitants had been sidelined from the country's growing prosperity; it is hard to see, though, how New Labour's subsequent 'regeneration programmes', which drastically reduced the number of homes available for social rent on the estates concerned, would ensure that prosperity was shared more equally. During his premiership, David Cameron promised to put estate redesign – and demolition – at the heart of his 'all-out assault on poverty and disadvantage'.[13] Although many communities were concerned about physical aspects of their estates, including enclosed stairwells that helped enable crime and the poor maintenance of common areas, Cameron went much further – characterising council housing as the preserve of 'gangs, ghettos and antisocial behaviour', and arguing it was no coincidence that three-quarters of those convicted for their part in the 2011 riots lived on estates. In many cases, he concluded, the best way forward would 'simply mean knocking them down and starting again'.

In the context of a prevailing political narrative that casts social housing as a problem, and bulldozers as a big part of the solution, it is little wonder that across the capital estate after estate has been knocked down over the past twenty years and replaced primarily by private housing units, many of which end up being purchased with buy-to-let mortgages and placed in the hands of global investors. The fate of the Heygate estate, just north of Aylesbury in Elephant and Castle, is typical: originally built to accommodate 3,000 social housing tenants, it was auctioned off by Southwark council in 2002 for £50 million – although the local authority then spent £44 million of that windfall pushing through its development plan.[14] Residents were promised that of 2,530 new homes to be con-structed on the site, 500 would be retained as social housing units, but by the time the successful bidder Lendlease – an Australian real-estate giant – unveiled its final blueprint, that number had been scaled back to just eighty-two. In 2017 it emerged that every one of the new private housing units sold so far had been bought by offshore capital. The old residential community at Heygate was broken up, with families offered alternative accommodation in different neighbourhoods all over London and beyond; some ended up as far west as Slough, and as far east as Thurrock – near Tilbury – and Sevenoaks in Kent.[15] 'I have been forced to give up my home to accom-modate the building of homes for overseas investors,' observed

Terry Redpath, a former Southwark housing officer and one of those evicted from the estate.[16] There are Terry Redpaths, and Heygates, all over London: the list of estates either already demolished or currently earmarked for full or partial demolition under a council 'regeneration' programme runs to eighty in all, from Aylesbury itself, where bulldozing began in 2009, all the way down the alphabet to Woodberry Down in Hackney and Wornington Green in Kensington, just over half a mile north-east of Grenfell. 'London's ruling elites are demolishing council estates like an occupying power toppling monuments from the old regime,' wrote sociologist David Madden in 2017. 'Except these monuments are also people's homes.'[17]

When social housing stops being seen as a place where real people live, and instead becomes either an issue to be tackled or a cash cow to be liquidated, the lingua franca of MIPIM UK – where councils come to 'sell their wares' – begins to make a lot more sense. Both Olympia, host of the conference, and Grenfell fall under the jurisdiction of the Royal Borough of Kensington and Chelsea. Its chief executive Barry Quirk – the man who was forced into an open-air negotiation on the picket line by striking cleaners and United Voices of the World – was seconded to the borough when its previous CEO resigned in the wake of the Grenfell fire. In his view, during the run-up to the fire the council was behaving like 'a property developer masquerading as a local authority'.[18] His remarks were met with outrage, but to anyone who has spent time at MIPIM, they would have come as no surprise. 'Think Like An Investor', the words written at the top of Deborah McLaughlin's PowerPoint presentation to local-authority representatives during the MIPIM panel discussion I attended, might as well have been the mantra of the entire conference. 'We hear a lot from cities about what they're up to,' observed Andrew Parker, chief executive of the Centre for Cities think tank and chair of that event. 'The question is whether it's relevant to the investment and to the development community. What do cities need to do to be more attractive to investors and developers?' John Miu, chief operating officer at ABP – a Chinese developer that is leading a mammoth real-estate project at east London's Royal Docks district – told me that in a world where buyers can pick between countries, cities and regions, what matters is how places mould themselves to the needs of foreign investors. 'Local governments and councils really need to have a more long-term view of the area, of their cities,' he said, 'of what they want to be.' In my conversation with Manchester's Richard Leese, he made several references not to England, Britain or the United Kingdom, but rather to 'UK PLC'.

The year before the Grenfell fire, Kensington and Chelsea council made more money out of the sale of just two social housing units than it spent on its fatal cut-price cladding for the tower; a chain of decision-making that is logical enough, perhaps, if you are thinking more like an investor, and less like the steward of a community. As Edward Daffarn, a Grenfell resident who wrote a blog predicting a calamitous fire in the tower, pointed out in its aftermath, the tale of what happened to this troubled corner of Kensington involved more than just building-regulation failures. It was about choices made by the local authority, like so many local authorities since the advent of austerity, to close or threaten a whole host of collective assets, including the local library, an adult education college, and a riding stables for children that is situated underneath the Westway. In Kensington and Chelsea's case, these choices included offering rebates to residents in the borough who were paying the top rate of council tax, all the while sitting on a budget surplus and reserves of more than a quarter of a billion pounds.[19] 'These things are linked,' Daffarn explained.[20] 'The things that were precious and mattered to this community were not respected and weren't protected.' The council insists that it understands the anger of Grenfell's community and has learned from its mistakes. But a few months after Rania, Fethia and Hania died, as part of its annual survey of local priorities, it asked residents to rate the importance of the Grenfell fire on a scale of one to ten, alongside other issues such as recycling, rubbish collection and congestion.[21] 'I don't want to give any personal opinion on this tragedy, it was clearly a tragedy, et cetera,' replied Ronan Vaspart, the director of MIPIM, when I asked him whether what happened at Grenfell just a few weeks earlier had changed the mood at this year's conference. 'We do see that the UK is still a really attractive place, and people are here to prove it.' It was a fortnight on from the Ibrahim family funeral, which took place at the al-Manar mosque only a few blocks away from where we sat; one adult-sized coffin and two smaller ones, each carried under the flyover by a throng of men in the driving rain. Vaspart told me that, as far as he could tell, there was nothing amiss with investor enthusiasm. 'All the feedback I got as of today is quite positive,' he reassured me. 'The meeting rooms are crowded ... People come here to attend the conferences, to learn more, to network and to do business.' London, I thought to myself. Where else?

And yet what Grenfell exposed, as much as the economic forces behind the marginalisation of social housing, was the readiness of communities – when pushed too far – to fight back. The evidence of that snapping point and the force of its reverberation was there in the immediate aftermath of the fire, when there were few representatives of local or national government to be found on the ground and it was volunteers who took on the task of responding to the needs of victims, all through those hours and days when broken windows in the tower were still discharging columns of ash, and the air in North Kensington lurched with fumes, stench and soot. 'People were hustling and bustling, the road was alive,' recalls Swarzy Macaly, a twenty-four-year-old from Ilford, on the other side of the capital, who travelled over to Grenfell as soon as she saw news of the fire and found herself leading efforts to organise and distribute donations to the newly homeless. 'They just came out of nowhere, from Birmingham, from Coventry, from all over London – it was that organic, that natural. There were pockets of everyone.' It was the Grenfell community, with help from arrivals like Swarzy, who directed traffic in that early period, who established a bedraggled grass-roots media to share information about what was going on, who walked the streets holding up posters they'd been handed of missing strangers. After helping to sort hundreds of boxes of supplies without any assistance from the council, Swarzy spotted a group of people who seemed to be officials, 'very glossy, very clipboard-ish', she said, 'not like me, raggedy, sweaty, and whatever'. She went over and asked for some details about how the donations were being processed, but was ignored. 'Not this girl, she's not with us,' she remembers one of the group saying, as another official turned up to hand out security wristbands. 'And I just thought, "I'm not wearing the same colour skin as you, I probably don't earn as much as you, and I'm not suited and booted like you." And I felt so deflated. I thought, "Why did I think I should have a say in anything?" So I just told them I wasn't there for a wristband, and left.' The streets themselves had a different vibe: Swarzy's phone contacts from that period are full of names like 'Andy with blue cap' or 'Faiza with red T-shirt', the mark of friendships forged swiftly in the heat of necessity. Overwhelmingly, those at the heart of solidarity actions reflected the make-up of Grenfell's community itself: first-, second- or third-generation migrants from Europe, Africa, Asia, the Americas and the Middle East. Just as Rania's had been, their reference points were global. 'If you believe you're a citizen of the world, you're a citizen of nowhere,' Theresa May had claimed in her Conservative Party conference speech the year before the fire. At Grenfell, while the state seemed nowhere, citizens of the world asserted their shared and vital ownership over somewhere that mattered so much to them. For Swarzy, being part of that story was painful, but exhilarating. 'I feel very privileged to be born at this time in history,' she told me. 'Young people went home thinking, "Oh my gosh, what was that? When can we do it again?"'

The fightback was visible, too, in the protests which erupted outside Kensington and Chelsea town hall later that week, as police formed protective rings around the entrance to the council chambers and a surging crowd bellowed, 'No justice, no peace.' Talking with demonstrators that day, it felt as if for many of them a dam had broken; the fire was the catalyst for anger, but it was an anger that grew out of connecting the dots which surrounded it. The trajectory of housing in London was addressed – 'They build luxury flats for the rich, and ovens for the poor,' said one speaker on the megaphone – but so too was inequality, attacks on migrants, race, class, policing, education, and the skewed loyalties and limitations of the mainstream media. 'What do you want to happen?' a journalist from Sky News had asked Ishmahil Blagrove, a local resident and co-ordinator of the Justice4Grenfell movement, the day after the blaze. 'What do I want to happen?' Blagrove replied, spinning round towards the camera. 'I want there to be a revolution in this country. I say fuck the media, fuck the mainstream.' Those around him broke into cheers. 'People actually believed your bullshit for a while,' continued Blagrove, pointing at the reporter. 'But [now] people are immune. They're wearing bulletproof vests ... they're immune to that shit now.' In the weeks that followed, council estates right across London – many of which were already home to vibrant anti-eviction movements – simultaneously hung 'Justice for Grenfell' banners from their tallest buildings. 'Justice will be yours, and because of that justice will be ours,' declared a joint statement from those involved, although the action received no coverage in the mainstream press.[22]

Like the catastrophic landing of Hurricane Katrina in the United States, for many in London Grenfell's devastation illuminated the rot of something larger. The state's inability to meet one fundamental demand – the desire we all share to feel safe and secure in a home that we can afford to live in – spawned many others, too many for the existing system to handle. Years later, toxins from the fire are still scattered around the Lancaster West estate and its environs, but so too are the seeds of something rebellious, something different.[23] 'Like a war-zone planted here in the city,' wrote the poet Ben Okri in response to Grenfell. 'A sword of fate hangs over the deafness of power / See the tower, and let a new world-changing thought flower.'

*

On a sunny September morning in 2018, two miles south-east of Grenfell, a group of young people in white shirts and red bow ties gathered on a lawn next to the Sherfield Building at Kensington's Imperial College, and began to play tiny violins. Inside, private landlords had gathered for a conference entitled 'Future Renting' – billed by the organisers, the Residential Landlords Association, as a response to the 'hostile environment' imposed on landlords by government regulation. 'With a tidal wave of legislation change on the horizon there are more tough times ahead for the PRS [private rented sector] landlord,' warned the association in a press release. 'The conference welcomes anyone with an interest in private rented housing, from landlords with just one property, to those with larger portfolios, letting-agency owners, local-authority councillors and officers, journalists, and housing charities.' Despite the day's keynote event being a panel discussion on 'Tenants As Consumers – The Future', tenants themselves weren't deemed to be among those with an interest in private rented housing, and didn't make the invite list. No matter. They wrote out a giant cardboard cheque for £22 billion – the amount private tenants would be paying to landlords in London over the coming year – and noisily turned up anyway. 'We need a lobbying-and-legal arm, and a direct-action-in-the-streets arm,' Anabel Bennett, a member of the London Renters Union – the organisation that arranged the protest – told me. She held up two fists as she spoke. 'But this one,' she said, raising her right arm further, 'the streets one, that's the strongest. It has to be. Because the law is not on our side. There are so few laws protecting private tenants that if you're going through a case with someone and trying to solve an issue for them, you very quickly exhaust all the legal avenues. So collective action isn't just a tactic, it's a necessity.'

Anabel is in her mid-twenties. If she had been born three or four decades earlier and reached this age during the mid-1980s, back when Margaret Thatcher was proclaiming her dream of Britain as a property-owning democracy, chances are she would have bought her own place by now or at least be on the cusp of doing so. At that time, it took the average young couple in outer London three years to save up a housing deposit, and more than half of twenty-five-to-thirty-four-year-olds owned their own home. Today it takes the average young couple nineteen years to save up a housing deposit, and just 16% of twenty-five-to-thirty-four-year-olds own their own home.[24] As late as 2002, the ratio of house prices to wages in London was 6.9 to 1; now it's more than double that, and across England home ownership is at a thirty-year low.[25] With the concurrent loss of social housing, Anabel, like millions of millennials, has been left with no choice but to rent privately. Having already spent most of her childhood dependent on the grace and whims of landlords – 'From the age of eight onwards, my family moved home pretty much every year because we were kicked out for some reason or another, or because the rent was raised so much that it became unaffordable,' she told me – she now lives in the knowledge that, on current trends, there is a good chance that the rest of her adulthood will look very similar. The number of privately renting households with children has tripled in just over a decade, from 600,000 in the mid-2000s to 1.8 million in 2016.[26] Half of Anabel's generational cohort will be paying private landlords well into their forties; one in three will still be renting privately when they are pensioners.[27] Like every private tenant in London, Anabel can trade rental horror stories for as long as you've got to spare. There was the place in Manor House that she got evicted from with no explanation; or the one in Kentish Town where the landlord announced that he was raising the rent by £100 per person, per month, just like that; or her most recent 'shitpit' property in Finsbury Park that featured no common space, no central heating, no protected deposits, and damp creeping up the walls.

'My current rental place is the fourteenth I've lived in, over a period of eighteen years,' she reflected. 'It affects you, more than you realise I think, not just because moving is always such an exhausting process, but because there is never anywhere you can simply just call, and feel, and be at home.'

In 1988, Section 21 of Britain's Housing Act came into force. It decreed that once the initial period of a tenant's contract had elapsed, landlords could evict them at any time with two months' notice and offer no reason whatsoever for doing so. That institutionalised precariousness on the part of the tenant not only encouraged property owners to repeatedly hike up rents, it also made tenants wary of questioning poor or unsafe living conditions. Nearly half of all private tenants who make a formal complaint about their housing are subjected to 'revenge evictions', and although local councils should theoretically help in these situations, in practice 95% of tenants are afforded no protection at all.[28] And so renters have been left to watch black mould bloom and swap tales of it on social media – via the popular #ventyourrent hashtag on Twitter, for example, where users post grim pictures of their homes and reveal the excuses landlords have given them for the poor living conditions (one was told that the reason for fungus growing on the walls was that the tenant was 'breathing at night'; another landlord blamed the presence of rats on 'tenants keeping food'). Since 2015, *VICE Magazine* has run a 'London Rental Opportunity of the Week' column on its website featuring real property listings for small, normally one-bedroom, tenancies: highlights include a shed in Sudbury Hill (£750 a month), a cupboard in Old Street (£1,785 a month), a 'three-storey petite studio' in Hammersmith that seemingly consists of nothing but interconnected well shafts (£800 a month), and several apartments with toilets placed inside kitchens, toilets placed inside showers, showers placed inside kitchens, and beds placed under stairs.[29]

With each passing year, the average size of Britain's housing units shrinks, and new-builds in the UK are now the smallest in Europe; official figures suggest that more than 2 million people live in privately rented homes that actively damage their health.[30] In desperation at rising rental costs, many have turned to alternative sources of accommodation that are shady at best, and abusive at worst. The 'live-in guardians' model, where those in need of housing are offered reduced rents on commercial sites in return for acting as 24/7 security guards, has come under fire for denying occupants even the paltry legal rights to which tenants are normally entitled; so too has the concept of 'lettings clubs' where occupants are technically 'members' rather than renters, and can be fined as much as £90 by managers for leaving a plate unwashed.[31] The housing organisation Shelter has reported a quiet rise of subsidised room rentals being offered in exchange for sexual favours to the landlord. 'Some people are desperate for housing,' observed Kate Webb, Shelter's head of policy. 'Others have the power to exploit that.' And yet despite their shared vulnerabilities and struggles, private renters are generally atomised from one another; they don't conceive of themselves as a collective economic entity, or political actor. 'Most people in London don't know their neighbours, never mind other private tenants in their area,' points out Anabel. So how do you begin to build a movement which enables them to assert power together? Over the past few years, several young organisations have been trying to find out. Acorn, a tenants union founded in Bristol in 2015, now has branches in Manchester, Brighton, Newcastle and four other cities around the country; Living Rent, a similar operation in Scotland, is active in Edinburgh and – as mentioned in the previous chapter – Glasgow too. But in London, where housing costs are highest and asymmetries between landlords and renters most extreme, the challenge of bringing the latter together has often felt insurmountable, at least until recently.

In the back room of a community centre near Bethnal Green, in March 2018, I watched Heather Kennedy – co-founder of a housing activist network called Digs in East London, and now a volunteer organiser with the London Renters Union (LRU) – ask a room full of private tenants where power lay within the housing system. 'Legislators!', 'Property developers!', 'Homeowners!' shouted various people in reply. Heather nodded. 'And what kind of power are we trying to build?' she continued. This time the answers were more hesitant. 'People power,' said one young woman. 'Relational power?' suggested her friend. Heather stuck a large piece of paper on the wall and wrote 'One-to-ones' at the top of it. 'One-to-ones are not interviews, or a chance to rant, or a date, or a counselling session,' she explained. 'They are a place to agitate someone, to find shared motivations and stories, to discover things you can do together.' We paired off with the person next to us and began practising these targeted conversations, guided by bullet points on the wall. 'What stories do people tell about what brought them here today? What questions will open up people's passions?' asked Heather, walking among the chairs that had been laid out on the carpet. It was a squeeze; the LRU had only formed a few months earlier, and this open meeting had drawn several dozen people, a bigger crowd than anyone expected. We were encouraged to ask each other what made us angry about our housing situation, how any housing problems we mentioned made us feel, and how we thought things might change. 'Listen, and discover people's skills,' Heather urged us. 'Don't try and do anything for someone that they're able to do themselves. Remember: we're a movement, not a service union.'

One-to-ones are at the core of the LRU's political model, because organisers like Heather, Anabel and Amina Gichinga – a singer, music teacher and community activist – believe that the only way to overcome the fragmentation of private renters is to build strong, geographically concentrated solidarity networks from the bottom up, rather than constructing a loose and diffuse association from the top down. One of their inspirations is the 'Plataforma de Afectados por la Hipoteca' ('Platform for People Affected by Mortgages') movement in Spain that developed in response to the financial crisis in the late 2000s and the mass repossession by banks of people's homes. Structured around hundreds of autonomous local assemblies,

PAH's manifesto explicitly distances itself from consumer associations and charities. 'We are a citizens' movement to defend
and conquer our rights,' it declares.[32] 'The PAH is a space of
encounter, mutual aid and trust in which anyone can help and
be helped.' Replicating that dynamic in London means ensuring
that the LRU looks like the communities it is building within,
communities that – as Amina pointed out – are typically less
white, less middle class and less immersed in the existing
world of left-wing London activism than those attending this
particular meeting in Bethnal Green. 'Strong, local networks
already exist in Newham,' she said, referring to the east London
borough where the LRU had just opened its inaugural branch.
'There are migrants' networks, movements against school acad-
emisation, movements to support the Roma people. These are
groups we want to reach out to, connect with and learn from.
It's not always clear on the surface, but this stuff is bubbling,
and I want you to know that.'

One-to-ones aren't instantly gratifying and effortless in the
way that signing a petition or joining a Facebook group can
be. They involve sitting down with someone from your local
area – Heather recommended a minimum of forty-five minutes – and giving yourself the chance both to discover current
communal connections and devise fresh ones. Anabel, whose
first experience in this sort of activism came when she helped
to organise rent strikes against her student-accommodation
provider while at university, recently travelled to Barcelona on
behalf of the LRU to make contact with PAH campaigners. 'In
Spain, a sense of community is much more central to people's
lives than here, and the assemblies work because they can be
so local, right down to the neighbourhood level,' she told me.
'People already know each other, they are already connected.
We're trying to work out how to translate that here, to a city
where the neoliberal economic model has hit people hardest,
and where we don't have that much of an existing community
base. That's why migrant networks are so important – because
there are links already there that can be built on – and why

it's so important to understand that people take on many identities. A tenant is not just a tenant: they are a worker, a mother, a carer, whatever, and right now the housing crisis is almost certainly affecting every element of their life. That's a challenge for us, but it's also a huge opportunity.'

I asked Anabel what aspects of the LRU's work she gets most excited about. In response, she didn't mention the big protest outside the Residential Landlords Association conference in Kensington. Nor did she flag up some of the other high-profile LRU campaigning events which have followed, such as the showdown with a letting agent in Romford accused of conning a vulnerable tenant and LRU member out of thousands of pounds, which prompted fellow LRU members to stage colourful protests outside the firm's offices, as well as to swamp them with calls about the issue as part of a highly disruptive, long-distance 'phone picket'. Instead, Anabel talked about the LRU members in Newham who have come together to help redecorate each other's flats, or to pack up boxes and lift furniture when one of their group is forced to move. 'Even when you join the union, you won't feel ready to truly get involved, to really take risks, until you've built up trust in people,' she said. 'You won't have that trust until you walk into a room and see a group of people around you, whether they are a working-class Muslim family or a young white renter from a middle-class background who looks like a gentrifier, and think "these are people who will support me"'. She brought up the case of one LRU member in west London who was facing eviction under Section 21 legislation, and turned to the union for help. The co-ordinators only had a few hours' notice of what was happening before the bailiffs arrived, and the member's home was a long way from the city centre, but they put a call out for solidarity on WhatsApp; the following morning, twenty people showed up at the crack of dawn to form defensive lines at the front and back doors. Unable to access the property, the bailiffs eventually gave up, and during the two weeks' grace that followed the member was able to find alternative housing in Newham instead of falling into homelessness. 'And now, he's super-involved in the union,' grinned Anabel. 'He comes to every meeting, gets stuck into every action, helps out others in the LRU with member support. That's what mutual aid looks like, and that's how we will grow this union. That's how we must fight for fairer housing in London.'

From Newham, the LRU has expanded into Leytonstone; from Leytonstone into Hackney; from Hackney over to Lewisham. Street by street, shopping parade by shopping parade, the union is knocking on doors and setting up stalls, slowly infiltrating a metropolis that, from above, can sometimes resemble an exquisitely wrought treasure chest: studded with shiny towers and sparkling shrubbery, but driven by little more than money and the interactions between those bending over backwards to hand it over, and those who receive it. 'The combination of global capital, government policies designed to kill off social housing and failures in housing benefit are reconfiguring the city,' writes housing academic Anna Minton.[33] 'The politics of space is replacing the traditional politics of class. The old hierarchy of upper, middle and working class, which ranked groups in society as workers and bosses, no longer holds up in the face of a property-based economy where the income from rent far exceeds economic growth and wages. There is more wealth coming into London than ever before, but these riches are not shared, with unaffordable property prices and rents making life worse for the majority.' Like that of central Manchester, London's housing market is no longer a market at all in the traditional sense; it now beats to the rhythm not of local supply and demand, but of international financial flows, and those who can't keep pace are finding themselves hollowed out from within. The café where Anabel and I first met, Pueblito Paisa – part of the eclectic indoor market known as the 'Latin Village' in Tottenham, north-east London – is set to be demolished soon as part of a council-supported redevelopment project led by Grainger PLC, the UK's largest professional landlord; mock-ups of the retail units that will replace the market feature branches of Costa Coffee and Pizza Express.[34] When I first started reporting on United Voices of the World, it was headquartered alongside a gaggle of small international solidarity organisations and obscure religious ministries up in Hannibal House, the tower that rises above the Elephant and Castle shopping centre; all of them have now been evicted as part of the Lendlease regeneration scheme. London is still one of the most electrifying cities on the planet, filled with cultural subspaces. But across the capital, quirky pubs, gay saunas, decades-old music venues, theatres and dog tracks – the crannies that cater to communities whose strength must be measured in something other than financial clout – are being gradually buried, often under identikit towers of new-build concrete: global bank accounts with walls and windows, stacked high atop one another to the sky.

Unaffordable housing and cultural stasis are symbiotic: more people are now leaving London than moving to it, with net outward migration up by 80% since the early years of the financial crisis.[35] The sociologist Saskia Sessen calls this process 'de-urbanisation', describing it as the haemorrhaging not just of residents themselves, but of the connective tissue that forms around them: the frontier zones, as Sassen puts it, 'where actors from different worlds can have an encounter for which there are no established rules of engagement, and where the powerless and the powerful can actually meet'.[36] Hyper-investment in London property and the private-developer-led regeneration model on display at MIPIM has resulted in not just buildings themselves but even the streets, parks and plazas in between them falling into corporate hands. There are now more than fifty large open spaces in the capital that appear to be public but are actually privately owned and run, and where landholders are permitted to employ their own security guards and police behaviour as they see fit. One of them houses London's seat of government: City Hall sits on an estate owned ultimately by the sovereign wealth fund of Kuwait, which forbids journalists and photographers from operating on their site without prior corporate permission.[37] Just as they are most likely to be excluded from new housing opportunities, it is London's most marginalised populations that tend to bump up hardest against these invisible fault lines: the rough sleepers moved on by a private security firm to preserve the aesthetic quality of a new set of 'public' squares in King's Cross, for example, or the housing complex in Lambeth where initially the playground was open only to the children of property owners, forcing those of the social housing tenants on the same site to go elsewhere.[38] 'We've gone from being ruled by Barclays bank to being controlled by Berkeley Homes,' Peter Rees, the City of London's former chief planner, proclaimed in 2014.[39] It is this London, at this time, that makes the LRU's alternative vision and form of organising feel so radical. It is this London, with all its epic and infinitesimal iniquities, that might just mean they win.

*

Kensington, home to MIPIM and to Grenfell, as well as to the LRU's first major public protest, is a barometer of the challenge facing those who seek a different kind of London: a gauge of the sheer scale of what they're up against, but one that offers some optimistic indicators too. Walking the streets here can be a disorientating experience. Of course, all of the capital's neighbourhoods are socially variegated; this is the city where wealth and poverty get lost most rapidly in one another, forming enclaves within enclaves as precise as they are dense. Yet even by London's standards, Kensington's shifts can give you whiplash. Blocks of social housing give way to genteel rows of cherry blossoms and white Regency villas worth millions; at the bottom of Kensington Palace Gardens, the most expensive street in Europe, stands a TK Maxx, where end-of-line products are sold at heavy discounts.[40] Just south of Kensington Palace Gardens is Heythrop College, an educational institution which will soon be knocked down to make way for a new private-housing complex consisting of a luxury spa, wine-tasting room, dog-grooming parlour, and apartments with a market value of between £3 million and £6 million each. Out of 142 properties built on the site in total, five will be classed as affordable. Yet travel a few stops north of Heythrop on the 452 bus and you'll come to St Marks, a housing co-operative that provides a not-for-profit alternative to the short-term 'live-in guardians' system. Right next to the Lancaster West estate, staring up at the smooth skin of the Westfield shopping centre, lies the remnants of the People's Republic of Frestonia: a squatters' community that declared independence from Great Britain in 1977 in protest against the planned demolition of their homes. Frestonia appointed its own foreign minister, and began issuing stamps; at one point during their struggle, several occupants changed their surnames to 'Bramley' – named after nearby Bramley Road – in an attempt to be legally recognised as a family unit, and thus rehoused together. Bailiffs and bulldozers have always threatened Londoners, and Londoners have always dreamt up unexpected ways of pushing back.

And then there is the Walterton and Elgin estate, the story of which is really the story of post-war housing in London – only, in this case, one that offers an alternative ending. Properties here, just north of the Paddington branch of the Grand Junction Canal on the other side of Kensington's border with Westminster, were built in the late nineteenth century. By the 1950s they were run-down and being bought out by unscrupulous private landlords, including the infamous Peter Rachman whose name became so synonymous with the mistreatment of tenants that it entered the *Oxford English Dictionary*. In the years that followed, all manner of misfits and bohemians made their homes around Walterton Road, including rock band the 101'ers (named after the door number of the house they squatted in) whose frontman Joe Strummer went on to form the Clash. In the 1980s, ownership of the estate passed to the local authority, which – presaging the London still to come – announced that it planned to 'create a new community' on the site, replete with a high-end hotel.

'I remember the phone call,' Jonathan Rosenberg, who was living on the estate at the time, told me. 'There was no consultation, no warning. They told us that our homes were being sold off and demolished, and something just went off in my head. I just thought, how dare they? That phone call changed the course of my life, and I've never stopped since. I simply can't stand bullies.'

Jonathan and other residents threatened with eviction formed the Walterton and Elgin Action Group, which waged a seven-year war with the council to halt their expulsion and secure control of the estate by its community instead. Members ranged from twentysomething 'soul poets' to grizzled octogenarians; together they lobbied council meetings, targeted potential private investors, and stencilled a huge 'Not For Sale' sign on top of one of the estate's tallest towers, Chantry Point. The local authority, led by Dame Shirley Porter (of homes-for-votes scandal fame), put up a ferocious resistance to the idea of community ownership, deploying an array of dirty tricks and at one point even housing homeless families on the estate in units that it knew were contaminated with asbestos. But in 1992, campaigners won the battle and the site was formally transferred to a new entity entitled Walterton and Elgin Community Homes (WECH) – a democratic body, run by its own residents. WECH is now one of the largest community land trusts in the country, responsible for over 600 homes. Community land trusts take different legal forms, but common to all of them is that they don't generate profit and are designed to benefit a particular local group, members of which all have an equal say when it comes to decision-making. 'Communities can own anything: housing, agricultural land, woodlands, ports, lighthouses, castles, you name it,' argues Jonathan, who has gone on to become a full-time advocate for the community housing model, and now advises residents' groups and local authorities all over the country. He pointed out that the majority of land has been held in common for much of human history. 'Private ownership of land is actually a very modern aberration,' he told me. 'Bullies started stealing from poor people a few hundred years ago, and they haven't stopped since.'

Community land trusts are not a panacea for the housing crisis. Lots of things have gone wrong along the line that runs from Grenfell to MIPIM, and the job of repairing them will require a number of different tools. Rent controls and more robust rights for private tenants may be among them, alongside a reversal in the decline of social housing and a dramatic rebalancing of the relationship between property developers and local authorities, all rooted in a reconceptualisation of housing as a fundamental social good rather than a global commodity to be gambled on. But to their supporters, community land trusts are key to providing a route not just away from the violence of estate evictions, but also towards a future that doesn't involve blandifying the city. 'Commodification only really became possible by stealing land out of community ownership,' argues Jonathan. 'Now if it can be said that the privatisation of land – taking land out of community ownership – is one of the major drivers of commodification, then putting land back into community ownership is an antidote to commodification: a very deep antidote too, not just something that treats symptoms but something that actually gets at the cause.' At WECH, a sense of communal ownership is woven into the fabric of the estate: when residents first won the right to take control of the neighbourhood themselves, a democratically elected management board ensured that friends and families were placed in refurbished units next to one another – compare that to the vast displacement of former residents on the Heygate estate – and the administrative office is located only a short distance away from anybody's home. 'A community land trust headquarters should be within fifteen minutes' walk of any property,' insists Jonathan, 'because residents need to be within walking distance of staff and more importantly staff need to be within walking distance of residents. If they can't walk to people's homes, they won't see them, and if they can't see them, how will they ever understand them and look after them?'

An independent study in 2010 designed to measure the impact of community ownership found that WECH residents, despite being more economically deprived than the regional or national average, reported a much stronger sense of belonging to their neighbourhood. Over 90% of WECH inhabitants felt secure in, and proud of, their homes – a rise of more than thirty percentage points compared to their previous, precarious, living situation under Porter's Westminster council. Jonathan showed me some of the old campaign posters produced during the battle against eviction, including designer John Phillips' iconic image of a figure in a hat, suit and tie with a face made out of a mechanical digger, and the strapline, 'We are a little worried about our landlord'. 'WECH residents have gone from a deep level of insecurity to an extraordinarily deep level of security,' concluded Jonathan. 'It's transformed us psychologically, because we don't have that fear or worry about the landlord any more. The landlord is benign, the landlord is amenable, the landlord is ourselves. There is no us and them. The landlord has a face at last.'

As of 2018, London councils have already granted planning permission for more than 26,000 new luxury apartments valued at over £1 million, most of which are yet to begin construction.[41] Council leaders cite the impact of austerity to justify these decisions, and it is true that the capital has been among the hardest hit by national cuts; local authorities in London lost, on average, a fifth of their budgets between 2010 and 2018, and in places like Hackney that equates to a reduction in spending power per household of nearly £1,500 each year.[42] Income from top-end developers helps make up for some of that shortfall. But that on its own does not account for councils' repeated refusals to hold developers to account for breaking their public commitments on affordable housing, nor for the hostility with which community-based alternative development proposals have routinely been met. At many councils it seems that the logic of late capitalism – of markets, ultimately, knowing best – is continuing to stifle political imaginations. If the housing needs of those who live in the city do remain subordinate to the interests of global capital, it is not hard to envisage what this next wave of de-urbanisation might look like: flats snapped up overwhelmingly by investment outfits, anonymous tax-haven addresses and absentee landlords, guarded by concierges who sit in a small pool of light on the ground floor at night, propping up towers of ghosts. Almost one in five MPs are landlords and nearly a hundred London councillors have links to the property industry; given the money already sunk into a perpetuation of the housing status quo, the prospects for change can often seem dim.[43]

And yet change is materialising. The LRU are already racking up successes, both for individual members and the renter community more widely: in April 2019, following sustained pressure from the union and other housing campaign groups, the government announced that – despite furious lobbying from the Residential Landlords Association – it would begin consultations on the scrapping of Section 21 and 'no fault' evictions. And to the south of Kensington at Earls Court, another attempt to 'decant' a social housing community in order to make way for a multibillion-pound redevelopment project – this time helmed by the global management and consultancy company Capco – has hit the buffers thanks to a concerted effort by residents of the imperilled estates to stand firm and insist on a community-ownership alternative instead. 'Grenfell has changed the mood, and a new political consensus is emerging,' says Jonathan Rosenberg, who is supporting the 'People's Plan' for the West Kensington and Gibbs Green estates. At least one of the local authorities concerned has now turned against Capco and is considering using compulsory purchase orders to force the company out; the current mayor of London, Sadiq Khan, has also declared his opposition to the original 'regeneration' plan, and is urging Capco to hand back the land to the local community.[44] 'Now that the dragon is on the ground,' observed Jonathan, 'the invitation to come and do some spearing has gone out, and there's a queue down the street.' In among the stalled cranes and CCTV-monitored construction hoardings encircling the site, there is a feeling that the tide might finally be turning against the sort of makeover inflicted on the Aylesbury or Heygate estates, the sort of makeover residents of the Walterton and Elgin estate battled so mercilessly to resist. 'We won', reads graffiti on some corrugated iron fencing in the area.[45] 'You should fight them too'.

Just before I left MIPIM, I tried out one of the conference's star attractions: a virtual-reality simulator created by the French bank BNP Paribas, who are heavily invested in property development projects and keen to position themselves as central to the 'future of real estate'. The company's head of digital innovation, Florian Couret, ushered me in to an eight-sided grey box spotlit by neon green lamps, and sat me down in front of a large flatscreen television displaying the words 'Bienvenue Sur Le Pod' ('Welcome to the Pod'), against a background of Chinese lanterns. He fitted a headset over my eyes, and I found myself in a digitally rendered skyscraper in Saint-Ouen, on the north side of the Parisian Périphérique. A shiny black table was in front of me, surrounded by office chairs; through the windows, the cityscape glowed in the early evening sun, and the names and location of other BNP Paribas construction projects shimmered on the horizon. A small digital maquette of the building I stood in was positioned at the bottom of my field of vision, and as I focused on it and nodded my head up and down, storeys melted away and re-formed accordingly. In its pixelated rigour, the world before me lost all distinction: three-dimensional blades of grass flickered in a non-existent wind, blocks of colour appeared and vanished, metal became wood, wood became glass, glass became cut-out people. 'The Pod is a marriage of start-up innovation that will enable clients to make even more informed and empowered decisions about their real-estate investments,' read the promotional material that BNP Paribas sent to me that evening. 'An investor can project himself into a building, even those that do not yet exist, in any city in the world … Or, a town-planning committee can envisage a new urban landscape, giving them the potential to truly embrace the concept of place-making.' It was the kind of language that has become commonplace among both developers and local authorities in Britain, and the thought of town-planning committees determining the future of our neighbourhoods by sitting in virtual-reality boxes mediated by BNP Paribas made my head swim all the more. 'The primary role of the council has become one of place optimisation and entrepreneurship,' claimed Lambeth officials recently.[46]

Soon after the end of my time at MIPIM, I visited a small art gallery near Waterloo which was displaying a series of artworks responding to the London housing crisis.[47] One of them, created by the artist Jasper Delamothe, was a virtual-reality experience shot inside the council flat of Aysen Dennis, a fifty-nine-year-old woman facing eviction from the Aylesbury estate.[48] Wearing a VR headset identical to the one installed in Le Pod, I was able to view a 360-degree panorama of Aysen's living room and watch her feed her cat, put the kettle on, and settle down to watch some tennis on TV. Nothing else happened: no disappearing floors or rising rebars, no pulsing dots indicating a portal to other real-estate projects, no marketing blurbs flashing down the left-hand side of the screen. All I could see was a person, sitting on a sofa in front of windows that looked out across her city, savouring the prosaic and dwindling wonder of feeling safe and secure in her home.

6

Parties

Brighton, East Sussex

There are three stages through which every new notion in England has to pass: 'It is impossible: It is against the Bible: We knew it before'.

—Sidney Webb

It takes less than five minutes to walk along the seafront from the Hilton Metropole to the Synergy Centre, but the distance feels like a country mile. At the Hilton, once you get past security, things are brisk and neatly organised; the air smells of time-tables and lanyards. The first time I entered the Synergy Centre, where there is no security, a stranger handed me a can of Red Stripe. Woven banners and tall posters tumbled down the walls, and a vapour machine pumped low clouds across the stage. At the Hilton, drinks receptions are sponsored by institutions like the Law Society, or Boeing, or NatWest, and advertised as a 'great opportunity to network'; at Synergy, nights tend to end with laser beams, ferocious dancing, and chants demanding the nationalisation of Greggs. 'When people ask you where you were at the end of neoliberalism,' cried a woman into the microphone at one of Synergy's events, 'you can tell them you were in a dark, dank club space in Brighton!' The crowd let out a euphoric roar.

The World Transformed, a festival of arts, politics, music and rupture, has taken place alongside Labour's annual conference every year since Jeremy Corbyn became leader of the party in 2015. Its big, official cousin always unfolds in a tight, semi-militarised zone guarded by armed police; by contrast, TWT, as The World Transformed is known, sprawls across the cities that host it, fizzing into gallery spaces, community centres, former homeless shelters and Regency churches. In Brighton, there were TWT sessions on the future of work, the rise of new media, reclaiming football from the clutches of corporate ownership, and luxury automated communism; there was a sensorial fashion workshop, a three-day hackathon inspiring young people to take on the tech giants at their own game, and a panel discussion entitled 'Acid Corbynism' in which a long-winded question from somebody representing the Psychedelics Society was interrupted by hecklers demanding that acid house be played without delay. I watched debates about the planet's future that referenced both loft insulation and Marx's *Grundrisse*, queues for a political pub quiz that stretched for block after block down Bond Street, and a rave finale featuring the Feminist Jukebox DJ collective, Horse Meat Disco, and gusts of dry ice. Anyone can come to TWT, and at every event, time permitting, everybody is encouraged to speak. Each September, the festival poses lots of questions about the moment we're in: questions about the economy, about how we conceive of care, about the lessons of history when it comes to social struggle, about internationalism, populism and repre-sentation. But the biggest question it asks is one that doesn't appear in the programme, and that's whether all this – TWT's messiness, and its massiness – is where politics is really at now, or whether, ultimately, power remains sealed inside the secure zone, 400 yards up the road.

That question has preoccupied the left for more than a century, but never with more urgency than today. TWT, and its main organisers Momentum, are positioned at the cross-roads of two very different political traditions: one formal, parliamentary and focused on electoral gains, the other grass roots and community-built, anchored in the language and culture of social movements.[1] As politics in Westminster jerks from crisis to crisis, patently unequal to our times, so a space has opened up for more radical currents to lap up against the citadel, potentially contaminating those within. In Brighton, a steady stream of the infected abandoned the comforts of the Hilton and made the short journey down Kings Road to Synergy, be it just to sate their curiosity about TWT and soak up some of its energy, or to proclaim, as several senior politicians did, that *this* was where the action was now, that what drove them forward was to be found not there but here. 'The cosy consensus in Parliament is beginning to crumble,' declared Clive Lewis, one of Labour's shadow ministers, at a TWT event. For a long time, he explained, those who shared the values of TWT had been on enemy turf in Westminster. 'We were facing uphill, and they were at the top of that hill,' he observed. 'Well now we're choosing the terms of battle!' He was buried in cheers, and nodded approvingly as he gazed around the room. 'It's about having local spaces where there's an alternative to the narrow confines of corporate consumerist culture, where we talk about things like solidarity and love and respect and community,' he went on. 'These aren't words that are normally associated with politics, but they should be.' On the same platform, a few days earlier, Corbyn himself had appeared to a pounding rendition of the White Stripes' 'Seven Nation Army' and the vapour machine on full whack. 'Through the fog and through the smoke, we can see the future,' he yelled, and the stage scaffolding shuddered with the applause. 'There is something happening here!'

And yet just as elected representatives were making the pilgrimage to Momentum's pulsating political carnival, so too were Momentum members heading the other way, up towards the Hilton Metropole and on to the official conference floor. There they were sent recommendations from Momentum's leadership via a mobile app regarding which way to vote on dozens of ballots each day, concerning everything from the topics that would be selected for 'contemporary motion debates' to byzantine procedural issues relating to the published agenda of the conference arrangements committee. Cans of Red Stripe were nowhere to be seen. The new politics, it seemed, involved stuff that looked quite a bit like the old. 'These things are interconnected, and they're all necessary,' Laura Parker, Momentum's national co-ordinator, told me. 'They involve very different ways of working, and depending on your background you might find one of them very didactic, or very woolly. It's a constant tension, and we'll never resolve it. It's not our job to resolve it, it's our job to be the bridge.' That bridge, in Momentum's eyes at least, will eventually connect groups like Demand the Impossible, United Voices of the World, the Unity Centre and the London Renters Union to the epicentre of government, and vice versa.

But building it is a hard task, especially when many of those active in social movements have good reason not to trust organs of the state, and view the Labour Party as one such organ. The success or failure of Momentum's project will help shape the future not just of Labour, but of institutional politics in Britain; it will help determine whether Westminster, after decades of technocratic stasis that have tipped into chaos, can be refashioned into something that citizens feel they have agency over, an entity that is meaningfully plugged into the politics of their daily existence. The great unknown is whether Momentum, throughout its fight to realise this, can maintain its proximity to institutional power without becoming institutionalised itself along the way. 'Have you heard of the Westminster Club?' Momentum asks in one of its wildly popular short videos, against a backdrop of foppish aristocrats enjoying a ball before a horse suddenly gallops in through one of the windows and sends the revellers flying. 'We're crashing the party.' The question is, what will the horse do next?

*

When Santiago searches back through his earliest memories, he mostly sees picket lines. He was seven years old when Augustus Pinochet, the Chilean military dictator responsible for thousands of brutal executions, was arrested by British police in 1998 at London Bridge Hospital while recovering from surgery. An eighteen-month legal battle ensued over whether Pinochet should be extradited to Spain to face trial on charges of torture, or be released on medical grounds. 'It kicked off every day after school,' remembers Santiago. 'Some days we would miss school altogether, and just head to wherever we needed to be: the Chilean embassy, Grovelands [Priory Hospital], [Pinochet's rented house in] Virginia Water, Margaret Thatcher's house in Belgravia. We were always moving, because we wanted to make sure that wherever Pinochet went, no matter what time of the day or night, there would be Chileans outside the window shouting at him. At that age, you don't understand all of the politics. You just know that Pinochet was a bad guy, and that he did bad things to your family.'

Santiago's father Jimmy was the son of a high-ranking political figure in the southern Chilean province of Ñuble under the socialist government of Salvador Allende, which was overthrown by Pinochet in a 1973 US-backed coup. Like many of Pinochet's political enemies, he was sent to a concentration camp for two years; other members of the family were killed or disappeared. Jimmy managed to get out, though, along with his mother Miriam and a scattering of relatives. 'They turned up at the airport and were just given different tickets,' said Santiago. 'None of them knew where they would be going.' Jimmy ended up in London, and then a school in Cambridge. 'He loved the sweets in Britain,' smiled Santiago. 'But he always thought it was temporary. The sad thing is that for literally decades there was always a bag packed by his bedside, so he would be ready to return home. He never did.' Instead, Jimmy stayed and started a family. Growing up among the vibrant, politicised Latin American community in London, Santiago was weaned on stories of the old country and the injustices inflicted both there and here. He can still recall the moment in March 2000 when then Home Secretary Jack Straw announced he had overruled a final court decision to extradite Pinochet, and would allow him to walk free instead. 'Everyone was crying,' said Santiago. 'I turned to my dad and said, why don't we just call 999 and ask for the police? We can tell them that Pinochet is a bad guy and then they'll have to go and get him. My dad told me that things didn't work like that. It made me realise what justice was, or at least what it wasn't.'

Fifteen years later, Santiago was working as a labourer when some curious news came through. It was the mid-2010s, and the explosion of wealth inside the capital's property market showed no signs of abating. Santiago, who lived with his family in an Islington council flat, was put to work renovating multimillion-pound houses in chic neighbourhoods like Belsize Park. 'You see the worst excesses from that angle,' he told me. 'Properties were being traded and flipped faster than we could keep up with. We'd be doing a building and halfway through the job the foreman would come in and say, "The house has just been sold, so strip out all the work you've done because the new owner has different ideas. Oh, but keep the spiral staircase and marble walls."' On one occasion, Santiago was told to take delivery of a small box of hand-painted terracotta tiles. 'The guy explained that this box of tiles cost more than they would be paying me in a year, and that my sole job for the rest of the day was just to sit next to it, making sure it wasn't damaged.'

The obscenity of London's inequalities gnawed at Santiago, but he wasn't sure what to do about it. A few years earlier he had joined Labour, but in truth he often found the party's incessant triangulation and lack of ambition to be uninspiring, and despite paying his membership dues he'd never really engaged. Those around him took little interest in electoral politics at all; their feelings towards Westminster tended to be resentful, and minimal. 'It was despairing,' he said. 'One of my biggest political wake-up calls was on the day of the 2015 general election when I was working on a building site. During the smoking break I asked all the young guys if they were voting. One by one, without exception, they all went round and explained that they would be voting for UKIP. And then one by one, without exception, they all went round and realised they hadn't actually registered, so couldn't vote for anyone after all. It was a microcosm of everything that was wrong.' It was a few weeks later that Santiago heard the news. Following the resignation of Ed Miliband, the Labour Party was having a leadership contest, and a left-wing backbencher named Jeremy Corbyn had just thrown his hat into the ring. Pundits thought it unlikely that he would garner enough nominations from MPs to even make it on to the ballot paper, and the bookies dismissed him as a 100–1 outsider. Most people hadn't heard of the man. But Santiago had. Not only did Corbyn represent one of Islington's constituencies in Parliament, but he had also been standing alongside Santiago at nearly every vigil, every protest, and every picket line that the Chilean solidarity movement in Britain had ever staged.

As the results were announced, Santiago's family were gathered together listening on the car radio. When Corbyn emerged victorious, with a staggering 60% of the vote, every one of them joined Labour there and then. 'We all need to commit to this thing,' said Jimmy. 'Santiago, you need to be involved.' They asked around to see if there were any volunteering opportunities available, and were eventually sent an address in Soho where, apparently, the seeds of a new political organisation, built out of the Corbyn leadership campaign, were being sown. 'I didn't know what it was,' remembers Santiago. 'The first day I turned up there, it was horrible. Four people I didn't know in a room, arguing about things I didn't understand: arguing in the morning, arguing over lunch, arguing when we came back in the afternoon. At one point they seemed to remember I was there, handed me a spreadsheet of local Corbyn supporter groups from the leadership election, and told me to ring them all up and ask if they wanted to become a Momentum group. "What's a

Momentum group?" I asked? "No idea," came the reply. "Just ring them."' When Santiago got home, he complained to his mum that the whole thing had been a waste of time. But later that evening he received a text from one of the four founders of the new group – Adam Klug, a teacher from Birmingham. 'I'm sorry today was so shit,' it read. 'We understand if you don't want to come back, but please give us another chance.' Fuck it, thought Santiago. One more day. Four years later, he had become one of Momentum's senior co-ordinators as well as an elected Labour councillor in Islington.

Momentum means different things to different people, which is the source of most of its strengths and many of its weaknesses. It has been called shady, suicidally inclined, deeply sinister, neo-Marxist, neo-fascist, and a cult, labels that all reveal a great deal about the labellers, and nothing whatsoever about Momentum.[2] In early 2018 the group released a loving, soft-focused video montage on social media featuring many of the insults that have been hurled in its direction by critics ranging from Labour Party grandees to Conservative Home Secretaries – which, from Momentum's point of view, is not much of a political range at all. Alongside each quote, it showed a steadily rising membership tally, all the way up to 40,000. 'Thank you to everyone who helped get us this far,' the video concluded, with a heart emoji. 'If we didn't count, if our ideas didn't count, no one would attack us,' Laura Parker told me. Joe Todd, Momentum's head of press, agrees. 'You have to understand that if the *Sunday Times*, for example, do a takedown on us, then on the Monday we will email that round to our supporters, we will publicise it, we will use it,' he explained. 'It's like proof of concept for what we're aiming to do.'

So what is Momentum aiming to do? Formally, the organisation operates on three levels: it works to defend Jeremy Corbyn and the wider leftist project within the Labour Party; it campaigns to ensure that a leftist Labour government wins power nationally; and it seeks to bring together autonomous, grass-roots movements and the Labour Party as a whole. Its tactics are wide-ranging, from attempting to win positions of influence inside the Labour apparatus to training left-wing activists in and around the party, as well as coming up with innovative campaigning methods to win public support – not only during national and local elections but all year round, and on an assortment of social and political issues. 'We are political outsiders inside a parliamentary democracy,' says Laura. 'To change this country you have to come through the floorboards and come through the ceiling, and we are doing both.'

For Laura, Momentum is the product of a double crisis: one of capitalism, which erupted so visibly in 2008, and one of the social-democratic left, which failed to provide a convincing narrative of why the crash occurred, or a vision of what lay beyond it – omissions which in the decade that followed wiped out support for major market-friendly, centre-left political parties across Europe. In its protean mission, and its relative flexibility about the tools and methods needed to implement it, Momentum also reflects many of the core dynamics of our political moment. A more insecure world, promising an uncertain future, and the erosion of material foundations – stable communities, stable jobs, stable homes – that might once have anchored us to certain political identities, has fuelled what the cultural theorist Jeremy Gilbert calls a new era of political 'reversibility', intensified by the rise of social media platforms that enable large numbers of people to swarm rapidly together around specific political flashpoints before dispersing. Swings between different parties at recent elections – Labour voters in Tilbury moving to UKIP, UKIP voters later swinging behind the Conservatives, the Conservatives haemorrhaging support to the Brexit Party, the fall and rise of the Liberal Democrats, or Scots handing the SNP a crushing victory at Westminster in 2015 only to swing back towards Labour and the Tories two years later – indicate that what were once enduring, tribal loyalties are now being replaced by political affiliations that are faster, looser and more contingent.[3] Momentum's approach

– speak to anyone, convince everyone – is designed to exploit the potential of this newly febrile political environment.

But since its inception, there has been persistent infighting within Momentum over what sort of organisation it should be: either a mirror image of Labour itself, with a traditional membership structure, policymaking bodies and lots of federated local groups that each send delegates to national meetings, or a more unconstrained and agile organising platform that can be used at different times for different objectives, with direct democratic input from its supporters: occupying banks in protest at fossil-fuel financing one day, for example, and ensuring that a left-wing slate gets elected to the Yorkshire and Humber branch of Labour's National Policy Forum the next. After a particularly intense period of turmoil in late 2016 and early 2017, marked by accusations of entryism and personal power struggles, a survey of all members on the issue helped the latter model win out, and it was quickly enshrined in a new constitution. That puts Momentum in the position of not just campaigning against what it regards as stale forms of politics, particularly within the Labour Party, but also being able to present itself as a living example of an alternative means of political organisation at a time when all traditional parties, not just Labour, are in desperate need of original thinking. Before 1997, modern general-election turnout in Britain had never dropped below 70%; since 1997, it has never exceeded it. 'People felt aggrieved that their communities and their lifeworlds were being transformed because of political decisions that had been taken by someone, somewhere, but not by them; decisions over which they had not been consulted and for which nobody seemed to be accountable to them,' says Gilbert of the popular disenchantment with formal politics which contributed to the EU referendum result. 'Unless Labour can really grasp the nettle of our democratic crisis, proposing new processes and new experiments which could build, at local, regional and national levels, democratic institutions worthy of the twenty-first century, then ultimately such grievances are only going to fester.'⁴ At its best, Momentum is what such an institution might look like.

Not that it felt like that in the beginning. 'We were making mistake after mistake,' said Santiago, 'learning everything the hard way and doing everything from scratch.' He was splitting his week now between construction work and Momentum, and although the scale of the organisation's aspirations was thrilling, the practicalities of getting it off the ground in the face of an unfriendly media and a largely hostile Labour Party bureaucracy took a heavy toll. 'There would be haggling for four hours over the wording of a single tweet; meanwhile all the basics of just registering ourselves legally as a company and so on got forgotten. The senior guys were careful not to give too many people access to the contact database at first, so we wasted enormous amounts of time having to get the most simple communications signed off and sent out by those at the top.' When I asked Santiago if it felt like the start of 'a new kind of politics' – Momentum's slogan – he laughed wryly. 'It's easy to forget how depressing it all was in those early months. Corbyn was getting slaughtered in the press each day, we were as well, and the money we needed to build Momentum wasn't there. At that point I think everyone was low and thought this could fail.' Rachel Godfrey-Wood, another early volunteer who went on to become Momentum's lead co-ordinator, also remembers that siege mentality. 'There was a strong sense of it being all on us, because we couldn't necessarily rely on anyone else,' she told me. 'It was clear that the project was in a very vulnerable position. But actually, that helped build a strong sense of collective support, a feeling of "this is it, we have to make it work". I actually found it an incredibly positive and inspiring atmosphere.'

What turned Momentum's fortunes around were events orchestrated over two successive summers by its political adversaries in an attempt to kill off the nascent rise of the Labour left. First, following the Brexit poll in June 2016, members of the Parliamentary Labour Party forced a vote of no confidence in Corbyn which triggered another leadership election; Corbyn won by an even bigger margin than before. Momentum was able to tap into the anti-establishment enthusiasm that had fuelled his original campaign, lobbying Labour Party members, conducting an impressive social media campaign, and staging a series of meetings and rallies; its membership rose to 20,000 people, with ten times as many registered supporters. Just under a year later, with her party posting double-digit leads in opinion polls, Theresa May went back on her word and called an early general election in the hope that it would dramatically increase her majority and wipe out Corbyn; instead Labour posted the biggest increase in its vote share since 1945, and May lost her majority. Momentum had a transformative impact on that election, and the result had a transformative effect on it in return. 100,000 people used the organisation's 'My nearest marginal' online tool to find out where pro-Labour campaigning would be most effective in their area; Momentum volunteers knocked on 1.2 million doors on polling day itself, and twenty-five out of the thirty constituencies that Momentum targeted were won by Labour, an astonishing success rate for an election in which the party were widely predicted to lose existing seats rather than gain new ones.[5] In the aftermath of the result, the organisation's profile rocketed, and its political rivals stared on with a mixture of horror, fascination and envy. The *Financial Times* noted that Momentum had 'outgunned the Tory press'; *Business Insider* claimed it had 'won the battle for the soul of the Labour Party'; the *New Statesman* suggested that it was 'the future of political organising'.[6] 'How Momentum delivered Labour's stunning election result,' declared a headline in the *Independent*, 'and how the Tories are trying to copy it.'[7]

More meaningful than the bald statistics was a vitality to Momentum's campaigning style that won plaudits across the political spectrum. Before the general election of 2017, Labour had to all intents and purposes given up on the notion of persuading citizens on the doorstep: the job of activists was reduced to merely asking select individuals who they planned to support on election day and mechanically recording the answers on a data sheet to enable an efficient 'get out the vote' effort when the time came. Borrowing directly from the 'big organising' tactics adopted by the Bernie Sanders presidential campaign in America, with whom the group has developed strong links, Momentum's alternative approach was to knock on every door and talk to every voter: an effort not just to reach people who had fallen through the cracks of Labour's record-keeping, but also to normalise the everyday practice of having political conversations, wrenching electioneering back from a distant, professionalised realm and replanting it in the day-to-day. As Becky Bond and Zack Exley, who both worked on the Sanders bid, explain, 'small organising', based around promises for change that are modest at best and an expectation of popular apathy among the target population, 'works well enough when incumbents want to maintain the status quo, but it isn't big enough to challenge the establishment ... When organisers figure out how to integrate the huge opportunities that new, social technology provides with effective peer-to-peer organising principles and practices as part of a smart, centralised plan – that's big organising. And it's the way we can win the political revolution.'[8] At the general election of 2017, Momentum put those principles into practice, and the influence its activism model had on those who witnessed it first-hand was lasting. 'More activists than I've ever seen in a constituency election were swarming around the place ... Feck me, they were young!' remembers Julian Jackson, who was based in Lewisham (a Labour stronghold) but encouraged by Momentum to campaign for the election in nearby Croydon, held by the Conservative housing minister Gavin Barwell.[9] 'We were laughing and bandying repartee between us. There were positive vibes all round. Horns honked. Passers-by demanded stickers. There was an incredible diversity of experience, life stories.' Labour ended up winning the seat from Barwell with a majority of over 5,000 votes.

And so from strife, Momentum swelled, with membership passing the 30,000 mark. Some of its new supporters were existing Labour members, already well versed in the often labyrinthine world of party administration. Many more were from a typically younger cohort that had come of age either in the New Labour era, when the closest most left-wing activists got to party conference was a heavily barricaded protest pen, or, slightly later, from those who were at university in the early 2010s – when the coalition government's tripling of tuition fees sparked a large, dynamic and confrontational student movement, one that dovetailed with waves of anti-austerity campaigning pioneered by imaginative new organising platforms like UK Uncut. This was a generation more familiar with direct action and being kettled by the police than it was with constituency meetings, minutes and minutiae. It was also a generation for whom the Labour Party's leftist leadership, despite their status as upstart interlopers among mainstream political commentators, was not an entirely unknown quantity. Very few Labour MPs ever took the trouble of standing by students who occupied their academic buildings, often at great personal risk, in protest at the financialisation of their education; Corbyn and Labour's shadow chancellor John McDonnell, however, were among them. 'You've sparked off a new generation of political activism,' McDonnell told students at University College London when he visited their occupation, lending its radicalism a degree of institutional legitimacy – albeit from a then-marginal corner of the parliamentary party. More than half a decade later, Momentum became the means by which some of that legitimacy was paid back.

*

As the influx of members continued and the organisation's core team outgrew its initial Soho home, so a nomadic march through unlikely office spaces began: from Soho to the Waterlily, a wedding venue and banquet hall in Stepney Green; from the

Waterlily to spare rooms at the headquarters of the Transport Salaried Staff's Association, a trade union based in Euston, which were temporarily available thanks to construction work being carried out at the station as part of Britain's high-speed rail project; from the TSSA to a few rooms at the back of Aldgate East station; and from Aldgate to the Cypriot Centre on north London's Green Lanes, up past the *ocakbasi* restaurants and the Wood Green retail ziggurats, all the way out towards Bowes Park and the thundering North Circular ring road. Officially, Momentum's home here comprises a pair of adjoining rooms at the back. One is laid out with two rows of desks and lap-tops, decorated by a Meghan Markle face mask propped up in the corner and a map of Cyprus painted on the wall. The other consists of a single desk wedged in the middle of five unused snooker tables, bordered by a parade of small, dreg-filled coffee cups from the basement canteen. Unofficially, the organisation often spills out across the building's maze of pale green hall-ways, and it's not unusual for meetings to creep into the dining hall, or the music room, or the smoking terrace overlooking the car park where some of the centre's regulars boom Greek clas-sics from their vehicles. When I sat down with Beth Foster-Ogg, who at the age of twenty-one is the lead organiser responsible for training Momentum activists up and down the country, it was in a large, echoey teaching space featuring an old-fashioned blackboard and a preacher's pulpit adorned with a Bible verse, 'Blessed are they that hear the Word of God and keep it.' Around it someone had written the words 'compassion, care, gratitude, appreciation'. Beth mulled on the vista for a few moments, then took a photo on her phone. 'I like that,' she concluded, after another pause. 'We should come to this room more often.'

In an organisation with a lot of overlapping missions on the go, Beth is uniquely placed to command a view of how they all, in theory at least, lock together. Like Santiago and Rachel, she was one of Momentum's earliest volunteers back in those heady, halting days when it was 'all energy, no plan'. The group formed a tight bond, she said, which helps explain why, after deciding to begin a university degree in September 2016, preceded by five weeks of backpacking around Cuba, she had an abrupt change of heart upon hearing news of the post-referendum leadership challenge to Corbyn. 'There aren't many places in Cuba with Wi-Fi,' she told me. 'It was a few days after the referendum vote, and when I found a hotspot and turned my phone on it just exploded with messages. I rang Adam [Klug, the Momentum co-founder], which cost me a fortune, and I was like, "What the fuck is going on?" He told me that it seemed likely there would be a leadership election, and I said to him, "Well if there is, then tell me, because I don't feel like I can miss this. If it happens, I'll come home."' Two days later, Beth was riding a horse through the tobacco plantations around Viñales, west of Havana, when her phone rang. It was Emma Rees, another Momentum co-founder. 'Yes,' she said. 'You need to come home.'

For Beth, who had spent some of her teenage years working with the community-organising movement Citizens UK in her home neighbourhood of Hackney, east London, the most interesting dimension to Momentum – and its most likely path to having a real impact – was always training, and she threw herself into it with zeal. 'One of the biggest problems we face in society is that generally we just don't know how to relate to other people in a non-friendship or non-work context,' she told me. 'The core training for community organising is essentially about how to hold those conversations: how we discover other people's interests and motivations and what we have in common, how we can channel that into projects, how people gain the confidence to take on leadership roles in their communities. And so training helps achieve specific goals, but it's also a catalyst for lots of other good things happening. It's about activating people.' Beth and Momentum try to activate people in different spheres, each of which offers a useful window on to what Momentum is trying more broadly to accomplish.

The first of these spheres is Labour itself, which accounts for much of the opprobrium the organisation receives from other wings of the party and regular headlines decrying the 'hard-left takeover' of constituency groups. One of Momentum's training sessions – delivered directly or, more commonly now, via Beth's 'train the trainer' events that teach activists how to go back and deliver the sessions themselves in their own areas – is called 'How the Labour Party works': it's billed as a guide to navigating this 'sometimes intimidating machine'. If Parliament, as Aneurin Bevan put it, acts as a 'a social shock absorber placed between privilege and the pressure of popular discontent', then the Labour Party – one of the two great forces that have shaped modern parliamentary history – can hardly be immune from the charge that it too is capable of functioning in such a way as to suppress radical change. Prominent political commentator and Labour member Paul Mason argues that 'One of the last-ditch trenches to defend the British elite has always been the Labour Party'; by equipping members with the tools necessary to influence and democratise the party's many complex institutions, Momentum's hope is that some of those trenches can be vaulted.[10]

The second sphere is general elections: Beth's training on 'persuasive conversations' – providing attendees with 'a simple framework for communicating political ideas with people who may have very different preconceptions and background knowledge', the bedrock of the 'big organising' model – reached more than 3,000 people over the six-week campaign in 2017, and many others since. It's based around a cycle of responses that Labour activists might elicit when beginning political conversations, be that on the streets in the run-up to polling day or in the pub with colleagues after work, and the best way to engage with them: acknowledging someone's initial reaction, isolating their specific political concerns, then addressing key issues associated with them before asking for support. Not everyone will be persuaded into supporting Labour, but the hope is that at the very least stock replies to political questions – 'I don't trust any politicians', 'I'm not interested in politics', and so on – progress towards something more insightful and potentially more empowering for all concerned. 'How the Labour Party works' and 'Persuasive conversations' are Beth's staple training sessions; what excites her now, though, is pushing some of their techniques in new directions that travel past both Labour and Westminster.

Hamilton House is a scruffy, sparky community space cum 1970s office block that lies in the Stokes Croft area of Bristol.[11] On a Saturday afternoon in August 2018, I sat in one of its upper-floor meeting rooms and watched as Beth addressed a group of about twenty current and aspiring local councillors from across southern England, and encouraged them to think about what power looked like in their communities. 'Who are the gatekeepers in your area?' she asked, pacing the stained carpet tiles with a casual, self-deprecating assurance. Alternating expertly between mild cajoling and intensive flipchart-scrawling, she divided the attendees into two sides and invited them to role-play a scenario which pitted community campaigners against elected councillors in a struggle over the rehousing of refugees. Most felt more comfortable in the former role; those playing the councillors seemed paralysed by bureaucratic restraints, and unsure about how far they were allowed to break them. 'In the past, when we've done this, I've seen people shouting at each other, walking out, coming close to tears,' Beth confided. 'It's about getting you to question how, as a councillor, you see yourself in relation to the community. Is the community a partner, something that is a part of you and that can direct you, or is it something separate?' She shared an anecdote about a campaign in Hackney that she had participated in regarding unsafe housing for children, and detailed how she had tried to get the local church on board. 'We had meetings with the priest and got nowhere,' Beth explained. 'One day as I was leaving, the woman who serves the tea and coffee at the church came up to me and said, "Why are you bothering with the priest? I'll sort this out for you." That woman knew all the parents, she knew all the kids through the Sunday school, and she knew how to tell the priest what to do as she had been working with him for twenty years. She was the real gatekeeper to that institution, and she had relational power there. When you map out power in your community, think of people like her.'

At Beth's instruction, each of the attendees drew stick figures on pieces of paper and used them to identify the building blocks of their personal stories. In the wrong hands this could have lapsed into a David Brent tribute act, but Beth was careful to avoid any hint of corporate away-day cringe. 'Some commercial training sessions are all about teaching you how to project your voice when speaking in public, or how to use confident hand gestures,' she said. 'But the best way to persuade someone of anything is to tell them your personal story. No one can argue with your personal story, and it's something that people remember, so draw on it.' I sat with a small huddle of Labour councillors, all of whom were very much part of the political minority in their respective regions, and watched as they wrote down sentences describing their values, their heritage, and their hobbies and interests, before linking these personal elements to sources of local power that lay outside of formal council structures. Among them was a twenty-six-year-old woman who represented a deprived ward near the racecourse in Newbury, one of the most affluent towns in Europe; every other member of the parish council that she now sat on was male, and over fifty. 'You have this feeling of powerlessness when you're surrounded by white-haired Tories,' observed another woman, who had recently won a seat on the Conservative-dominated borough council in Worthing. 'What I've realised, and what this training has helped accentuate for me, is that there's all this power that resides outside the town hall, and that we need community activism to change things.' She told us that she had been forming a tentative relationship with Acorn, the communal tenants' union. 'We need partners like that to stir up trouble with,' she concluded. 'In a nice way.'

Finding partners to stir up trouble with, in a nice way, could be the unofficial motto of Momentum. It's especially important for those in the movement who, like Beth, are interested in stuff that currently happens outside of the Labour Party – the solidarities formed and battles waged inside workplaces, schools, universities, hospitals, housing estates, small towns and city neighbourhoods across Britain – and want to embed some of that within the party's internal infrastructure and sense of purpose. 'My life mission within Momentum is to build an activist base that is highly educated, skilled and engaged, and just does things,' Beth told me. 'It's about politicising people but not in the sense of getting them to just vote Labour or even jump on a bus down to London to join a protest. Politics is a mum having a picnic in their local park with other mums from the area, and talking about how to change things. It's about people becoming activists who are already embedded in their communities. It's basically about becoming an active citizen, which is something that as a generation we don't have a lot of experience of.'

That third sphere of Momentum training that Beth was concentrating on in Bristol – local councillors – is really about finding a way to reach across into a fourth sphere, a far more amorphous one, where people are organising politically in ways that have nothing directly to do with either democratising Labour or winning elections, people like the ones already mentioned in this book. Most of Momentum's members have lived through thirteen years of Labour government under Tony Blair and Gordon Brown, and recognise that having a Labour prime minister is simply not enough if your aim is to build a new kind of politics; according to Momentum's internal mission statement, the group cannot hope to 'transform Britain only through policy at the top – we also need a direct, bottom-up politics which empowers individuals to take power for themselves and make a difference in their communities now'.[12] And across the country, there are already projects under way by local Momentum groups that in their scope and structure bear more resemblance to a movement like the London Renters Union or a political education programme like Demand the Impossible than they do to other organisations traditionally affiliated to national political parties. In Lancaster, for example, Momentum members have founded a club that enables locals to access affordable food that would otherwise have been thrown away. In Doncaster, Momentum has thrown its weight behind campaigns against exploitative loan practices by the 'rent-to-own' appliance retailer Bright House, and in Chorlton, as Beth Redmond recounted in Chapter 1, local Momentum members are now organising film nights, football games and karaoke – a recognition of the fact that politics is culture and, as Raymond Williams put it, 'Culture is ordinary: that is where we must start.'[13] Momentum has launched a mass email initiative enabling members to share campaigning advice, supported Picturehouse cinema workers fighting for a living wage in south London, and collaborated with the food workers' union, the BFAWU, on its McStrike protests; Momentum's video on the subject, in which McDonald's staff complained of inadequate first-aid procedures and revealed the burns they'd received while cooking burgers, was watched by over 2 million people including a quarter of the company's UK workforce.[14]

Digital campaigning – short films, viral social media posts, comic memes – is a big part of how Momentum tries to intervene in broader 'movement-building' issues, be that confronting the rise of the far right (Momentum recently released a video charting the history of the '43 Group', for example, a movement of Jewish ex-servicemen who broke up Oswald Mosley's fascist rallies in the late 1940s) or challenging different forms of social discrimination. Anti-Semitism, an issue where the response of the party's leadership has been poor, is a particular focus. 'The first three to five seconds are the most important, because you've got the whole Internet to compete with,' said Paul Nicholson, who makes up one half of Momentum's video team alongside Emile Charlaff; they describe themselves as being among the most apolitical staffers in the office. 'But what really pushes the film, much more than how nice or pretty it looks, is the argument. You want people to connect with that strong idea and then feel the urge to share it with friends and say: "You see? This is what I'm talking about. It's *this*."' With the help of a volunteer database of supportive production experts, the pair have scored some spectacular viewing figures: during the general-election campaign, one video – an imagined conversation between a parent and daughter in the 'Tory Britain of 2030' that culminates with the child asking, 'Daddy, why do you hate me?' – was watched 8 million times alone, and on average their clips reach about 11 million unique users of Twitter and Facebook every month.[15] 'We're offering people a tool to help them express their political opinions, rather than trying to force our message down their throats,' said Emile. 'What made me happiest with that particular video,' added Paul, 'was that people were sharing it by tagging their parents and adding comments like "That's why I'm voting Labour, wow."'

A few days after meeting Emile and Paul at the Cypriot Centre, I travelled down to the banks of the River Lea, near London's Olympic Stadium, to watch them shoot their latest video. This one wasn't about Labour, Westminster or elections; instead its subject was to be transphobia, and a comparison between the frenzied discourse around trans issues now and the moral panic about gay rights whipped up several decades earlier. Many of Momentum's films rely on amateur actors – the young star from that 'Daddy, why do you hate me?' clip was the flower girl at Paul's wedding – but this one was being anchored by a celebrity face: Juno Dawson, the bestselling young-adult fiction writer who came out as a transgender woman in 2015. Juno carried a salad packed inside a Haribo box ('My dad used to work for Bassetts, so I do have a crazy sweet tooth,' she admitted), and picked at it thoughtfully on a canal-side bench as she read through the script and tried out different tones of voice for the narration. 'We're going for mildly exasperated,' suggested Paul. 'Imagine you're speaking to your slightly racist grandma.' I was handed a light reflector to hoist aloft and we attempted a few takes, each of which was swiftly interrupted by either passing cyclists, passing boats, inquisitive security guards or strong gusts of wind. 'It's a gentle pace,' said

Emile. 'Sure,' nodded Juno. 'A dawdle.' She began another walk to camera and delivered the opening lines: 'With the current debate around trans issues, is anyone else getting a sense of déjà vu? Like haven't we done all this before? For years there was scaremongering about gay people. That they would "come for your children". That it was a mental illness. That if we let gay people marry, next we'd be marrying animals. And don't those people look ridiculous now? Same-sex couples can get married and – spoiler alert! – the world didn't end ...' Juno's hair blew into her face, and so she stopped and asked Paul if they were supposed to be aiming for the reverse-Beyoncé look. 'That's fine, we've got it,' he said. 'Let's finish off the rest of the script up on the bridge.'

Later, when I saw the finished video, I was impressed.[16] Juno's lines had been spliced with a rapid-fire showreel of snippets from talk shows, news programmes and popular culture: *Question Time, Groundhog Day*, Margaret Thatcher and Homer Simpson all made an appearance. 'Can we not waste time creating material for, you know, those montages that we'll look back on in twenty years' time and think "what the hell were they thinking?"' she asked viewers, with not a hair out of place. The film then cut to a red-faced Piers Morgan fulminating about whether recognising trans identities was equivalent to him declaring that he was an elephant and going off to live in London Zoo. Coming in at just over two minutes, the whole thing was short, funny and persuasive; perhaps most importantly, it was also grounded in a recognisably online visual culture that was instantly familiar to its target audience. 'Often, TV adverts don't transfer well to the Internet,' said Emile. 'We're coming from the starting point of "what would a good video on this topic look like if it was made for social media?"' Within a few months of its release, Juno's film had been watched nearly half a million times on each of Facebook and Twitter.

The problem is that, video viewing figures aside, measuring Momentum's impact on the battle against transphobia, or, for that matter, on food poverty in Lancashire, loan sharks in Doncaster, or any of the 'movement-building' side of the organisation's activities, is a great deal harder than counting the number of seats they've won on Labour's National Executive Committee or the votes their motions have secured at party conference. Those relatively intangible goals of organising around and intervening in broader issues – of finding partners to make trouble with – are always in danger of being sidelined in favour of immediate challenges which are more quantifiable, and seemingly more urgent. 'If you don't do the long, slow-build movement stuff, if you don't try to spread that cultural hegemony, then when a future left-wing government marches to the top of its hill and turns around, it will find that no one is there to defend it,' says Laura Parker. 'So education and movement-building isn't separate from our ultimate purpose, it's part of that purpose. The thing is that hegemony is like tomorrow. It never arrives.'

In the late nineteenth century, the modern labour movement recognised that progressive politics had to stretch beyond the confines of a monthly meeting or occasional election campaign: more than a hundred years ago cycling groups, rambling clubs and socialist choirs all formed part of the radical firmament.[17] But these initiatives were often paternalistic rather than democratic, a trend that deepened with the development of local Labour groups into highly tuned polling engines. 'On the whole,' argues Tom Blackburn, a Momentum member in Manchester, 'Labour's constituency parties (with honourable, if usually isolated exceptions) have served primarily as narrowly focused electoral machines for getting out the vote – very often controlled with a stifling iron grip by MPs and their allies – rather than taking on the mantle of organising and solidarity work among the local community ... and addressing how working and marginalised people might free themselves from the fetters that constrain their personal development and deny them the opportunity to meet their full human potential.'[18] Decades of late-capitalist logic and many years of austerity have served to atomise communities and intensify those fetters, but for many on the left, Momentum – forever seduced by relatively more straightforward tasks – is not doing enough to reverse the trend. 'I came from a social movement background, not an internal Labour Party one, and I'm still very social-movementy,' Santiago told me. 'We need to guard against being more and more internal. All of the crises over the last few years – the general election, the leadership elections, Labour committee votes, the really antagonistic internal debate over how Momentum is organised – they have all forced us in that direction. Those things always feel so precarious and down to the wire, and so we're always being pressured to turn inwards.' While lavishing effusive praise on the digital team, he flagged up Juno's transphobia video as a perfect example – not of Momentum reaching out into an ambitious new world of grass-roots organising, but of the group's limits being revealed. 'We've become excellent at doing certain things, like putting out funny, snappy videos that engage people on difficult topics, and so the temptation is to keep doing it – we've got that bit nailed,' Santiago argued. 'But it's on the surface level, and the question is how do we do the more time-consuming job of actually building links with the communities who are leading these discussions, how do we get to the point where, if a community has a problem, the Labour Party becomes their first port of call? It's really difficult, and at the moment I think nobody has the answer.'

A praetorian guard for Corbyn's inner circle, or a transformational outrider, enlivening politics from below?[19] 'Momentum is the consequence of the tension between those two things,' says Rachel. 'Without it, we wouldn't be Momentum.' But maintaining a balance isn't easy, and the nearer the Labour left inches towards formal power, the more often that tension will reach boiling point. In 2018 Momentum released a video calling for more police officers on the streets, a response to Labour's leadership announcing that reversing austerity-driven police cuts would be a key plank of its policy programme. On the 'social-movementy' side of Momentum's support base, where experiences of the police have often been marked by racism and violence and where many believe a drastic reduction in the policing of marginalised communities is necessary, there was immense disquiet; after a noisy backlash, Momentum quietly deleted the film. In Haringey, London, where Momentum now dominates the Labour-controlled council, campaigners fighting to save the Latin Village at Seven Sisters were infuriated when council leader Joseph Ejiofor – who also sits on the National Co-ordinating Group, Momentum's highest organ of authority – insisted that the demolition and redevelopment of the market area would continue as planned, and refused to consider an alternative community blueprint for the area. Local activists, many of whom are members of Momentum, demanded to know why the organisation's most prominent faces seemed to be maintaining a conspicuous silence on the matter.

'Some of the most exciting ground-level activism right now is rooted in opposition to state logics of power, and those people are not excited about Corbyn or Labour,' says Ewa Jasiewicz, a writer, union organiser and campaigner involved in an array of social movements and who has also worked with Momentum; she describes herself as having a 'foot in both camps'. 'It's problematic because there's a danger that Momentum just comes to be seen as this golden treasure trove of activist capital or a supply line for disputes, something that can be called upon whenever bodies are needed for a picket line. But that's not how you build relationships, it's not how you organise.' Ewa fears that with its strong links to the Labour Party and heavy focus on internal reform, Momentum may at best have enabled a sort of fast-track route for activists into representative politics, which is not the same thing as helping to reshape politics from the bottom up. 'The kind of community organising Momentum talks about is already happening, independently of Momentum or Labour, and what it needs is solidarity, not co-optation by a political party; once something becomes branded by an institution, institutional needs will always dominate,' she told me. 'Momentum says it wants to bring the grass roots up to the seat of power. But if you don't trust that seat of power in the first place, that doesn't feel very encouraging.'

That last point goes to the heart of a bigger question facing both Momentum and the party it is trying to transform: just how renegade does Labour's leftist leadership really want to be, and will it prove renegade enough for Momentum's supporters – never mind those grass-roots activists outside of Momentum that the organisation hopes to connect with? Current evidence is mixed. When Labour's manifesto for the 2017 general election was unveiled, the Institute for Fiscal Studies described its proposals as the most radical tax and spending reforms in more than seven decades. The research outfit claimed that Jeremy Corbyn's wing of the party was offering not just an alternative to austerity, but 'something much, much more dramatic than that – an alternative to the form of market capitalism practised in this country for at least the past forty years'.[20] This was true, although how profoundly different that alternative looked depended very much on your starting point: scrapping university tuition fees, renationalising railways, and raising taxes on corporations and high-earners was radical by the standards of Britain in the late 2010s, but not by the standards of many other European countries in the late 2010s, nor indeed by those of Britain itself before the 1980s. In some ways, the manifesto's fairly unremarkable social-democratic policy suggestions exposed nothing more than the radicalism of late-capitalist norms; as Lorna Finlayson, a lecturer in philosophy at Essex University, contends, 'the significance of Corbynism has less to do with Corbyn or his politics than with what it discloses about the political system in which we live, widening an already growing gap between the reality of that system and the story it tells about itself'.[21] Arguably the most militant aspect of Corbyn's election campaign was the one he identified himself in his 2017 Brighton conference speech, when he observed that the political centre of gravity 'isn't fixed or unmovable, nor is it where the establishment pundits like to think it is. It shifts as people's expectations and experiences change and political space is opened up.'

But plenty on the Labour left, and Momentum, want more: not merely a return to social democracy, but a new politics, as revolutionary in its own way as Thatcher's disembowelling of social democracy was forty years ago. Partially foreshadowed in 'Alternative Models of Ownership', a report unveiled by shadow chancellor John McDonnell a few days after the 2017 vote, this new politics has more ambitious components: a shift away from financialisation towards a more co-operative economy, for example, an embrace of automation in the workplace, and the equitable distribution of subsequent productivity gains through the means of a shorter working week and a universal basic income.[22] Some have called this 'incremental utopianism': an attempt to shape the future rather than to 'resurrect a discredited pre-Thatcherite corporatist past'.[23] These kinds of forward-looking ideas, whether one agrees with them individually or not, should be a vital part of our public discourse as Britain looks beyond late capitalism, as should the question of whether such transformations can be achieved within our traditional political system at the hands of traditional political actors – or whether the institutions and participants of formal politics in Britain need to be reimagined from the ground up. But despite commentators often asserting that the rise of Corbyn since 2015 was solely a function of him being in the right place at the right time, implying correctly that deeper socio-historical forces are at work here, most media coverage of the Labour left rarely finds room for any such debate. We get told a great deal about Corbyn's allotment, his past associations with foreign figureheads, and his sartorial choices. We hear much less about the extent of his political aspirations, and – more importantly – the aspirations of those who propelled him to the leadership.

Despite being a parliamentarian, Corbyn's own roots lie in grass-roots campaigning: from anti-apartheid activism to the Palestine solidarity movement, as well as the protests against

Latin American dictatorships that brought him into contact with a young Santiago all those years ago. In 1983 he was elected as representative for Islington North and swiftly set up shop in the caretaker's flat above a former co-operative music hall named the Red Rose on Seven Sisters Road, which hosted bawdy music and comedy nights; in order to reach his office, Corbyn often had to jostle his way through a group of drunks to climb the stairs.[24] He gradually gained a reputation as an outspoken backbencher, but was always at his most comfortable far away from the bars and benches of SW1A, ideally traipsing the back alleys and council estates of his constituency and getting waylaid by impromptu encounters with residents. 'Every single person you meet knows something you don't,' he once claimed, and that mindset has persisted throughout his ascension to leader of the opposition, even as the trappings of state – the Privy Council, weekly knockabouts at Prime Minister's Questions, state banquets with the queen – have rarefied his professional surroundings beyond recognition.[25] Of the two occasions upon which I've met Corbyn for any significant length of time – once by chance when he knocked on the door of my rented flat while canvassing for the 2018 local elections, and the other when we sat down for a scheduled interview in his Westminster office – it was the first that made him far more comfortable. Having walked up three flights of stairs bathed in flickering municipal disco light, he bumbled into our tiny living room with no introduction and cheerfully plopped himself down on a manky second-hand chair matted with cat hair, complimenting everything and politely ignoring both the large damp patch above his head and a lingering smell of weed. His wife, Laura Alvarez, who owns a fairtrade coffee business, followed soon after, and the pair plunged into an easy, free-ranging discussion about Middle Eastern politics, social care and the British media while glugging cups of tea. Corbyn seemed relaxed and entirely without airs, graces or awkwardness, a long way from the tetchy mood that sometimes characterises his broadcast interviews. Whereas most politicians, especially very senior ones, have to perform a clumsy, ersatz authenticity when meeting members of the public in their own realms, I got the sense that if Corbyn had the choice he would always rather be here: enquiring about the pot plants and scribbling earnestly in his notebook, rather than being stuck in the House of Commons where the ambience and rituals reek of institutional power on somebody else's terms.

A few weeks later, when we sat down at his desk in the Norman Shaw buildings overlooking Victoria Embankment, Corbyn was in high spirits. In the news that day, the grilled-chicken chain Nando's was furiously denying reports that the Conservative Party had been planning to offer young supporters a discount card for their restaurants in an attempt to compete with Labour's membership growth, prompting much mirth on social media.[26] 'I can officially confirm that Nando's haven't offered *us* a sweetheart deal,' he grinned, passing me a bowl of fruit. 'The Nando's question is now closed.' He leaned back in his chair and grew more serious. 'It's about offering young people some hope,' he told me, when I asked why younger demographics were overwhelmingly abandoning the Tories and embracing Labour under his leadership. 'I grew up in an age where I had free healthcare, free education, and most of my generation never had any real concerns about housing – we thought "well, we'll get somewhere". We didn't feel that housing was something that we would never be able to sort out. I now meet forty-year-olds who wonder where they are going to live.' Corbyn's Labour Party, he told me, was one that recognised not just the limits of market forces but the corrosion their logics can induce. 'I don't use the words "competition in education", I use the words "inclusivity in education", as with health and other things, and that is a deliberate and very conscious choice,' he said. 'New Labour was very much about the Third Way, which was essentially a gigantic accommodation with financial interests.' He insisted that making an accommodation of that sort shrinks the scope of political possibility. 'We don't triangulate. We don't spend our whole time sitting around working out some mathematical equation: if I hack off X, that will please Y, which will irritate Z, but Z will support me because I've hacked off X,' Corbyn explained. 'We've managed to reach beyond the notion that it's all about managerial ideas.' I asked him for examples of how a new political settlement, orientated away from perpetual competition, would feel different to those who lived under it, and after running through a fairly predictable checklist of investment, jobs and economic progress, Corbyn's eyes lit up with genuine enthusiasm. 'Music, art, dance, theatre,' he concluded, naming aspects of our lives that can, or in his opinion should, exist beyond the market. 'Human beings are naturally inquisitive and creative. And [at the moment] we stifle it out of them.'

It's a line that could have been lifted straight from Momentum's mission statement, or the programme for The World Transformed. Given that Momentum emerged out of Corbyn's initial leadership campaign, it's no surprise that the organisation's belief in pushing politics beyond Westminster – indeed beyond conventional electoral strategies at all – should harmonise so closely with Corbyn's vision, nor that both are rooted in that 'big organising' model of change. When I asked him about this, Corbyn reminisced on his teenage years in the 1960s devoted to the painstaking production of anti-racism literature. 'I would stay up all night at home with a hand duplicator, and I could produce 2,000 or 3,000 leaflets, or more than that if you halved the paper,' he said. 'I would hand-guillotine them after I'd rolled them off the machine, or put them through twice if it was a two-sided leaflet, then keep adding in the ink. If I was really good, I could probably turn out 6,000 leaflets overnight. And we'd then go and deliver them, or give them out in shops or pubs, as our way of mobilising people. Now I have 1.7 million Twitter followers.' He looked out the window, and shook his head incredulously. 'Today we have a combination of cutting-edge social media and public rallies which would have been pretty much the norm in the nineteenth century,' he smiled. 'We can organise a demonstration, tweet it out, and people come.'

Elliot Dugdale grew up in Chippenham, the same Wiltshire town in which Corbyn was born and spent his early years. The twenty-six-year-old found it a politically lonely place, with 'no visible trade union movement, none of those institutions of the left that connect you with the cultures of socialism and the labour movement'. Like Santiago, Elliot joined the Labour Party in the pre-Corbyn era because he thought it would be a transmission line to radical action, particularly regarding the iniquities of the financial crisis. 'I couldn't have been more wrong,' he told me. Instead, in common with so many of those at the heart of Britain's new left politics, Elliot found his political home in the student movement of 2010, and the way it brought together different strands of progressive thinking, organising outside of party politics. 'There was a lack of dogmatism, a tendency to experimentation,' he remembers. 'Politically, people aren't satisfied any more with standing aside and letting other people do things on their behalf.' Today, Elliot is one of the main organisers behind TWT, and views it as a means of not just exposing ordinary citizens to the formal Labour Party, but also exposing the formal Labour Party to ordinary citizens. 'TWT is about raising the collective knowledge of our movement through people coming together and engaging with each other,' he claimed. 'But it's also about ensuring that ideas generated at the grass roots have a forum in which they can be raised with those who have power and authority, who are actually making policy decisions. If we do an event on housing, for example, and we have a big speaker from the shadow Cabinet involved, we will put them on a platform with people who know about housing in Britain today – and that doesn't just mean housing experts, it means those who are living the reality of housing and are involved in struggles on the ground around it, because they have knowledge that academics won't. So it's a political education event, but the education runs both ways.' Hope Worsdale, another senior member of the TWT

team, told me that the festival pointed towards a politics that
was less transactional. 'For years party politics has been dominated by a certain way of doing things that is all about votes,
and about data sheets, and about short-term election cycles,'
she said. 'Something different like this is quite alien to people,
but if we don't build a grass-roots movement that creates and
sustains a new political culture, then ultimately there is no
point in Labour winning.'

Does Corbyn see things the same way? Recently, in a huge
nod to Momentum, the party announced that it was setting up
a 'community campaign unit' to help organise political movements at the local level, and funding it to the tune of several
million pounds. The hope, explained Labour official Richard
Power Sayeed, was that eventually 'when you think of Labour,
you won't imagine rows of MPs on green leather benches, or
a smartly suited minister chatting to a reporter. Instead, you'll
think of activists reinvigorating their estate's tenants association, while others organise their co-workers and stand with
them on picket lines.'[27] Under his watch, Corbyn told me,
'the Labour Party will increasingly become involved in a lot
of things that we would never have been involved in before.'
He pointed out that the party was established 'as a coalition
between intellectual socialists, community activists and trade
unions', and declared proudly that 'Labour today is a mass
organisation in a way it hasn't been for a very long time.'

But for all that, there remains the contradiction at the heart
of the party's messaging regarding just how radical a Labour
left government might be: is it a 'common sense' revival of
social-democratic principles, or something bigger? Momentum,
which at the time of writing has fifteen paid members of staff
and derives 95% of its income from members, is trying to tip
the balance in ways that go well beyond Corbyn, McDonnell
and the individuals surrounding them, ensuring that Labour
remains a vehicle for radical economic and political transformation – for something more than centrist consensus with a
kinder face – long after the current generation of leaders have

departed. In May 2019, it announced that for the first time it would start directing its campaigning muscle towards persuading senior figures to adopt more ambitious pledges in its next manifesto, including a green new deal for the economy; 'Radical and transformational policy can't only come from the halls of Westminster,' a spokesperson for the organisation insisted.[28] Their pressure may be paying off. When Conservative chancellor Philip Hammond warned that Labour was an 'existential challenge to our economic model', for example, Corbyn responded that Hammond was 'absolutely right'.[29] But while common-sense economic reforms are achievable through Parliament and politics as we know it, a truly existential challenge to our economy, and the wider social and cultural structures that underpin it, will not be. Labour should be 'in and against the state', John McDonnell has argued, implying both confrontation with institutional power and at least some adaptation to it. Where that adaptation leaves Momentum – and TWT, and all the social movements from which Labour's young left flank have arisen, and which, as Ewa Jasiewicz pointed out, remain wary of state institutions and the hierarchies and bureaucracies they wield – remains to be seen. Will a meaningfully 'new kind of politics' ever really be possible, after all?

*

On a bright Saturday lunchtime in spring 2019, a couple of blocks north of the Synergy Centre, two people in their mid-twenties climbed the facade of a Barclays bank branch on North Street, and used string and gaffer tape to affix a large black banner across the entrance. On it were printed the words 'STOP FUNDING FOSSIL FUELS' and a bastardised version of the Barclays logo – a reference to the fact that Barclays is the worst bank in Europe when it comes to environmental finance, funding £67 billion worth of fossil-fuel projects over the previous two years alone.[30] A staff member scurried out to investigate, peered up at the banner, and then swiftly withdrew back into the building, locking the large double-fronted glass doors behind her as she went. The banner-hangers, who were both members of the climate action movement Extinction Rebellion, let out a cheer, as did an older man with a drum set who had maintained a faintly ominous beat throughout proceedings, and a young girl who was dancing with no little panache to the beat and helping scrawl chalk slogans on the pavement. So too did Amelia, a musician, teacher and single mother, and an organiser with a nearby branch of Momentum.[31] Amelia had driven a bunch of 'Stop Funding Climate Change' placards over from Hove for the event; the leaflets which were supposed to accompany them, she explained bitterly, were currently marooned at a Parcelforce depot in Crawley. That misfortune aside – 'Bloody privatisation,' she muttered, with feeling – Amelia seemed delighted. 'To be honest I didn't know if they would turn up today,' she confided, gesturing at the Extinction Rebellion activists who were now eagerly engaging in conversation with curious passers-by and disgruntled Barclays customers searching out a side entrance. 'All these kids, they've put us to shame. They're the real leaders.' She told me that when she had first suggested partnering with Extinction Rebellion on an action like this, some other Labour members had looked askance at her, arguing that the upcoming local elections were a higher priority. Amelia snorted. 'We have to do both,' she retorted. 'There's no point fighting to get social-ist candidates on the council if the whole planet is about to go up in smoke.'

As we spoke, other Barclays branches in more than thirty towns and cities across the country, from Edinburgh to Falmouth, Norwich and Merthyr Tydfil, were being similarly breached, bedecked and occupied by an alliance consisting of Momentum, Extinction Rebellion, and People and Planet, a network of anti-poverty and pro-climate-justice student campaigns. In Salford, activists staged a 'die-in' outside the Barclays entrance; in Plymouth, protesters sang a rewritten version of the Supremes' 'Stop! In the Name of Love' as they set up camp at the front door. 'Who would have thought you'd ever see these guys together on the streets,' mused Jake Woodier to me in Brighton, with a satisfied smile. Jake is the campaign co-ordinator for the UK Student Climate Network, the organisers behind a rolling wave of walkouts by schoolchildren to demonstrate against climate change, and he had spent a lot of time thinking about the nexus between institutional politics and direct action. 'Bankrupt Climate Change' was Momentum's biggest effort to date at showing it could operate in both domains and serve as a useful bridge between them, and the Extinction Rebellion activists I spoke to were suitably impressed – especially by a public intervention from John McDonnell the previous day urging all Labour members to participate. 'The shadow chancellor of the exchequer just called on people to occupy branches of one of Britain's biggest banks,' reflected one of them.[32] 'I mean, that's quite something when you think about it. Labour's climate policies are not good enough, but perhaps they're moving in the right direction, and you've got to salute Momentum for helping to make that happen.' But he went on to tell me that he was not a member of the Labour Party and still refused to see Labour politics or Westminster as an effective route to change. 'I don't think they'll ever be as radical as we need them to be, and I'm not going to spend the limited time I've got in the evenings trying to move pro-Corbyn motions in my local Labour Party,' he said. Amelia, for her part, insisted that a Labour left government was exactly what change looked like. 'For me, the purpose of Momentum remains the same as it was on day one, which is very simply to put JC in Number 10,' she told me. 'That has to be the ultimate goal.'

As things fall apart, Momentum's greatest potential lies in proving that politics can flourish in the gap between Amelia and the Extinction Rebellion activist; that alongside the inhabitants of all the other crevices neglected by market liberalism, the denizens of this one can play a leading role in the fight to remake the future. Their aim is not to convince social movements that institutional politics is the answer, nor to persuade

Labour devotees that elections are meaningless, because neither claim stands up to any scrutiny. It is to retool everyone within those two poles in order to help them better navigate a new political landscape, one in which the distinctions between them will perhaps feel less significant than they do now. Along the way, like a horse bursting through a window and landing in the middle of a genteel get-together, they hope to illuminate the absurdity of what came before. 'Down by the seaside,' wrote journalist Marie Le Conte, in a piece about the moderate, centrist Labour politicians in Brighton who found themselves left behind in the shadows of TWT's energy and ideas, 'these MPs and fellow travellers ... had their drinks receptions and cosy dinners, and made peace with their own irrelevance.'[33] Elliot, the TWT organiser, said that coverage of the festival in the traditional media is growing more positive every year, as journalists on the party-conference circuit adjust to a new reality. 'The fact that it's not just the same familiar seven faces on a stage doing the same thing again and again with complimentary wine at the back, most of them haven't seen anything like it in their lives before,' he told me. 'They see the excitement at our events, and the numbers, and the fact that it's this place where grass-roots activism is being platformed, and they just think "what the fuck is going on!", and that works for us. It helps send the message that the centre is dead, and it won't be coming back in the way that it was.'

At the London Marathon in 2019, a runner dressed as Big Ben got stuck as he reached the finish line. A video clip on BBC News, which lasts for forty-two painful seconds, shows volunteers attempting to bend and manoeuvre the man's outsized costume under the last set of overhead advertising hoardings, as the Palace of Westminster's famous spire smacks repeatedly, and futilely, against a plastic board. For the past few years, the real Big Ben has been clad in scaffolding, while the House of Commons is intermittently disrupted by water leaking into the chamber; as our old politics crumbles, the gods are writing the metaphors for us. 'The kids who are walking out of school on climate strikes have a hugely radical understanding of the way that politics works, and they recognise that our democratic processes and structures as they stand are designed to uphold the status quo,' said Jake. 'These are the children of the financial crisis, who know that they will be worse off than their parents, know that they'll never own a home, and know that on current trends they will probably live to see the end of humanity. So for them, for us, politics is not a game, it's reality, and that's reflected in the way we organise – relentlessly, radically, as if our lives depend on it.' For Momentum, 'a new kind of politics' must mean a politics that speaks to the generation Jake is talking about; anything less would fly in the face of simple, pragmatic common sense.

7

Futures

Wallsend, Newcastle

That's what the babies did, after all, when they were born. They looked a look at the world as if they could see something that your own eyes couldn't, or had forgotten how to.
—Ali Smith, *There but for the*

The future lies in a black box off the A19, ringed by a handful of car-dealership forecourts and pointless mini roundabouts. Everything is neat here, and drawn in straight lines: trim grass banks, abbreviated trees, and a double fence with a strip of no man's land between it, the sort of unplace that belongs to nowhere and leaves you feeling lost. But nothing is as neat and straight as the black box itself, as big as an aircraft hangar, or the cluster of slightly smaller grey boxes that surround it. I had to show my passport at the gate, and then drive slowly up the approach road while my car and face were repeatedly filmed, scanned and processed, shredded into data packets that blazed through wire coils and server racks and cooling tanks the size of houses before looping their way round and triggering a dull green light. The structures up ahead had no windows, and no personality. This land wasn't made for people. Apart from the solitary guard back in the security booth, there wasn't another human being in sight.

The Stellium data centre lies about five miles east of Newcastle city centre, and just north of what remains of Segedunum, a Roman fort that once protected the easternmost edge of Hadrian's Wall. Covering more than 10,000 square metres of floor space and capable of drawing on 180 megawatts of power – that's the equivalent of more than 25 million household light bulbs – there is nothing else quite like this, according to Stellium's chief technology officer Gerry Murray, in the country. From here, he explained to me, beams sent down fibre-optic cables should reach anywhere in the UK in less than seven milliseconds, all of Europe in under fifteen milliseconds, the east coast of America in about fifty milliseconds, and Australia in 259 milliseconds: that's half a second to span the entire globe. 'We are part of a virtual marketplace,' said Murray. 'But rather than a traditional market defined by the buildings around it and the stalls within it, this marketplace is not bound by walls, or rules, or anything. It's defined by light.' From its stronghold on the Tyne, Stellium is in a race to fling and fetch light through its pipelines faster than its rivals can, and to store the information conveyed by that light more securely and efficiently than anyone else. It seems ironic, then, that when Murray gives me a tour of the facility, we end up walking predominantly through darkness. 'When you arrive here as an outsider and you travel around the town, you see the legacies of the industries that were in this region: the coal, the steel, the shipbuilding, all of that,' Murray observed as we navigated halls of massive, blank proportions, stacked with sterile air and electric hums. 'You see the things that were built in the boom times, all the old banks, office blocks and working-class housing estates, all these rows and rows and rows of houses, and you say to yourself, "Where did all those people go?"' He fumbled his way along a pitch-black corridor and then through a set of doors out into the open, and we found ourselves in a vast yard hemmed in by high walls and red alarm beacons, standing among backup generators and 20,000 litres of diesel held in vats. 'Now you see the new Newcastle, the new north-east,' Murray, who moved here from Ireland a couple of years ago, concluded with a sweep of his arm. 'And you just try to figure it all out.'

At the end of one Britain, and the fitful beginnings of another, the landscape surrounding Stellium is as good a place as any to try to figure it all out. There are gatherings here, of people trying to work different things into shape from the shreds and splinters of the present. Some of the gatherings take place on the ground – by the River Wear, for example, about fifteen miles south of where we were standing. Others unfold inside the data centre itself, in strings of ones and zeros. How we think about these gatherings will determine what sort of paradigm comes after this one; indeed, it is how we conceive of our own capacity to gather, and to act collectively, that will decide our collective future.

*

In the old days, when he was just a bairn, David Brown would wake up on the morning of the Big Meeting and run down Saddler Street from Market Place, darting and slaloming through a forest of grown-up legs. There were thousands of legs, packed into the narrow alleyways that slope to Elvet Bridge, and on the other side there were many thousands more: filling the pavements, filling the roads, filling the paths that led into the racecourse and spilling out across the green. His uncle Tommy – the best trumpeter in Craghead, as anyone who heard him will tell you – was in the colliery band, and what David wanted on those mornings more than anything in the world was to find him among all the legs and bustle and beer cans and brass, and then follow as he marched past the Royal County hotel, his lodge's blue and yellow banner proudly thrust aloft. David is retired now, and Uncle Tommy is on life support; Craghead colliery closed in 1969. Still, David keeps coming to the Big Meetings, just as his dad did, and his dad's dad before that. 'I would sit up there from half-eight in the morning until God knows what time,' he told me, pointing at a scrabbly ledge overlooking the racecourse. 'It was brilliant, completely brilliant. I just sat there, loving it, and watched.'

It's been a quarter of a century since the last pit in the Durham coalfield was shut for good, but every summer, at the annual miners' gala, more than 100,000 people still gather to drink, dance, and sing; to just sit there on the racecourse, loving it, and watch. The Big Meeting, as the gala is also known, has been called an ancestral procession and an almighty piss-up, and when you're in the middle of it all, encircled by concentric rings of noise and colour – the stage set and the speakers, the wire fences where the banners are hung, the stalls and tents beyond them and the fairground rides past that – both those descriptions sound about right.[1] There's a defiance to the nostalgia here, writ large on the Orgreave placards and the 'Blacklisted' T-shirts, and on the red blimp that flies high above the river reading 'Never on our knees'. It used to be the miners who dominated the gala, and then, after Thatcher, the ex-miners. These days, more and more, those making up the crowds are the ex-miners' children, who know better than anyone the ways in which economic shock gets passed down the generations, poisoning each one anew. 'The people who really struggled were those like myself,' said Darren, the son of a miner who went down the pits in Boldon at the age of fourteen and worked there at the face all his life. 'It was always assumed that we would follow in our fathers' footsteps, so we didn't get no career advice at school, no forward-planning, no path to anywhere else where our lives might end up. And so when the colliery closed as I left school, I had no idea what to do next.' A group of women walked past us clutching trays of chips and gravy, and wearing T-shirts that proclaimed 'The North Remembers'. Darren smiled, nodded, and addressed no one in particular as we soaked up the sun. 'You took all the apprenticeships away, you killed the shipyards, you killed the pits, you killed the steelworks, you killed the heavy industry,' he murmured. 'You gave us a call-centre job and some bookies and said there you go, thank you very much, have fun.'

Later, I went up to Durham Cathedral to observe the Miners' Festival Service, where new trade union banners are dedicated – a ritual which goes back to the earliest days of the gala. As each intricate square of fabric was carried into the transept to be blessed, including the first-ever official women's banner, the band struck up the haunting miners' hymn, 'Gresford', which commemorates the Welsh mining disaster in 1934 that claimed 266 lives.[2] 'In the words of St Paul,' intoned the bishop, 'we are hard-pressed on every side, but not crushed; perplexed, but not in despair; persecuted, but not abandoned; struck down, but not destroyed.' The bishop's assessment seemed correct. As much as a remembrance of something lost, the Durham Miners' Gala is a celebration of endurance, and of a culture of political organising reinvented to fit the times. From the main stage of the gala, İbrahim Doğuş, the son of a Kurdish miner who arrived in Britain as a refugee, declared: 'The Big Meeting is not just big because of its numbers; it's big because of its big values, its big vision, its big heart.' During the departure procession from the racecourse along Old Elvet that marks the end of the Big Meeting, ageing trade union bosses sashayed with teens from Unite's Young Members division as the brass bands pumped out 'I Predict a Riot' and gullies of liquor drenched the gutters. A woman in her twenties twirled past with a sign bearing the words 'Miners' grandchild against transphobia', and the throng around her cheered. 'It's about the collective strength of a working-class community,' David Brown had answered when I asked him what the gala was ultimately for. 'I was going to say "a community that has died off", but look around you. It hasn't. It's just changed a bit.' In the late 2010s the gala has evolved into an expression of the new left almost as much as the old: international, diverse and precarious, bringing migrants in Manchester together with zero-hours contract staff in Sunderland, queer kids in London and working-men's clubs in Carlisle. And perhaps befitting a political moment in which so many communities – especially post-industrial ones – have turned their backs on an imploding centre ground in search of alternatives, standing among a thicket of anti-Trump posters that had been pinned to the racecourse railings was an ex-miner wearing a 'Make America Great Again' cap, watching it all, loving it, unapologetically taking everything in. It emerged afterwards that a number of supporters of 'For Britain', the far-right Islamophobic movement, had attempted to join the Big Meeting that day, which they praised as embodying 'the very essence of being an Englishman in our free and pleasant land'.[3] After a series of altercations, the group were escorted out of the city by police.[4] Out of all this history, and all this injustice, and so very many grievances, something fractious and volatile is being constructed here, as it is in every corner of Britain, and it's still not clear in what direction that something will go off. 'The past we inherit, the future we build', runs the National Union of Mineworkers' slogan. But there are myriad ways to make sense of that inheritance, and from them many different futures to be built.

Peter and Baz know this.[5] I met them a few days later on the first floor of a Caffè Nero in central Newcastle, where we talked about the far right over cappuccinos while Peter's kids clambered on the sofas and chased each other around our table. As administrators of the 'Northeast Frontline Patriots' (NFP) Facebook page, the pair had noticed the high volume of anti-Trump imagery associated with this year's Durham Miners' Gala, which coincided with Trump's first visit as president to the UK. They were determined to push back. 'Some of the miners past and present will be shocked,' they posted, alongside an image of a 'Trump Not Welcome' banner being unfurled at the Redhills Miners Hall. 'A waste of money and an insult to all.' In response to the 'lefties', they had mocked up a picture of Trump on horseback dressed as St George; in it, he is holding a Northeast Frontline Patriots flag, next to a sign stating 'Welcome to England'. Underneath, in capital letters, was a caption: 'Expect a reaction from the ordinary people! We are no longer silent', it boomed. 'He gives me hope,' explained Peter, highlighting some of the economic similarities between north-east England and the American rust-belt states from which Trump drew critical support. 'We need people like him.' Baz agreed. 'We're up against it here, aren't we,' he ventured. 'Things are collapsing from the inside. Most of these politicians, they don't know what to do.'

Neither Peter nor Baz hail from mining families themselves, though they both claim an affinity with the ways in which the industry has shaped the landscape of the north-east, and with the insecurity that has attended its demise. Peter, now in his late forties, is from Morpeth, a market town about fifteen miles north of Newcastle. 'I grew up in a family of criminals, to be honest,' he told me. 'My ma was into all sorts, and she married seven times. I left home at sixteen and I've worked ever since.' Baz's story is more complicated, and painful; his childhood in the Newcastle care system was marked by sexual abuse and violence. 'We was just passed about,' he said. 'It led us into a different life, into crime. I ended up in prison for a lot of my adult years.' The pair met through the English Defence League (EDL), the proto-fascist street movement most strongly associated with hard-right provocateur and convicted fraudster Stephen Yaxley-Lennon, who goes by the name Tommy Robinson. 'He stands up and tells it like it is,' insists Peter. 'It doesn't matter how bad things get for Tommy, he's still there.' Peter used to be the main EDL organiser for Northumberland, but fell out with other senior members of the organisation when he used its social media pages to flag up stories about white paedophiles, stories that complicated the EDL's relentless warnings about 'Muslim grooming gangs'. He and Baz, who sat on the EDL's national committee, subsequently split off to form the breakaway NFP, and took many others in the region with them. Before its account was eventually removed by Facebook for violating the company's terms of use, the NFP page had almost 10,000 followers and a total reach, according to Peter, of half a million users (it has since reappeared on the platform under a slightly different name).[6]

Each day, the pair post about seventy updates between them, ranging from far-right memes to excoriating takedowns of left-wing social media content and a running commentary on the news. Most attract a string of responses from NFP supporters. 'It's like a full-time job,' said Baz, who is now in his sixties. The majority of the content is focused on three themes, which in the NFP's imagination are often smudged and interlinked: sexual violence, particularly by child molesters; the problems associated with immigration to Britain; and the menace posed by Islam and its adherents. 'Oh dear how sad never mind,' wrote one NFP fan, below a link to a news story about thousands of migrants being expelled by Algeria and left to fend for themselves in the Sahara. 'They're illegal immigrants terrorists rapists & paedophiles hell bent on the destruction of our countries, they're dangerous & unwanted.' That comment was fairly typical of interaction on the NFP Facebook page in the days leading up to my meeting with Peter and Baz. Another popular post consisted of a single photo of an anti-Trump protester – a person of colour dressed in a flamboyant leotard and dazzling jewellery – which prompted dozens of enraged responses. 'If this is British future [*sic*],' read one, 'have mercy on our souls.' A headline about a Leicestershire police officer charged with the sexual assault of a seventeen-year-old girl drew a similarly furious reaction from the NFP community. 'Hang the c**t,' insisted one follower. 'What chance has a white girl got now,' complained another.

The NFP do sometimes try to hold rallies and marches in Newcastle's city centre, though they are always heavily out-numbered by anti-racist counter-protesters. But it is online, and particularly on social media channels, where people who already think like Peter and Baz tend to discuss and discover one another, and where curious doubters are radicalised into viewing the world through a similar lens. 'The Internet is like that now,' Peter told me. 'You can post a picture, and that's then law: it's true, because it's up there. Or at least it's true to a lot of people, is what I'm trying to say.' He took a sip of his drink, and tried in vain to get his children to settle down for a while in front of a tablet screen. 'It gives you power, I suppose, to manipulate.' For the NFP, digital technologies are a vital tool in the effort to promote a specific vision of the future, one that has far more in common with that of the ex-miner wearing the MAGA hat and the For Britain supporters who tried to crash the Durham gala than it does with the one envisaged by most of those taking part in that event. To Peter and Baz, Stellium's data centre is where their own Big Meeting takes place; deprived of one world, they have gained – redemptively – another in which to rise again. 'British history and culture is being taken away from us,' said Baz. 'It's lost. You've lost your community. But with the Facebook page, and how powerful that is, you do have that control.'

The chaos which has ripped through our politics in the years since the financial crisis has been thoroughly mixed up with the rise of new digital technologies. The chain of causation is often murky, but the Internet, we are repeatedly told, is embolden-ing people like Peter and Baz, and as a result imperilling the very survival of liberal democracy. 'Can democracy survive the Internet / social media / Facebook / digital technology?' has been a headline, in one form or another, at the BBC, *The Economist*, the *Spectator*, *Forbes*, the *New York Review of Books*, the *Washington Post*, the *Journal of Democracy* and the Harvard Kennedy School in recent years, to name but a tiny handful. The impulse behind that question is understandable. Although the idea that we all now live in unprecedented infor-mation silos is hard to justify historically – almost everybody in Britain today accesses a wider range of news sources than almost everybody in Britain sixty years ago – it is true that the mushrooming of social media feeds driven by personalised search histories and confirmation bias has fragmented the media landscape, limiting our exposure to alternative perspectives and fuelling an intellectual flight to the extremes. 'We don't trust the mainstream media, on the left or the right,' said Peter. 'Those journalists don't care that Joe Bloggs has had to shut his shop down, because they're still going home to their big houses and loads of pay.'

Facebook allows the NFP to create and share their own framing of reality without mediation, in a setting where hierarchies appear flattened, barriers to participation are levelled, and credibility is crowdsourced rather than imposed unaccountably from above. In such an environment, scepticism about claims made by the authorities, any authority – the ones, as NFP supporters regularly remind each other, who lied about Iraq, crashed the economy and bailed out the bankers – becomes a form of defiance in its own right, and can quickly give way to credulity. 'We always do our research, and we'll remove any fake news from the page,' Peter told me, citing several recent occasions where this had happened. But as just one example among many of verifiably false information that was posted by the NFP in the run-up to our meeting and hadn't been taken down, I pointed to a series of screenshots that Peter himself had uploaded a few days earlier purporting to show that the LGBTQ+ community were campaigning to legalise paedophilia and add 'P' – for paedosexual – to their initialism. This is a hoax that originated on far-right Internet forums back in 2016 and has been repeatedly debunked by the Snopes website.[7] Despite going back and forth on the matter for some time, it proved impossible for me to get Peter to acknowledge that regardless of all the other political disagreements we had, the 'paedosexual scandal' simply wasn't true. As far as he was concerned, the facts on this were fundamentally unknowable. It was, like everything else, just one more contested claim in a whole galaxy of contested claims: claims that could be right, or could be wrong, but which ultimately – if they chimed with the mood music of the online spaces that enveloped him – had a ring of authenticity to them that no fact-checking team would ever overcome. It might be a hoax, he admitted, or the accusation that it was a hoax might itself be a hoax by the liberal media establishment. And just as I could point to what I considered to be inconvertible proof of it being the former, including links to the Reddit forums in which those behind the hoax openly laid out their plans, so he could show me a hundred examples of things on the Internet that would disprove my beliefs and contradict my facts, on this topic or any other; what else therefore, when all is said and done, do we have to go on but our instincts? 'I'm 50–50 on it, whether it does [turn out to be genuine], or whether it doesn't, we just don't know,' he offered, magnanimously. A few moments later, that ambivalence had already recrystallised into certainty, as if our entire conversation on the subject had never happened. 'I believe this paedosexual thing,' Peter said in passing, definitively. 'And it's a big problem, giving people like that the green light to go and do whatever.'

When we retreat into online echo chambers, it is those whom the political sociologist Paolo Gerabudo calls hyperleaders – including authoritarian populists like Trump – who are best placed to capitalise. At the core of any demagogue's appeal lies a claimed moral monopoly on representation; they, and they alone, speak on behalf of the silent majority, rendering other political actors illegitimate. Such characters have always circled the fringes of democratic systems. But the walled gardens of social media platforms now create microclimates that can accommodate physically scattered millions, in which simmering resentments are amplified and authoritarians can offer a fantasy of liberation from them without biased brokers getting in the way. Belief in the existence of widespread voter fraud hardens when every news item appears to confirm it; do a web search for one racist theory and you will see pages with racist content soar up the rankings next time round. From inside the morass, benevolent strongmen appear to offer a direct line between aggrieved subjects and organs of power. As the political scientist Jan-Werner Müller argues, anti-democratic figureheads invariably promise a facsimile of direct democracy while in reality cleaving to a strongly representative model – one in which they, uniquely, are the genuine representatives.[8] To Peter and Baz, that apparent clarity – Trump or Tommy Robinson 'telling it like it is' – is precisely what they crave. And services like Facebook enable anti-democratic forces, be they authoritarians or just your common-or-garden plutocrat, to capitalise on that desire in other ways as well. Most notably, they offer political campaigns a means of micro-targeting selected segments of the population with divisive messaging that might play badly if subjected to the scrutiny of an entire electorate, but which can prove highly effective – and incendiary – when appearing only in the social media feeds of particular voters identified through data profiling. Facebook has been blamed for fanning outbreaks of political violence in the Philippines, Turkey, Kenya and Myanmar; in Italy, right-wing populists Lega dominated the social media battlefield on their road to power.[9] In 2019, the campaign group Avaaz identified more than 500 different far-right Facebook pages spreading false news across Europe, generating more than half a billion views between them.[10]

If this trajectory continues, then it would seem that we are drifting towards a dystopic politics in which untruths, hyperbole and hatred are more powerful than their opposites, a politics that will privilege Peter's and Baz's form of gathering over others that are less conducive to private profit. Social media products are designed to ensure that we spend as much time as possible within their platforms generating data trails, which in turn means providing us with content that will maintain our attention, which in turn encourages the sharing of information that either reconfirms our existing prejudices or makes us apoplectic. It is this particular business model that has given us the digital universe we inhabit today. Despite an EU package of General Data Protection Regulations coming into force in 2018, and a small but high-profile political backlash against Facebook in the wake of the Cambridge Analytica scandal, so far both governments and the citizens who elect them have, with a few notable exceptions, appeared generally content to allow digital technologies to grow and govern along existing lines rather than recalibrating them to serve a wider, nonmarketised interest. The senior corporate figureheads behind such technologies show no compunction at ignoring subpoenas by democratic parliaments; 'old institutions like the law', complained Google co-founder Larry Page in 2013, impede the company's freedom to 'build really great things'.[11] We view with alarm the former company-towns, designed and dictated entirely by coal barons or other industrial magnates for their own purposes. Yet to date we have acquiesced in the construction of a far larger digital metropolis in which the notion of public accountability is assumed, almost by default, to be inapplicable, to the point where Apple has the chutzpah to rebrand its private retail outlets as 'town squares'.[12] Maybe future generations will chastise our own for so passively accepting the enclosure of our digital commons as the long, late twentieth century drew frenetically to a close. Maybe, in defence, we will tell them how unremarkable that choice felt at the time; how its very mundanity rendered it almost invisible.

We already have a decent idea of where, on current trends, that invisible choice will lead. In its never-ending quest for competitive advantage, capitalism is necessarily extractive: it continually seeks to identify new resources that others have yet to recognise and exploit. Big Tech is merely another extractive industry. The resource it mines is data: those information signals that emanate from all of us as we speak, move, think, feel and make decisions, and which, if collated and interpreted correctly, enable others to predict how and when we might speak, move, think, feel and make decisions – especially purchasing decisions – in the future. As of now, Silicon Valley has grabbed at the low-hanging fruit, such as the search terms we use in our web browsers or the products we look at online before parting with our cash. But just as our economic system has always evolved via the commodification of new materials, absorbing things that were once outside the marketplace – water, woodlands and meadows, for example – and transforming them into tradable assets, so capital now seeks to do the same with our private thoughts and inner lives, creating proprietary material out of everything from our use of exclamation marks in an email to the slope of our shoulders as we walk.[13] Facebook's machine-learning system already generates 6 million predictions per second, and as the American scholar Shoshana Zuboff has demonstrated, the more that it and other technology platforms can fine-tune and herd our behaviour rather than simply observe and record it – a shift that data scientists describe as going from 'monitoring' to 'actuation' – the more accurate, and lucrative, those predictions will become.[14]

This drive to find or create new markets is intensified by the vast cash piles that technology giants have amassed, money that demands something to invest in. As of 2016, Apple had reserves of $216 billion, the vast majority of which it holds offshore, while Google is so cash-rich that it could, if it wished, buy the whole of Goldman Sachs outright.[15] That is the reason Amazon runs its 'Prime' membership at a notional loss – the scheme's value lies in the data it provides, not its next-day deliveries – and is aggressively marketing its facial 'Rekognition' software, which under the right conditions can track the eye movements and diagnose the emotional state of anyone caught on camera.[16] It is why Amazon is also competing so heavily with Google to get its smart speakers (another loss leader) into as many homes as possible, and why we are constantly being ushered towards a modernity made up of smart fridges, smart thermostats, wearable tech and the 'Internet of things'.[17] 'It will be ubiquitous,' Gerry Murray, the chief technology officer at Stellium, told me. 'Where a place like this comes into its own is in the aggregation and manipulation of all that data mining, using it to profile clients.' There is an echo of colonialism in this scramble to capture 'uncharted' territory, and it's unsurprising that in its hunger for supremacy, Facebook has built a 'Free Basics' program, providing a pared-back and carefully controlled form of Internet connectivity for large numbers of people in countries such as Ghana, Mexico and Pakistan.[18] 'From a data-production perspective, activities are like lands waiting to be discovered,' observes Nick Srnicek, author of *Platform Capitalism*.[19] 'Whoever gets there first and holds them gets their resources – in this case, their data riches.' Facebook's public mission statement is to 'give people the power to build community and bring the world closer together'. But community and closeness only really matter to Facebook as far as it results in data resources flowing back to the company, as Mark Zuckerberg himself confirmed privately in 2012 when asked about the possibility of applications utilising the data of Facebook users without producing useful Facebook data trails themselves. 'That may be good for the world,' he wrote in an internal email, 'but it's not good for us.'[20]

Amazon is already a military behemoth; it manages cloud computing on behalf of America's intelligence agencies, and is currently the leading contender for a new $10 billion contract with the Pentagon.[21] Via its purchase of a smaller tech company that had previously struck a deal with the British health authorities, Google now has access to more than a million NHS patient records.[22] Uber, with its unparalleled insights into where and when we want to travel through our cities, is positioning itself as best placed to own and operate the transport systems of tomorrow.[23] The danger is that these firms, while remaining largely immune to democratic accountability, develop beyond mere market participants into gargantuan market-makers: the gatekeepers of huge swathes of human existence, left free to regulate themselves and discipline the rest of us. Facebook has developed systems to measure its users' 'trustworthiness' and the company's insights are now exploited by third parties to determine personal credit scores.[24] China offers a glimpse of how this technology could intersect with authoritarian governance: its 'social credit' scheme – which will eventually combine data from private entities and government departments to assign every resident a dynamic score that determines individual access to all sorts of economic and social opportunities, consumer products and physical places – is currently in its planning stage and set to be launched within the next few years.[25] But for examples of social marginalisation via algorithms that cannot be seen or challenged, we don't have to wait until then. In several US cities, artificial-intelligence programs are already being used to guide law and order operations and criminal sentencing, and have been shown to replicate racist human prejudices; Kent constabulary are one of fourteen police forces that have been trialling the same 'predictive policing' software in the UK.[26] The notion that we could ever ask, persuade or 'nudge' technology companies into doing a shuddering about-turn and scaling back their levels of digital surveillance is as ludicrous as the idea of asking a shopkeeper to stop selling goods: the act of mining data and producing behavioural predictions from that data is the essence of the tech giants' business model, and privacy is entirely antithetical to it.

And yet. Social media, smartphones and Google's information empire have positively enlivened our world in innumerable ways, and they are the outcome of immense human ingenuity. The same technologies that enable Facebook to profile our credit worthiness, and which allow the Northeast Frontline Patriots to hurl abuse at people dying of starvation in the desert, can also be designed for very different purposes – creative, democratic and humane. Wikis, open-source software and the Creative Commons licence are all digital commons in their own right. Amazon's 'Mechanical Turk' is a marketplace for casual labour; 'Turkopticon' is an initiative by two design activists at the University of California, San Diego, which 'hacks' the Amazon software to provide workers with better information and more power when navigating potential employers. These illustrate how common endeavours can disrupt digital infrastructure from within. At the local level too, examples of radical technological potential abound. In Beijing, residents are collecting air-quality data from the ground up. More than two dozen campaign groups have come together to form an 'Open Data Tax Justice Network' which crowdsources investigations into high-end financial improprieties in offshore tax havens. In Barcelona, the authorities have designated data a 'public good'. Reporters have been using digital tools to collaborate on maps of migrant routes across the Mediterranean so that more stories can be told, and more lives, sometimes, can be saved. Meanwhile, academic researchers and rebel developers are working on creating new online domains like Indienet and Indiephone, designed to circumvent the collection of data by private entities; distributed web infrastructure that makes commercial data-harvesting impossible is already available; decentralised artificial-intelligence systems and blockchains have been built that serve a wider cause than the bloating of Apple's offshore cash reserves.

As the nascent fightback by sections of the Silicon Valley workforce against their employers' enabling of censorship, racism, state violence and border enforcement has shown, people can be motivated towards innovation for reasons other than the pursuit of profit.[27] If the current model feels like an inevitable outgrowth of technological progress, it is only because we are making the category error of conflating digital technologies with the logics of capitalism that currently control them, and of viewing ourselves as merely economic consumers rather than political subjects; only because our political imaginations have been foreclosed. 'Technology is neither good nor bad; nor is it neutral,' runs the historian Melvin Kranzberg's first law of technology. It is a caution against both fatalism and banal techno-optimism. Digital advancements do not come preloaded with a moral status; their impact depends on the nature of the world in which they land, and the systems that determine their ownership and usage. These factors are not immutable. 'Reclaiming the emancipatory potential of technology will require prising it from the clutches of capital,' argues Wendy Liu, the former software developer and start-up founder who now writes about the politics of technology.[28] 'But that is a worthy fight. If the task of politics is to imagine a different world, then the job of technology is to help us get there. Whether technology is developed for the *right* ends – for the public good, instead of creating a privatised dystopia – will depend on the outcome of political struggles.' The question that the BBC, *The Economist*, the *Journal of Democracy* and all those other publications should be asking is not whether democracy can survive the Internet, but whether democracy can survive an Internet subordinated to the demands of the market; or, to put it more succinctly, whether democracy can survive the elevation of market logics over humanity. And the answer is that we don't have to risk it. The collapse of technocratic authority that has been precipitated by the financial crisis and furthered by the rise of digital technologies has, if nothing else, exposed a stubborn determination on the part of many citizens to defy the old political status quo and see themselves as agents of their own future rather than captives of somebody else's. To arrest a drift towards dystopic politics, our best hope starts here.

*

Like Peter, Jamie Driscoll was born in the early 1970s and left school at the age of sixteen. Like Peter, he has strong views on education, and home-schools his two children. And like Peter, he thinks something has gone profoundly wrong with life in the north-east, something you can feel in the texture of the place and hear in the timbre of its people. I met Jamie in the café of the Tyneside Cinema, a former newsreel theatre and art deco masterpiece that first opened in 1937. It's just around the corner from the Caffè Nero where I'd sat down with the NFP; the whole area falls within Monument ward, which Jamie represents as a councillor. 'It's not uniform,' he told me, when I asked him how he'd characterise Newcastle and its hinterlands. 'The population in this neighbourhood speaks about thirty different languages, from Bosnian to Somali. You've got financial institutions here in the city centre that have done well, especially through property speculation, and you've also got council estates where residents are living in the same homes that their grandparents did. And then if you travel just a few miles out in any direction, you sense the shift – to a fear and anger among pretty much everybody about the fact that their kids are going to be worse off than they are.' As in Tilbury, what's been lost here is more than jobs: it's something deep and vital and intangible, something to do with the links between person and person, and between people and place. 'When I was growing up, everyone's mam or dad worked at Sterling Organics,' said Peter, referring to a pharmaceuticals firm founded in 1969 that has since passed between the hands of many different global investment outfits, 'and if you lived in Dudley or Annitsford you'd join the Christmas parties there each year. You knew the shops, like Mr Ahmed's on the corner who you could go to with a note from your mam, you had your butcher's, you had your fishmonger's, you bought your Craster kippers. But you don't need to leave the house now. On the Internet you can do your shopping and top your gas and leccy up, you can charge your phone. You don't need to talk to anyone, because the web is like a big shop for relationships.'

Both Jamie and Peter have inherited a sense of displacement and loss within their community, but what they have done with that inheritance is very different. In a life that has so far included software development, engineering, and a rise through the ranks to achieve a black belt in jujitsu, most of Jamie's energy has been poured into left-wing politics – particularly anti-fascist organising, and working to stop groups like the NFP from building a street presence in Newcastle and surrounding towns. 'If you get out to County Durham or go further along the Tyne, you'll find lots of people who agree with you that the rich should pay more tax, that there should be more council homes, and that we should stop exploitation at work,' he said. 'But hardly anyone has ever come along to them and really talked about those ideas; they've left a space open for others to come in and say yes, your life is hard and you're getting ripped off, and it's because these guys who look different from you are taking your jobs.' For Jamie, that narrative chasm has been widened and heightened by the financial crash. 'Neoliberalism broke in 2008, and it can't be fixed,' he insisted. 'This is the moment of breakdown and transition, and it will be a patchwork process. We'll see new ideas, and backlashes; time periods and places that are marked by bloody conflict, and other time periods and places that are peaceful.'

As we are regularly informed by pundits, these are polarised days for Britain. We appear to view the world in ways that are more divergent and impassioned than before; any assumed infrastructure of broadly shared values and opinions has been exposed as rickety at best, and at worst illusory. We are angrier at each other, and our anger has lent a different tone to our political discourse, to our online interactions, to the curiosity and understanding we feel capable of extending to those who possess contradictory viewpoints to our own. But this polarisation is not the outcome of some sudden and regrettable failure of etiquette on a mass and mystifying scale: it's a by-product of the breakdown this book has been exploring, and will subside only if and when that breakdown is fixed. That will not happen quickly. Our economic system is now working almost completely in the interests of those who live off existing wealth rather than those who survive by earning wages; ownership and the power that accompanies it are overwhelmingly concentrated in the grip of a very few. The richest 10% of households in Britain now control about half of the country's aggregate wealth, while the poorer half of the country can lay claim to just 10% of its riches; within that poorer half, the median person's net worth is £400, when debt is taken into account, and the value of their property holdings is zero.[29] Under economic decline and austerity, the middle classes too have been impoverished by the erosion of socialised healthcare, libraries, pools, parks and welfare; as the journalist John Harris observes, 'their councils have no money left, and the public realm is decaying in front of their eyes'.[30] Is it any wonder we are getting irritable with one another on Twitter?

Fragmentation and uncertainty have also disordered those at the top. Our governing class has itself been a victim of the breakdown, not necessarily financially but in terms of the indignities that popular opinion in the post-crash era has inflicted on them in the form of both Brexit and Corbynism, and those accustomed to the job of ruling have experienced both phenomena as a trauma. The violinist Yehudi Menuhin once suggested that Britain, 'with her great administrative experience and remarkable achievement in the Civil Service, should offer a worldwide service called "Rent-a-Government"'.[31] Such a service would have very few customers today. When we talked, Jamie used the analogy of an office block whose ground floors are on fire while those at the top carry on working as if nothing untoward was happening, blithely ignorant of the bangs and crashes, the teetering walls and floors, and the rising fumes from below. A few months later, running on an unabashedly radical manifesto, he was elected by a landslide as the very first mayor for the North of Tyne region, which encompasses the area from Newcastle all the way up to the Scottish border. To get there, Jamie had to first defeat Newcastle council leader Nick Forbes in a Labour primary, and few initially gave this anti-establishment insurgent any chance of winning. Forbes is known locally as the 'heir to Blair' and 'Slasher' due to his role in implementing local spending cuts, and he ran a campaign based on politics as safety first. 'This is no time for a novice,' he claimed, in the run-up to the primary vote.[32] 'I know the business community are looking anxiously to make sure Labour chooses a candidate who has credibility and experience in the region.' Both Labour voters and the wider electorate told Forbes in no uncompromising terms what they thought of those who boasted of governing credibility and experience. In his acceptance speech, Jamie called the result a verdict on a derelict politics. 'All of these crises have the same cause: a dog-eat-dog ideology,' he declared from the stage in a Northumbria University sports hall. 'You cannot outsource democracy,' he added. 'If we're going to unite as a country, we will need to win the trust of those who have disengaged with politics ... Because that's what real democracy is, it's the citizens of our country taking part in public life and actively deciding our collective future.'

This region is the first in Britain to directly elect a mayor standing on an explicit platform of municipal socialism. It is also the region in Britain responsible for the highest number of people classified by the government's 'Prevent' scheme as being at risk of far-right radicalisation; despite accounting for just 4% of the UK population, the north-east is the source of 21% of all right-wing extremism referrals under the programme.[33] 'It's such a weird time to be alive,' Sara Bryson, a Newcastle-based community activist, told me. 'It's hard because everything is so intense day-to-day, but if you take a historical step back from it all, it does feel like the death of something, like we're witnessing an ending of sorts.' Like Baz, she grew up in poverty here – in her case in Cowgate, the huge 1920s housing estate that dominates the north-west corner of the city. Her family were soldiers, shopworkers and pitmen; she received her education at what Channel 4 described as one of the worst schools in the country. And yet working for a local children's charity over the past few years, Sara was exposed to levels of destitution that felt viscerally shocking even to her. 'Something different has been happening,' she said. 'When I was a kid, you were poor if your parents didn't work, but all these kids were in working households and yet hardly any of them had three meals a day. When I was a kid, hard as it was, I could go from Cowgate to university at the LSE and a secure job on the other side, whereas now the rungs on the ladder are so enormous, how do you climb them? When I was a kid, people could say with some honesty: go to school, work hard and you'll be alright. You can't tell kids that any more, because it's not true. These are unmet needs, and people are open to anyone who promises to meet them. My parents still live on the same council estate, and the feeling there is: "Something has to change. I don't care what it is, but something has to change."'

There is a danger, when trying to unpack the rise of hard-right sentiment, of stumbling into claptrap clichés regarding 'legitimate grievances'. Peter and Baz have a great many legitimate grievances about the inequalities that have afflicted them, the economic processes that have atomised them, and the political ideologies that have marginalised them; legitimate grievances that are shared by millions of people in Britain of different skin colours and religions. There is nothing legitimate about framing those grievances through the lens of a racialised white oppression; by 2020, women of colour will have lost nearly double the amount of money than white men have from the cumulative impacts of austerity.[34] But nonetheless, out of those grievances, a battle is under way over who can tell a more persuasive story of resolution: people like Jamie or Sara, who is now the north-east organiser for Citizens UK, working to bring communal institutions and faith groups together for progressive ends, or people like the Northeast Frontline Patriots, and the political elites that inflame and court them. 'We need to explain how we will build a stronger society that can hold the market in check and make the state accountable,' argues Sara. 'Because markets have been unfettered, and the mechanisms of limiting them have become unclear. The only way we can do that is to organise ourselves.' That is exactly what the organisations and movements explored in these pages – from Demand the Impossible to United Voices of the World, the London Renters Union to Momentum and Glasgow's Unity Centre – are doing.

There is a word, coined in 2005, to describe homesickness for a place that remains one's home: 'solastalgia', a combination of 'solace', 'desolation' and 'nostalgia'. It refers to the seeking of comfort in the face of distressing forces, and the suffering of abandonment and loneliness as one's space in the world alters beyond recognition. As climate change speeds up, all of the places explored in this book are mutating, and all of their occupants are negotiating that change alongside the economic impulses propelling it. Scotland, according to the nation's natural heritage organisation, is facing a 'climate apocalypse'.[35] Parts of the south coast of England are at risk of being 'swallowed' by the sea.[36] In London, the Thames Barrier is already in operation twice as often as expected when it was built, and 1.25 million people are believed to be at risk of severe climate-change impacts by 2050.[37] In Greater Manchester, Saddleworth – the hill near Oldham with the desirable homes that Kyle looked up to with envy – has been devastated by wildfires, as have other local moorlands.[38] Layla has been politicised in part by the threats posed to Congo and other nearby countries by soaring heat; a reminder that it is communities in the global south that have been suffering from the twin forces of market liberalism and ecological violence for the longest, and which have been leading the resistance to them too. 'It makes me so angry,' Layla told me. 'My environmentalism is about where I'm from, there and here.' A study by Oxford University has predicted that on current trends, temperature changes in the north-east could contribute to sand eels dying out, which in turn would devastate kittiwake bird colonies and Northumberland's famous puffin population; increased winter rainfall as a result of extreme weather events will cause water to run off blanket bogs into surface streams, releasing carbon, while wildfires will destroy upland heaths.

Nearly 200 miles to the south-west, on the edges of the Snowdonia national park, local authorities have already announced that due to coastal erosion an entire community will, over the next quarter of a century, be officially 'decommissioned'. By the time young adults like Layla, Kyle and Hannah reach middle age, many more towns, villages and city neighbourhoods on these islands will have followed suit. Late capitalism has helped get us into this mess – perpetual economic growth is simply incompatible with avoiding ecological catastrophe – and our reverence for or willingness to subdue market logics will determine just how far that mess spreads, and what emerges out of it. We are haunted by the spectre of dual and interlocking directions of travel: one towards scarcity, in the shape of environmental disaster, and one towards abundance, in the shape of technological strides towards automation. Who benefits from these transformations will not be resolved by robots or ice sheets, but by the choices we make – choices regarding who owns the robots, and whether or not the melting of the ice sheets is confronted for the good of us all.

In 2019, the IPPR think tank warned of a gathering storm of human-made threats to both nature and the economy. 'In the extreme, environmental breakdown could trigger catastrophic breakdown of human systems, driving a rapid process of "runaway collapse" in which economic, social and political shocks cascade through the globally linked system,' its report stated, comparing the level of risk to the 2008 financial crisis.[39] The mobilisation of resources required to confront this threat is likely to be of a magnitude rarely seen in the past outside of periods of war, or revolution; which of these ruptures will more closely characterise our future remains to be seen. The longer that climate change is permitted to advance unchecked, the harder collective solutions become to implement, and the more likely it is that a resentful, defensive and fascistic world turns in on itself. The NFP have posted links to stories claiming that climate change is a 'UN-Led Ruse To Establish A New World Order'; it is telling that their spiritual cousins in Germany, the AfD, have embraced climate denial and turned on the Swedish schoolgirl and climate activist Greta Thunberg, dismissing her as 'mentally challenged' and a fraud.

Unlike in Hollywood disaster films, the real danger ahead is not a total collapse of humanity, but rather a slow, bitter and steadily escalating struggle over dwindling space and resources as landscapes degrade and bits of the planet, piece by piece, gradually become uninhabitable. The apocalypse, if it comes to pass, will lie not in a human failure to adapt to climate catastrophe altogether, but in a human failure to prevent a privileged elite from asserting control over those vanishing spaces and resources, and cocooning themselves off from a realm of deprivation left behind. Some members of the super-rich are already shelling out down-payments on mountain bunkers; meanwhile UVW, LRU and the others are striving for the kind of economy that neither creates nor maintains a super-rich at the expense of others, and the kind of politics that could mean the bunkers are never needed after all. As the novelist William Gibson observed, 'The future is already here, it's just unevenly distributed.' Stellium's light beams can span the planet in half a second: it's up to us, and our political choices, to establish in whose interests those light beams will flash in the years to come, and what kind of planet they will illuminate.

*

The old railway line runs a few metres to the east of Stellium's data centre, winding north through the pit villages of the Tyne lowlands before striking out across the coastal plain towards Blyth, a medieval port town with its face set against the sea. The 'waggonways' network once bore horse-drawn coal loads along these tracks, to the keelmen who would row their freight out to collier ships anchored in deeper water, waiting to set sail for London. In the nineteenth century, the horses were replaced by steam engines; in the twentieth century, the steam engines were replaced by weeds. Soon, in our own century, the weeds will be joined by tight bundles of silica clad in multiple layers of protective sheathing and reinforced with Kevlar, all gathered together in a plastic tube and passed carefully through the earth below the train tracks. When the tube reaches Blyth, it will plunge down through the harbour wall and hug tight to the seabed for more than 400 miles, all the way to the town of Esbjerg on Denmark's Jutland peninsula. This new underwater cable will be part of a huge subsea communications network carrying data traffic from North America across the Atlantic to Europe, and connecting Internet users everywhere with enormous server-banks built by social media companies up in Scandinavia's coldest reaches. The name of the network is Havfrue, the Norwegian word for 'mermaid', and Facebook and Google are two of its principal investors. The western end of its North Sea section will terminate here, among the huddle of mini roundabouts, right inside the black box of Stellium. 'In the Middle Ages, people went to sleep when it fell dark and woke with the sunrise,' said Gerry Murray. 'When the canals arrived, life changed because people and things could go further, quicker. Then it was the railways, and then the roads. Now there's this.' He told me that he sometimes got to walk bits of the cable route between Stellium and the coast as part of preparations for construction work, treading all that way upon past and future. 'It's an expression of the transition,' he reflected. 'I think it's marvellous.'

Today, most of what remains of the railway track is a half-forgotten bridleway, fringed by gorse and nettle embankments. Pylons stand sentry over nearby shrublands, feeding power into small cul-de-sacs of suburban homes. Past the site of what was once Prospect Hill station – now just ruts and grooves on a muddy floor, clogged with beer cans and crisp packets – things get more scraggly. The old colliery at Backworth is being slowly reclaimed by lichen-crusted trees and a cool, damp carpet of pine; Seghill, the next stop along, is a low-rise edgeland, pebble-dashed and furrowed-green. It was among pitmen here, during the lockout by mining companies in 1844 and the mass evictions of unionised workers that accompanied it, that the seditious folk song 'Blackleg Miner' originated, celebrating the community's determination to chase out strike-breakers. 'So, divvint gaan near the Seghill mine,' goes the most famous stanza, 'Across the way they stretch a line / To catch the throat and break the spine / Of the dirty blackleg miner.' At Seaton Sluice, the road curves suddenly to reveal a vast expanse of sea up ahead, perfectly flat but for the hulking silhouettes of Blyth's offshore wind farms, and a few hard, tiny pencil-lines on the horizon where container ships were passing in the distance. The dunes are soft and the sand dark, like demerara sugar. It was early evening by the time I reached the waterfront, and the slate-grey Northumberland sky was shot through with ribbons of pink and golden-yellow.

The renewable energy industry here is one of the great economic hopes for the region; there are huge turbine halls and research centres built at the mouth of the Blyth river, right next to where the Blyth and Tyne train line reached its end, and where Stellium's fibre-optic cables will sink down on to the ocean floor. 'I'm optimistic,' Sara Bryson had told me as we said goodbye, 'because the problems we face can also be solutions. You had industries here that people organised around, and then those industries were decimated and those ways of organising were decimated with them. Now we have new industries, new ways of working, and new opportunities to organise.' She paused, and a half-smile played upon her lips. 'I don't want to have to look my child in the face when they ask me what I did in the late 2010s, at the time when the world went mad, and reply, "Well, I just kept hoping for the best." I want to be able to say that I knew it was a time when the future was up for grabs, and that I didn't watch it unfold passively.'

The former railway terminus is now a car park for a shopping centre and a Mecca bingo hall, and from there it was just a short walk out on to the harbour wall. A squabble of gulls was tussling over some mackerel discarded by a solitary fisherman, while the rest of the colony lined the fences around an old radio mast on the edge of everything, taking refuge from the waves. I stood at the end of the wall and thought about the words Nigel Farage had used during a recent campaign speech made 250 miles south of here, gazing across at the same body of water. 'Just look out there,' he told supporters. 'It's called the North Sea – and half of it should be ours. Not to be shared with the Dutch or the Danes or anybody else. It's ours. It's our birthright.' I thought about all the mental processes that went into making, and believing, such a statement: the possessive nationalism, the resentment, the toxic entanglement of hereditary entitlement and commercial competition. I thought about how powerful those words were, and the size of the silences that sat between them. I thought, most of all, about what the North Sea and the land adjoining it will eventually look like if, from the chaos and the tumult that roils our age, it is Farage's philosophy that wins the day, if it is his future that is screeching down the tracks towards us, rather than that of the teenagers on the Demand the Impossible course in Ancoats, or Fatima at the Ministry of Justice, or Yusra up in Glasgow, or Jamie Driscoll here. The fisherman's small shelter buckled against the rising wind, and he began packing up his gear. I turned to go as well, drawing my jacket tight around me. The tide was coming in.

Acknowledgements

Trying to write a book about a moment in which things are falling apart is hard; doing so while living through that same moment has often felt like madness. More than anything else, I'm stupendously grateful to all the people who gave up their time to sit down and talk with me about their lives during a period when, as the poet Louis MacNeice put it in 'Snow', 'World is suddener than we fancy it / World is crazier and more of it than we think'.

In the final chapter I refer to the extractive impulses of Big Tech. At its worst, which is frequently, journalism can also operate as an extractive industry, displaying insufficient curiosity about the way its own cogs work and little regard for those caught up in their teeth. Many of the individuals interviewed for this book had good reason to distrust reporters and yet were generous enough to share their stories with me, describing past or ongoing traumas with a clarity, dignity and agency that left me humbled. This is as true for those whose tales didn't end up making it on to the page as it is for those whose did. I hope that, in a small way, this book does those tales some justice.

I owe a great many thanks as well to the organisations that let me in to their inner circles, their planning meetings and their marches on the streets. Their energy and vision have helped me to make some sense of late-capitalist Britain, and to discern the fuzzy outlines of what might come next. Raymond Williams argued that to be truly radical is to make hope possible, rather than despair convincing, and – with one obvious exception – all of them are engaged in struggles for a future that does exactly that for me.

Spending time with people fighting against the odds to change things has made me better appreciate the role played by the invisible support crews that orbit each of us. My own is vast, and without their love and encouragement this book would never have materialised. Foremost among them is Amy Horton, who restores and inspires me daily. I'm grateful to all my friends and family, especially Issy and Gabriel for their critical manuscript work, Shelley for everything, Jack and Nabs, Skye and her family, Caroline, and Dora. My agent Karolina Sutton and the amazing publishing team at The Bodley Head and Vintage have been a relentless source of professional encouragement – I owe a particular debt to David Milner, Aidan O'Neill, Chloe Healy, Sophie Painter, Stuart Williams, and above all Will Hammond, who is the kind of editor that authors can normally only dream of.

Parts of Chapter 2 are based on a long read of mine that was originally published in 2017 by the *World Post*, and it is thanks to Rob Stothard that I ever went to Tilbury at all. Parts of Chapter 7 are based on an essay about digital technologies that I produced for *Aeon* magazine, and Sam Haselby offered invaluable assistance in making it somewhat readable. The writing of this book was aided by a generous grant from the K Blundell Trust and the Society of Authors, and by a Carlyle Membership at the London Library.

As well as my own reporting, I relied on a huge number of existing sources to provide crucial background details, and to help shape my thinking about the issues I was exploring. Wherever possible I have tried to credit them in the main text or endnotes; if there are any omissions, please accept my apologies and let me know so that I can put them right. The work of a few people has been especially useful in clarifying my ideas: Will Davies on neoliberalism, the late Mark Fisher on capitalist realism, Wendy Liu on Silicon Valley and workers' resistance, Callum Cant and Jamie Woodcock on organising in the precarious economy, Anna Minton on housing, Jem Gilbert on platform politics, Tom Blackburn on political education, Satnam Virdee, Michael Richmond, Alex Charnley and Arun Kundnani on race and empire, Natalie Bloomer and Samir Jeraj for their vital investigations into the impact of the hostile-environment regime, and Peter Frase on futures.

If the book deserves any credit it is due to all of those mentioned here; the mistakes and missteps are my own.

Notes

Prologue

1 Nosheen Iqbal, 'Divided, pessimistic, angry: survey reveals bleak mood of pre-Brexit UK', *Observer* (16 June 2019)

2 David Runciman speaking on 'What Now?', a Talking Politics podcast episode (16 January 2019)

3 Edward Luce, 'Tony Blair warns US Democrats against supporting Bernie Sanders', *Financial Times* (23 February 2016)

4 John Harris, 'Britain is in the Grip of its Most Turbulent Political Time in More Than 30 Years', *The Nation* (27 July 2017)

5 Joan Didion, *The White Album* (Weidenfeld & Nicolson, 1979), pp. 12–13

6 Aditya Chakrabortty, 'Britain's real democratic crisis? The broken link between voters and MPs', *Guardian* (20 March 2019)

7 The American author Matt Taibbi expands on this in 'Hey, MSM: All Journalism is Advocacy Journalism', *Rolling Stone* (27 June 2013)

8 Rebecca Solnit, *Hope in the Dark: Untold Histories, Wild Possibilities* (Nation Books, 2004), p. 6

Chapter 1

1 At her request, Layla's name has been changed.

2 John Lanchester, 'After the Fall', *London Review of Books* (5 July 2018)

3 Sean Coughlan, 'Student debt rising to more than £50,000, says IFS', BBC (5 July 2017); 'Student debt "tops £10,000"', BBC (22 April 2002)

4 Kevin Peachey, Clara Guibourg and Nassos Stylianou, 'Where does rent hit young people the hardest in Britain?', BBC (3 October 2018); Robert Booth, 'Millennials spend three times more of income on housing than grandparents', *Guardian* (20 September 2017); Helen Pidd, 'Housing crisis: 15,000 new Manchester homes and not a single one "affordable"', *Guardian* (5 March 2018)

5 Robert Darnton, *The Kiss of Lamourette: Reflections in Cultural History* (W. W. Norton & Company, 1990), p. 18

6 Caroline Mortimer, 'Socialism "more popular" with British public than capitalism, survey finds', *Independent* (24 February 2016); Matthew Elliott and James Kanagasooriam, 'Public opinion in the post-Brexit era: Economic attitudes in modern Britain', Legatum Institute (October 2017)

7 'Theresa May defends free market economy', BBC (28 September 2017); 'THE *SUN* SAYS: As Corbynistas descend on London for Day of Rage, they're not remotely ready for the revolution they want', *Sun* (21 June 2017); 'Why we're launching a new campaign for capitalism and free markets', *Telegraph* (29 September 2018)

8 Emily Dugan, 'Young people suffering their "worst economic prospects for several generations"', *Independent* (30 October 2015); Sally Weale, 'Young adults most pessimistic on UK social mobility – poll', *Guardian* (11 December 2018)

9 'Most deprived town in England is Oldham, ONS study finds', BBC (18 March 2016)

10 'One in 25 people homeless in England's worst-hit areas', BBC (8 November 2017)

11 Jennifer Williams, 'Manchester's homeless crisis is about to get much, much worse', *Manchester Evening News* (8 February 2018)

12 George Hammond, 'Manchester's high-end boom runs risk of flooding market', *Financial Times* (9 March 2018)

13 Dominic Smithers, 'It's official – Manchester is at the very centre of Britain's property boom', *Manchester Evening News* (24 March 2017)

14 Dianne Bourne, 'How to win on Manchester's booming property market according to *Location Location*'s Phil Spencer', *Manchester Evening News* (29 April 2017)

15 George Hammond, 'Manchester's high-end boom runs risk of flooding market', *Financial Times* (9 March 2018)

16 John Harris, 'The great reinvention of Manchester: "It's far more pleasant than London"', *Guardian* (3 November 2015)

17 John Harris, 'Sir Howard Bernstein on reinventing Manchester: "Remarkable things have been achieved"', *Guardian* (18 April 2017)

18 John McDermott, 'Manchester: UK's new order?', *Financial Times* (20 February 2015)

19 Jonathan Silver, *From Homes to Assets: Housing Financialisation in Greater Manchester* (2018)

20 Ibid.

21 'Oldham among 10 areas "hit hardest by austerity"', *Oldham Times* (17 October 2018)

22 'Condemnation from town's political leaders in wake of austerity study', *Oldham Times* (17 October 2018)

23 'Mind charity in Oldham has its budget cut by 80%', BBC (18 November 2010)

24 'Exclusive: More than 2,000 charities and community groups face cuts', False Economy (2 August 2011)

25 Todd Fitzgerald, 'Oldham hikes council tax as mental health services and social care bear brunt of devastating £16m cuts', *Manchester Evening News* (24 February 2016)

26 Jennifer Williams, Charlotte Green, Lisa Meakin, Mari Eccles and James Illingworth, 'Children in care crisis: Councils are struggling to cope with huge rise in number of youngsters needing support', *Manchester Evening News* (29 August 2018); Tom Crewe, 'The Strange Death of Municipal England', *London Review of Books* (15 December 2016)

27 Sophie Norris, 'Oldham Council cuts: Have YOUR say on finding £20m after budget slashed again', *Mancunian Matters* (9 September 2016)

28 Andrew Oxlade, 'How QE affected your wealth: a snapshot', *Telegraph* (3 March 2016)

29 Juliette Garside, 'Recession rich: Britain's wealthiest double net worth since crisis', *Guardian* (26 April 2015); 'Wealth of people in their 30s has "halved in a decade"', BBC (30 September 2016)

30 Aditya Chakrabortty, from the foreword to William Davies, *The Limits of Neoliberalism: Authority, Sovereignty and the Logic of Competition* (SAGE, 2016), p. x

31 Jennifer Williams, 'Families are "being made homeless" by Universal Credit – but its rollout will continue', *Manchester Evening News* (18 October 2017); Patrick Butler, 'Call for universal credit overhaul amid fears of looming evictions crisis', *Guardian* (6 February 2019)

32 Helen Thompson, 'It's Still the 2008 Crash', *Political Quarterly*, Vol. 88, Issue 3 (July–September 2017)

33 Moya Sarner, 'The age of envy: how to be happy when everyone else's life looks perfect', *Guardian* (9 October 2018)

34 Quoted in ibid.

35 Chelsea Ritschel, 'Dating app Once gives users an attractiveness rating on a scale of one to five', *Independent* (20 June 2019)

36 Robert Booth, 'Anxiety on rise among the young in social media age', *Guardian* (5 February 2019)

37 Nicola Davis, 'Loneliness linked to major life setbacks for millennials, study says', *Guardian* (24 April 2018)

38 Denis Campbell, 'One in three young people have mental health troubles, survey finds', *Guardian* (18 October 2018); Nicola Slawson, 'Young Britons have never been unhappier, research suggests', *Guardian* (5 April 2018)

39 Mark Rice-Oxley, 'Austerity and inequality fuelling mental illness, says top UN envoy', *Guardian* (24 June 2019)

40 Mark Fisher, 'Reflexive Impotence', *k-punk* (11 April 2006)

41 Jim Waterson, 'This Was The Election Where The Newspapers Lost Their Monopoly On The Political News Agenda', BuzzFeed (18 June 2017)

Chapter 2

1 Daniel Defoe, *A tour thro' the whole island of Great Britain, divided into circuits or journeys*, Vol. I (1724)

2 'Full text of Tony Blair's [Labour Party conference] speech', BBC (27 September 2005)

3 Charles Leadbeater, *Living On Thin Air: The New Economy* (Viking, 1999)

4 Lynsey Hanley, 'Why class won't go away', *Guardian* (27 September 2016)

5 Joe Steeples, 'AGGRO BRITAIN', *Sun* (26 August 1980)

6 Lizzy Davies, '"It's one big cesspit here": Thurrock, the country's capital of misery', *Guardian* (25 July 2012)

7 Bagehot, 'The trials of life in Tilbury', *The Economist* (16 August 2014)

8 Camilla Hodgson, 'English councils face cash crunch as social care costs bite', *Financial Times* (12 April 2018)

9 Juliana Lucas, 'The Nigerian Way Is Essex', *The Voice* (9 November 2013)

10 'More policing after race attacks', BBC (22 August 2007)

11 Paul Tobias-Gibbens, 'Tilbury property prices are on the up', *Your Thurrock* (26 April 2018)

12 Tweet by Tim Aker (@Tim_Aker) on 5 October 2018: https://twitter.com/Tim_Aker/status/1048152189124972545

13 Laura Pitel, 'National Front activist hired by Ukip's rising star', *The Times* (7 April 2015)

14 Gabby Jeffries, 'UKIP deputy leader: "We face problems caused by migrants with HIV"', *Pink News* (14 October 2014); Matthew Weaver, 'Paul Nuttall stands by Ukip MEP who called Islam a death cult', *Guardian* (11 May 2017)

15 David Goodhart, *The Road to Somewhere: The Populist Revolt and the Future of Politics* (Hurst, 2017)

16 'Tilbury container stowaways included 13 children', BBC (17 August 2014)

17 Kim Moody, 'Who Put Trump in the White House?', *Jacobin* (1 November 2017)

18 Lorenza Antonucci, Laszlo Horvath and André Krouwel, 'Brexit was not the voice of the working class nor of the uneducated – it was of the squeezed middle', LSE 'British Politics and Policy Blog' (13 October 2017)

19 Mohsin Hamid, 'Mohsin Hamid on the dangers of nostalgia: we need to imagine a brighter future', *Guardian* (25 February 2017)

20 'Thurrock Council ends services contract five years early', BBC (23 July 2015)

21 Gill Plimmer, 'Carillion collapse set to cost taxpayer at least £148m', *Financial Times* (7 June 2018)

22 Tom Crewe, 'The Strange Death of Municipal England', *London Review of Books* (15 December 2016)

23 Patrick Maguire, 'Socially isolated voters more likely to favour Brexit, finds think tank', *Guardian* (17 December 2016)

24 William Davies, *The Limits of Neoliberalism: Authority, Sovereignty and the Logic of Competition* (SAGE, 2016)

25 John-Paul Ford Rojas, 'Ten million jobs could be replaced by robots in next 15 years', *Sky News* (24 March 2017); Larry Elliott, 'Robots threaten 15m UK jobs, says Bank of England's chief economist', *Guardian* (12 November 2015)

26 Mathew Lawrence, *Future proof: Britain in the 2020s* (IPPR, 2016)

27 Mathew Lawrence, 'Robots, Brexit and the Anthropocene – welcome to 2020s Britain', *New Statesman* (4 January 2017)

28 'Amazon to create more than 1,500 new permanent jobs with the opening of a fulfilment centre in Essex in spring 2017', Chartered Institute of Logistics and Transport (24 August 2016)

29 Mark Sweney, 'Amazon paid just £15m in tax on European revenues of £19.5bn', *Guardian* (10 August 2017)

30 Hilary Osbourne, 'Amazon accused of "intolerable conditions" at Scottish warehouse', *Guardian* (12 December 2016)

31 Jamie Grierson, 'Amazon "regime" making British staff physically and mentally ill, says union', *Guardian* (18 August 2015)

32 Michael Sainato, 'Amazon training videos coach Whole Foods staff on how to discourage unions', *Guardian* (27 September 2018)

33 John Harris, 'Britain's shared spaces are vanishing, leaving us a nation of cliques', *Guardian* (4 September 2018); Benedicte Page, 'Latest CIPFA stats reveal yet more library closures and book loan falls', *Bookseller* (7 December 2018)

Chapter 3

1 Details of Fatima's pay at the Ministry of Justice were correct at the time of writing. Cleaning subcontractors at the Supreme Court do currently pay their staff the London Living Wage.

2 Hilary Osborne, 'UK workers' wages fell 1% a year between 2008 and 2015, TUC says', *Guardian* (27 February 2017); 'UK workers experienced sharpest wage fall of any leading economy, TUC analysis finds', press release by the Trades Union Congress (27 July 2016); 'UK wages worth up to a third less than in 2008, study shows', *Guardian* (31 January 2019)

3 Bhrmie Balaram and Fabian Wallace-Stephens, 'Seven portraits of economic security and modern work in the UK', RSA (25 January 2018)

4 David Metcalf, 'United Kingdom Labour Market Enforcement Strategy 2018/19', UK Government (May 2018)

5 Elle Vickery, 'Theresa May: Work is the best route out of poverty', *Daily Express* (24 January 2018); 'Theresa May on not raising VAT, tax pledges, welfare and Brexit', ITV News (30 April 2017); '"Work is the best route out of poverty" – May and Corbyn debate Universal Credit', Conservative Home (12 September 2018)

6 Patrick Butler, 'Record 60% of Britons in poverty are in working families – study', *Guardian* (22 May 2017); 'Seven million UK workers living in poverty', *The Week* (7 December 2016)

7 Andrew Haldane, 'Pay Power', speech given to the Acas 'Future of Work' conference (10 October 2018); Amelia Hill, 'Seven in 10 UK workers are "chronically broke", study finds', *Guardian* (25 January 2018)

8 Nick Srnicek, *Platform Capitalism* (Polity Press, 2016)

9 Richard Partington, 'Gig economy in Britain doubles, accounting for 4.7 million workers', *Guardian* (28 June 2019)

10 Owen Boycott, 'Junior judges face zero-hours working conditions, say lawyers', *Guardian* (30 June 2019)

11 Sarah Butler, 'Nearly 10 million Britons are in insecure work, says union', *Guardian* (5 June 2017)

12 Graham Ruddick, 'Number of striking workers now lower than ever', *Guardian* (2 August 2016)

13 Sean O'Grady, 'Strikes are at an all-time low – and that's because we don't really need trade unions any more', *Independent* (30 May 2018)

14 Jonathan Maze, 'McDonald's CEO Steve Easterbrook was paid $21.8m last year', *Restaurant Business* (12 April 2018). The sterling calculation is based on currency exchange rates at the time of writing and assumes a forty-hour working week.

15 Donald Hirsch, 'Two-thirds of single Britons in their 20s now live with their parents. Here's what that means', CityMetric (4 February 2019)

16 'Ferrovial reports 454 million euro net profit in 2017, a 21% increase', press release by Ferrovial (28 February 2018)

17 My interviews with Fatima were conducted with the assistance of a Portuguese translator.

18 Form AR21 Annual Return for Unite the Union (2017); Form AR21 Annual Return for United Voices of the World (2017)

19 'What is the Origin of the Term Wobbly?', Industrial Workers of the World

20 'Unison Actively Undermining IWW Living Wage Campaign At St George's', Industrial Workers of the World (24 May 2012)

21 Alexandra Rucki, 'Medical school cleaners secure London living wage', *Wandsworth Times* (29 May 2012)

22 Upton Sinclair, *The Jungle* (The Jungle Publishing Co., 1906), p. 38

23 Ibid., p. 163

24 Callum Cant, 'The wave of worker resistance in European food platforms 2016–17', Notes From Below (29 January 2018)

25 Beverly J. Silver, *Forces of Labor: Workers' Movements and Globalization Since 1870* (Cambridge University Press, 2003), p. 47

26 Sarah Butler, 'Amazon accused of treating UK warehouse staff like robots', *Guardian* (31 May 2018)

27 Matt Novak, 'Amazon Patents Wristband to Track Hand Movements of Warehouse Employees', Gizmodo (31 January 2018)

28 Trent Gillies, 'Why most of Three Square Market's employees jumped at the chance to wear a microchip', CNBC (13 August 2017)

29 Emine Saner, 'Employers are monitoring computers, toilet breaks – even emotions. Is your boss watching you?', *Guardian* (14 May 2018)

30 Ibid.

31 Jamie Woodcock, 'Automate This! Delivering Resistance in the Gig Economy', *Mute* (10 March 2017)

32 Sinclair, *The Jungle*, p. 70

33 Woodcock, 'Automate This! Delivering Resistance in the Gig Economy'

34 Saner, 'Employers are monitoring computers, toilet breaks – even emotions. Is your boss watching you?'

35 Woodcock, 'Automate This! Delivering Resistance in the Gig Economy'

36 Ibid.

37 Ibid.

38 Amy Walker, 'Hospitality abuse: new website to encourage workers to speak out', *Guardian* (31 January 2019); see the 'WorkIt' app, available on iOS and Android app stores; John Evans, 'An introduction to Wobbly: an app for 21st century workers' power', Notes From Below (16 August 2018); Tim Lezard, 'Unite launches online pay tool to counter bosses' money lies', *Union News* (17 January 2018)

39 Alex Rosenblat, 'The Network Uber Drivers Built', *Fast Company* (9 January 2018)

40 Cara McGoogan, 'Uber drivers gang up to cause surge pricing, research says', *Telegraph* (2 August 2017)

41 Adam Barr, 'Microresistance: Inside The Day of a Supermarket Picker', Notes From Below (30 March 2018)

42 Ibid.

43 Kim Moody, *On New Terrain: How Capital is Reshaping the Battleground of Class War* (Haymarket Books, 2017)

44 Robert Wright and Camilla Hodgson, 'Foreign cleaners expose lack of protection in UK labour market', *Financial Times* (2 May 2019)

45 Callum Cant discusses this further in 'McStrike and Unions in the Precarious Economy', a podcast episode published by Novara Media (5 October 2018)

46 Ibid.

47 Steven Parfitt, 'Labour history shows us where workers "took back control" without building walls', Open Democracy (9 November 2018)

48 Ibid.

49 Zachary Young, 'French Uber Eats, Deliveroo, Foodora workers strike during World Cup final', Politico (11 July 2018); 'Food delivery riders protest against "wage theft" by Deliveroo, Foodora and UberEats', *Guardian* (16 May 2018)

50 Eric Hobsbawm, *Labouring Men: Studies in the History of Labour* (Weidenfeld & Nicolson, 1964), p. 139, quoted in Moody, *On New Terrain*, p. 75

51 Moody, *On New Terrain*

52 'Quentin Marshall steps up to head Weatherbys Private Bank', Weatherbys (6 July 2017); 'Meet the Private Bank Team', Quentin Marshall profile on Weatherbys' website: https://www.weatherbys.bank/about-weatherbys/team/private-bank

53 'Company History', IDM ('Intelligent Debt Management') Group website: https://www.intelligentdebtgroup.co.za/timeline.php

54 Wendy Liu, 'The Inevitability of the Gig Economy', *New Socialist* (19 November 2017)

55 Tim Lezard, 'We are going up! Trade union membership on the rise again', *Union News* (30 May 2019); Alice Martin, 'Young climate

strikers could achieve even more by joining a union', *Guardian* (30 May 2019)

56 Tweet by Jason Moyer-Lee, general secretary of the Independent Workers of Great Britain union (@MoyerLee) on 31 May 2018: https://twitter.com/MoyerLee/status/1002157038120652801

Chapter 4

1 Theo's and Shirley's real names have been changed to preserve their anonymity.

2 In a letter the Home Office recommended to Theo that he leave the UK and travel to his birthplace of Kenya, a country he had not visited for over fifty years, and then apply for some form of leave to remain in Britain from there. The Kenyan embassy, however, refused to recognise Theo as a citizen. When Theo pointed out to the Home Office that he did not own a passport, could not travel abroad without one, and was effectively being made stateless, officials said they would print him an emergency travel document entitling him to depart Britain for Nairobi – but not necessarily to come back.

3 James Walvin, *Black And White: The Negro and English Society 1555–1945* (Allen Lane, 1973), cited by Stuart Hall, 'Racism and Reaction', in Sally Davison et al (eds.), *Stuart Hall: Selected Political Writings* (Duke University Press, 2017)

4 Malcolm James and Sivamohan Valluvan, 'Left Problems, Nationalism and the Crisis', *Salvage* (27 November 2018)

5 Bastian Vollmer, 'Irregular Migration in the UK: Definitions, Pathways and Scale', Migration Observatory at the University of Oxford (11 July 2011)

6 Carlos Vargas-Silva and Madeleine Sumption, 'Net migration in the UK', Migration Observatory at the University of Oxford (24 August 2018); 'The Truth About Asylum', Refugee Council

7 'The truth about ... refugees', Amnesty International UK (4 April 2019); Adrian Edwards, 'Forced displacement at record 68.5 million', UNHCR (19 June 2018); 'More than half of British public overestimate number of immigrants in the UK', press release by Refugee Action (9 January 2012)

8 James Kirkup and Robert Winnett, 'Theresa May interview: "We're going to give illegal migrants a really hostile reception"', *Telegraph* (25 May 2012)

9 Natalie Bloomer and Samir Jeraj, 'The real Theresa May: How the PM tried to introduce immigration checks in schools', Politics.co.uk (5 October 2017); Natalie Bloomer, 'Panic, fear, confusion: Inside the hospitals piloting migrant ID checks', Politics.co.uk (13 October 2017)

10 Natalie Bloomer and Samir Jeraj, 'Single parent families could be left "destitute" as Home Office accesses child maintenance records', Politics. co.uk (8 November 2017); Diane Taylor, 'Homeless charity aided deportation patrols in search for rough sleepers', *Guardian* (5 March 2018)

11 Natalie Bloomer and Samir Jeraj, 'Revealed: MPs using immigration enforcement hotline to report people to the Home Office', Politics.co.uk (1 September 2017)

12 Samir Jeraj and Natalie Bloomer, 'Woman reports rape to police – and is arrested on immigration charges', Politics.co.uk (28 November 2017)

13 Ashley Cowburn, 'Theresa May's "hostile environment" policy seen as "almost reminiscent of Nazi Germany", says former Civil Service chief', *Independent* (19 April 2018)

14 Jamie Grierson, 'Number of *Windrush* cases passes 5,000', *Guardian* (25 May 2018); Diane Abbott, 'We still do not know the true scale of the *Windrush* Generation scandal', *New Statesman* (22 November 2018)

15 Robert Wright, 'The roots of *Windrush* scandal: "They saw enemies everywhere"', *Financial Times* (20 April 2018)

16 In response to an enquiry from the author about Theo's case, the Home Office provided the following statement in April 2019: 'The Home Secretary and the Immigration Minister are committed to righting the wrongs experienced by the *Windrush* generation and launching the Compensation Scheme is a crucial step in delivering on that commitment. In the cases of vulnerable individuals, our Commonwealth Citizens' Taskforce works with partners across government, including DWP [the Department for Work and Pensions], to secure access to benefits and housing support.' The DWP declined to comment on Theo's story.

17 David Wearing, 'Stephen Lawrence and the Hostile Environment', *New Socialist* (24 April 2018)

18 'GB Eurotrack Poll', YouGov (May 2014)

19 Jason C. Anthony, 'The importance of eating local: slaughter and scurvy in Antarctic cuisine', *Endeavour*, Vol. 35, Issue 4 (June–September 2011)

20 Essay by Geoff Manaugh, published in David Maisel, *Black Maps: American Landscape and the Apocalyptic Sublime* (Steidl, 2013)

21 Blind Harry, *The Actes and Deidis of the Illustre and Vallyeant Campioun Schir William Wallace* (believed to have been written around 1477)

22 Niamh McIntyre and Diane Taylor, 'Britain's immigration detention: how many people are locked up?', *Guardian* (11 October 2018)

23 Diane Taylor and Niamh McIntyre, 'Revealed: sick, tortured immigrants locked up for months in Britain', *Guardian* (10 October 2018); Liam O'Hare, 'At least one person a day is self-harming in UK detention centres', *Independent* (2 April 2018)

24 Liam O'Hare, 'MP slams UK Government detention policy as "absolute disgrace" after Dungavel suicide watch figures are revealed', *Herald* (8 April 2018)

25 'Because of detention / In spite of detention', Unlocking Detention (11 December 2018)

26 Yusra's name has been changed to preserve her anonymity.

27 Martin Moore and Gordon Ramsay, *UK Media coverage of the 2016 EU Referendum campaign* (Centre for the Study of Media, Communication and Power at King's College London, 2017)

28 Macer Hall, 'REVEALED: Shock £29bn migrants bill for Britain's crammed schools', *Daily Express* (22 June 2016); Giles Sheldrick, 'HALF of all rape and murder suspects in some parts of Britain are foreigners', *Daily Express* (23 May 2016); Giles Sheldrick, 'MIGRANTS PAY JUST £100 TO INVADE BRITAIN', *Daily Express* (1 June 2016)

29 Moore and Ramsay, *UK Media coverage of the 2016 EU Referendum campaign*

30 Arj Singh, 'Nigel Farage says controversial anti-migrant poster "won the referendum" for Brexit', *Yorkshire Post* (19 October 2018)

31 Scott Blinder and Mariña Fernández-Reino, 'Non-European Student Migration to the UK', Migration Observatory at the University of Oxford (5 October 2018); 'Reality Check: How many people seek asylum in the UK?', BBC (31 December 2018)

32 Jennifer Scott, 'Ann Widdecombe's EU slavery remarks branded as "disgusting"', BBC (4 July 2019)

33 Boris Johnson, 'Boris Johnson's victory speech: "we can find our voice in the world again"', *Spectator* (24 June 2016)

34 Jessica Elgot, 'Theresa May's "hostile environment" at heart of *Windrush* scandal', *Guardian* (17 April 2018)

35 Erica Consterdine, 'How New Labour made Britain into a migration state', The Conversation (1 December 2017)

36 David Blunkett, *The Blunkett Tapes* (Bloomsbury, 2004); Roy Hattersley, 'Home Truths', *Guardian* (7 March 2004), both cited in Richard Power Sayeed, *1997: The Future That Never Happened* (Zed Books, 2017), p. 32

37 Satnam Virdee, *Racism, Class and the Racialized Outsider* (Palgrave, 2014)

38 David Rosenberg, 'Immigration: Media Frenzy', from the Channel 4 web series *Origination* (2007)

39 Michael Richmond and Alex Charnley, 'Race, Class and Borders', Base (2 May 2018)

40 'National Statistics Returns', UK Government (23 February 2017)

41 Arun Kundnani, 'Disembowel Enoch Powell', *Dissent* (18 April 2018)

42 James Slack, 'ENEMIES OF THE PEOPLE', *Daily Mail* (4 November 2016); Andrew Pierce, 'ONE BY ONE, TRAITORS PUT THE KNIFE INTO THERESA MAY', *Daily Mail* (13 September 2018); Steven Swinford, 'The Brexit mutineers: At least 15 Tory MPs rebel against leave date with threat to join forces with Labour', *Telegraph* (14 November 2017)

43 Kundnani, 'Disembowel Enoch Powell'; Christopher Hope, 'Nigel Farage and Enoch Powell: the full story of Ukip's links with the "Rivers of Blood" politician', *Telegraph* (12 December 2014)

44 'BBC defends Rivers of Blood broadcast', BBC (12 April 2018)

45 Ash Sarkar, 'The BBC is wrong to broadcast Enoch Powell's speech – it's not a historical artefact, it's a living tradition', *Independent* (13 April 2018)

46 Libby Brooks, 'Glasgow council warns of humanitarian crisis over asylum-seeker evictions', *Guardian* (1 August 2018)

47 'Statement on Serco evictions', Living Rent Glasgow (30 July 2018)

48 'Child refugees "still being held" at Dungavel centre', BBC (1 June 2019)

49 Phil Miller, 'Dungavel detention centre in slave labour shame as asylum seekers paid just £1 an hour for work', *Daily Record* (15 January 2018);

'Detention Centre Profits: 20% and Up For The Migration Prison Bosses', Corporate Watch (18 July 2018)

50 Madison Pauly, 'Trump's Immigration Crackdown Is a Boom Time for Private Prisons', *Mother Jones* (May 2018)

51 'Deutsche Bank warning over Scottish independence', BBC (13 September 2014); 'US slams Deutsche Bank for financial crisis role', *The Local* (15 April 2011)

52 Virdee, *Racism, Class and the Racialized Outsider*, p. 164

53 Image of Sarah Boris's artwork available at Eye on Design: https://eyeondesign.aiga.org/sarah-boris-on-the-importance-of-personal-projects-and-designing-for-art/

54 Artwork by Ian Hamilton Finlay (1990)

Chapter 5

1 Oliver Wainwright, 'Walkie-Talkie tower: stark reminder of forces that rule the City', *Guardian* (27 July 2017)

2 James Warrington, 'Landsec profits rise despite retail's property slump', *City A.M.* (13 November 2018)

3 From the Yara Capital website: https://yaracapital.com/#About; prices taken from the Yara Students website: https://yarastudents.com/yara-central-holland-park/

4 This line and subsequent quotes from Hassan Awadh Hassan are taken from his testimony to the Grenfell Tower Inquiry at Holborn Bars, London (29 May 2018)

5 'KCTMO – Playing with fire!', Grenfell Action Group (20 November 2016); Adam Lusher, 'Grenfell Tower residents complained two years ago of "cheap materials and corner cutting" in block's refurbishment', *Independent* (16 June 2017); Konstantinos Daniel Tsavdaridis, 'What caused the Grenfell fire? Here's what we know', *CityMetric* (14 June 2018)

6 'CLADDING APPROVALS', a report commissioned by the Association of British Insurers and carried out by the Fire Protection Association (22 February 2018); Andrew O'Hagan, 'The Tower', *London Review of Books* (7 June 2018)

7 'Mayor Boris Johnson tells opponent to "get stuffed"', BBC (11 September 2013)

8 Dominic Gilbert, 'Legal aid advice network "decimated" by funding cuts', BBC (10 December 2018)

9 Dave Smith and Phil Chamberlain, 'On the blacklist: how did the UK's top building firms get secret information on their workers?', *Guardian* (27 February 2015)

10 Lisa Mckenzie, 'People shouldn't have to feel grateful for social housing – it's a basic human right', *Guardian* (11 August 2017)

11 Rowan Moore, 'Council houses were once a glory of the public realm. Let's return to those days', *Guardian* (20 January 2019)

12 'Income and repairs expenditure for Grenfell tower', Royal Borough of Kensington and Chelsea, (June 2017). RBKC released these figures under a Freedom of Information request (FOI2017-0777) made by Tom Keene. In addition to rental income, RBKC also received an additional £1.2 million in service charges, but some of this latter figure will have been paid by private leaseholders. Repair costs here do not include the contentious one-off refurbishment project that has been implicated in the fire, as RBKC itself categorises that separately.

13 David Cameron, 'Estate regeneration', UK Government (10 January 2016)

14 'Selling Heygate flats to overseas buyers "is insult"', *Evening Standard* (22 April 2013)

15 'The Heygate Diaspora', 35% Campaign (8 June 2013)

16 Andy Jones, 'Every Flat in a New South London Development Has Been Sold to Foreign Investors', VICE (13 April 2017)

17 Tweet by David Madden, a sociologist at the London School of Economics (@davidjmadden) on 17 November 2017: https://twitter.com/davidjmadden/status/931477559002484736

18 Robert Booth, 'Grenfell Tower borough "behaved like a property developer"', *Guardian* (20 June 2018)

19 Rajeev Syal and Harrison Jones, 'Kensington and Chelsea council has £274m in reserves', *Guardian* (19 June 2017)

20 Amelia Gentleman, 'Grenfell campaigner calls for return of local assets as reparation', *Guardian* (13 September 2017)

21 Paul Waugh, 'Tories Under Attack Over "Crass" Survey Asking Residents To Rate Grenfell Fire With Marks Out Of Ten', HuffPost (13 November 2017)

22 Farzana Khan, '"We are with you": 22 East London housing estates stand in solidarity with Grenfell', *New Internationalist* (29 June 2017)

23 Nick Hopkins, '"Huge concentrations" of toxins found in Grenfell soil, study finds', *Guardian* (12 October 2018)

24 Michael Savage, 'Millennial housing crisis engulfs Britain', *Guardian* (28 April 2018)

25 Larry Elliott, 'The UK housing market's perfect storm, and five steps to avoid it', *Guardian* (8 October 2017); Isabelle Fraser, 'London house prices now a record 14.5x average earnings, as Barclays reveals the fastest-growing areas', *Telegraph* (28 November 2017); Rupert Jones, 'Home ownership in England at a 30-year low, official figures show', *Guardian* (2 March 2017)

26 Patrick Collinson, 'One in three UK millennials will never own a home – report', *Guardian* (17 April 2018)

27 Ibid.

28 Patrick Collinson, 'Nearly half of tenants who make complaint face "revenge eviction"', *Guardian* (24 August 2018); Simon Goodley, 'Tenants in England not being protected from revenge evictions, study finds', *Guardian* (18 March 2019)

29 Joel Golby, 'London Rental Opportunity Of The Week', VICE (2015–19)

30 Savage, 'Millennial housing crisis engulfs Britain'; Simon Usbourne, 'Shoebox Britain: how shrinking homes are affecting our health and happiness', *Guardian* (10 October 2018); Robert Booth, 'Bottom of the housing ladder: "I feel like a squatter in my home"', *Guardian* (28 January 2018)

31 Anna Tims, 'The lettings club where tenants are fined £90 for leaving dirty dishes', *Guardian* (14 May 2018)

32 *The PAH Green Book*

33 Anna Minton, *Big Capital: Who Is London For?* (Penguin, 2017), p. 111

34 For more on the Wards Corner redevelopment controversy, see Anoosh Chakelian, 'How a Latin American market became the battleground for Corbynism's soul', *New Statesman* (20 February 2019) and a series of excellent articles on the subject available at the Novara Media website. Details of the campaign against Grainger PLC's proposals can be found at: http://savelatinvillage.org.uk/

35 Robert Booth, 'Bloated London property prices fuelling exodus from capital', *Guardian* (24 July 2017)

36 Kate Hardy and Tom Gillespie, 'London's exodus offers a stark warning to other UK cities: your culture is at risk', *Guardian* (4 August 2017); Saskia Sassen, 'Who owns our cities – and why this urban takeover should concern us all', *Guardian* (24 November 2015)

37 Jack Shenker, 'Revealed: the insidious creep of pseudo-public space in London', *Guardian* (24 July 2017)

38 Aamna Mohdin and Harriet Grant, '"Why can't they come and play?": housing segregation in London', *Guardian* (26 March 2019)

39 Oliver Wainwright, 'The truth about property developers: how they are exploiting planning authorities and ruining our cities', *Guardian* (17 September 2014)

40 Jonathan Prynn, 'Revealed: Britain's most expensive street … but prices have slumped to a mere £35m', *Evening Standard* (27 September 2018)

41 Rupert Neate, 'Anger over glut of "posh ghost towers" planned for London', *Guardian* (4 February 2018)

42 William Eichler, 'London council budgets slashed 17% over last decade', *Transport Network* (13 May 2019); 'Have the poorest councils had the biggest cuts?', BBC (23 April 2019)

43 Martin Williams, 'Almost one in five MPs are landlords', *Channel 4 News* (21 July 2017); Robert Booth and Frankie Crossley, 'Nearly 100 London councillors have links to property industry', *Guardian* (29 April 2018)

44 Jonathan Prynn, 'Council may "land-grab" in row with company behind £12bn Earls Court scheme', *Evening Standard* (20 February 2019); Dave Hill, 'Earls Court: Sadiq Khan "patience is wearing thin" with Capco over stalled scheme', *On London* (20 February 2019)

45 A photo of this can be found on p. 10 of *Against the Odds: Walterton and Elgin from Campaign to Control* (Walterton and Elgin Community Homes, 1998), which also contains many more details about the community's long struggle with Westminster Council.

46 'Senior Management Restructure Update Report', Lambeth Council (21 March 2019), referenced in a tweet by People's Audit (@PeoplesAudit) on 13 March 2019: https://twitter.com/PeoplesAudit/status/1105912859480023041

47 In an irony lost on no one except perhaps the developers, the gallery on Lower Marsh is now being demolished to make way for a new sixty-six-room hotel; other businesses that have been shut down to clear the site for construction include an independent bookstore, a knitting club, a branch of the gay sauna Chariots, and an independent fashion boutique named What the Butler Wore whose owners left behind a handwritten sign in the window reading: 'Enjoy dunking your gourmet sausages in your flat white.' At the time of writing, two other large hotels were also under construction on the same street. For more details see James Hatt, 'Another hotel for Lower Marsh gets Lambeth approval', *London SE1* (5 April 2017)

48 Jasper Delamothe, *Hell's Waiting Room: Aylesbury Estate* (artwork displayed as part of the 'A Rock and a Hard Place' exhibition at the V3 Gallery in 2017)

Chapter 6

1 Although Momentum still plays a major role in organising The World Transformed, the two are technically separate entities.

2 Tristram Hunt speaking on *Channel 4 News* (3 December 2015); John McTernan, quoted in Matt Dathan, 'So, who are the "moronic MPs" who nominated Jeremy Corbyn for the Labour leadership contest?', *Independent* (22 July 2015); Michael Portillo speaking on the BBC's *This Week* (17 January 2018); Toby Young speaking on the BBC's *Sunday Politics* (10 December 2017); Sajid Javid speaking in the House of Commons (28 March 2018)

3 Jeremy Gilbert, 'An epochal election: welcome to the era of platform politics', openDemocracy (1 August 2017)

4 Ibid.

5 Internal Momentum data shared with author.

6 David Bond, 'Labour's slick online campaign outguns Tory press', *Financial Times* (9 June 2017); Adam Becket and Adam Bienkov, 'Pro-Jeremy Corbyn group Momentum has won the battle for the soul of the Labour Party', *Business Insider* (25 September 2017); Jason Murugesu, 'Is Momentum's M.app the future of political organising?', *New Statesman* (22 September 2017)

7 Casper Hughes, 'How Momentum delivered Labour's stunning election result – and how the Tories are trying to copy it', *Independent* (19 July 2017)

8 Becky Bond and Zack Exley, *Rules for Revolutionaries: How Big Organizing Can Change Everything* (Chelsea Green, 2016), p. 4

9 Julian Jackson, 'How Croydon Went Red', Novara Media (18 June 2017)

10 Tweet by Paul Mason (@paulmasonnews) on 16 January 2018: https://twitter.com/paulmasonnews/status/953364895432626181

11 At the time of writing, tenants of Hamilton House were facing eviction as part of a controversial redevelopment plan pursued by the building owners Connolly & Callaghan. For more details, see Matty Edwards' excellent reporting for the *Bristol Cable,* including 'Hamilton House evictions begin as controversial development looms' (14 March 2018) and 'Bristol City Council to look into buying Hamilton House' (16 January 2019). Information on the campaign to save Hamilton House can be found at: https://www.hamiltonhouse.org/

12 Internal Momentum literature shared with author

13 Julia Kollewe, 'Rent-to-own retailer BrightHouse ordered to repay £14.8m to customers', *Guardian* (24 October 2017); Raymond Williams, 'Culture is Ordinary', in Jim McGuigan (ed.), *Raymond Williams on Culture & Society: Essential Writings* (SAGE, 2014)

14 Jessica Elgot, 'A quarter of McDonald's UK workers have seen viral Momentum video, Facebook data shows', *Guardian* (8 September 2017)

15 Internal Momentum data shared with author

16 Video available at the Momentum Facebook page: https://www.facebook.com/watch/?v=1934599106834234

17 Tom Blackburn, 'A Revolution of Souls: Culture Wars vs. Cultural Renewal', *New Socialist* (30 April 2018)

18 Ibid.

19 Angus Satow, 'Corbynism at a Crossroads', *New Socialist* (14 March 2019)

20 Paul Johnson, 'Labour is planning the most radical tax and spending reforms in over 70 years', Institute for Fiscal Studies (1 October 2018)

21 Lorna Finlayson, 'Corbyn Now', *London Review of Books* (27 September 2018)

22 'Alternative Models of Ownership', Labour Party (2017)

23 George Eaton, 'Corbynism 2.0: the radical ideas shaping Labour's future', *New Statesman* (19 September 2018)

24 Andy Beckett, 'The wilderness years: how Labour's left survived to conquer', *Guardian* (3 November 2017)

25 Ibid.

26 Maya Oppenheim, 'Nando's rejects Conservative Party member discount card idea', *Independent* (22 May 2018)

27 Richard Power Sayeed, 'Jeremy Corbyn is about to transform the Labour Party – again', *Independent* (9 January 2018); 'Labour bets millions on community organising to win next election', *Red Roar* (22 September 2018)

28 Heather Stewart, 'Momentum urges Labour to adopt "radical" pledges in next manifesto', *Guardian* (16 May 2019)

29 Jessica Elgot, 'Corbyn: Hammond right to say Labour threatens whole economic system', *Guardian* (13 October 2017)

30 'Banking on Climate Change – Fossil Fuel Finance Report Card 2019', BankTrack (2019). The sum of £67 billion has been converted from the $85 billion cited in the report.

31 At her request, Amelia's name has been changed.

32 At their request, the activist's name has not been used.

33 Marie Le Conte, 'Purgatory at the Hilton: what's happened to the mood at party conference?', *Prospect* (26 September 2017)

Chapter 7

1 Kieran Dodds, '"The Past we inherit, the Future we build": Lessons from the Durham Miners' Gala', *New Socialist* (12 July 2017)

2 Although women's banners had featured in previous galas, this one – commemorating the hundredth anniversary of some women gaining the vote, and their contribution to the region's mining industry and annual gala – was the first to be officially affiliated to the Durham Miners' Association.

3 Jeff Wyatt, 'My day at the historic Durham Miners' Gala', For Britain (23 August 2018)

4 Gavin Havery, '"For Britain" supporters led from Durham Miners' Gala "for own safety"', *Northern Echo* (17 July 2018)

5 At his request, Baz's name has been changed.

6 The claim that NFP's Facebook page has a reach of half a million users could not be independently verified.

7 Dan Evon, 'Is "LGBT" Adding a "P" for Pedosexuals?', Snopes (7 December 2017)

8 Jan-Werner Müller, 'Capitalism in One Family', *London Review of Books* (1 December 2016)

9 Jacob Weisberg, 'The Autocracy App', *New York Review* (25 October 2018); Ammar Kalia, Caelainn Barr and Angela Giuffrida, 'Revealed: how Italy's populists used Facebook to win power', *Guardian* (17 December 2018)

10 Emma Graham-Harrison, 'Far-right Facebook groups "spreading hate to millions in Europe"', *Guardian* (22 May 2019)

11 Donie O'Sullivan and Paula Newton, 'Zuckerberg and Sandberg ignore Canadian subpoena, face possible contempt vote', CNN (28 May 2019); Shoshana Zuboff, 'It's not that we've failed to rein in Facebook and Google. We've not even tried', *Guardian* (2 July 2019)

12 Henry Grabar, 'Apple Is Building "Town Squares" Now, Because Somebody Has To', Slate (12 September 2017)

13 Shoshana Zuboff, *The Age of Surveillance Capitalism: The Fight for a Human Future at the New Frontier of Power* (Profile, 2019)

14 Ibid.

15 Srnicek, *Platform Capitalism*, p. 31

16 'Losing to Win: The Truth About Amazon Prime', Engine (5 November 2018); Kate Fazzini, 'Amazon's facial recognition service is being used to scan mugshots, but it's also used to track innocuous things like soccer balls', CNBC (6 December 2018)

17 'Amazon and Google are losing money in a speaker price war', *New York Post* (3 January 2018)

18 Olivia Solon, '"It's digital colonialism": how Facebook's free internet service has failed its users', *Guardian* (27 July 2017)

19 Srnicek, *Platform Capitalism*, p. 6

20 Julia Carrie Wong, '"Good for the world"? Facebook emails reveal what really drives the site', *Guardian* (6 December 2018)

21 Frank Konkel, 'The Details About the CIA's Deal With Amazon', *The Atlantic* (17 July 2014); Lee Fang, 'Amazon Promises "Unwavering"

Commitment To Police, Military Clients Using AI Technology', The Intercept (30 July 2018)

22 Chris Stokel-Walker, 'Why Google consuming DeepMind Health is scaring privacy experts', *Wired* (14 November 2018)

23 Andrew J. Hawkins, 'Uber to open Advanced Technologies Center in Paris focused on flying taxis', The Verge (24 May 2018)

24 Leo Kelion, 'Facebook gives users trustworthiness score', BBC (21 August 2018); Karissa Bell, 'Facebook data reportedly helps companies guess your credit score', Mashable (20 May 2019)

25 Nicole Kobie, 'The complicated truth about China's social credit system', *Wired* (7 June 2019)

26 Daniel Cossins, 'Discriminating algorithms: 5 times AI showed prejudice', *New Scientist* (12 April 2018); Caroline Haskins, 'Dozens of Cities Have Secretly Experimented With Predictive Policing Software', Motherboard (6 February 2019); Leo Kelion, 'Crime prediction software "adopted by 14 UK police forces"', BBC (4 February 2019)

27 Cameron Bird et al., 'Silicon Valley revolt: meet the tech workers fighting their bosses over Ice, censorship and racism', *Guardian* (29 March 2019)

28 Wendy Liu, 'Abolish Silicon Valley', *Tribune* (10 January 2019)

29 Ronan Burtenshaw, 'The Old and the New', *Tribune* (26 November 2018)

30 John Harris, 'The Tories have forgotten their pro-EU voters. And they'll pay for it', *Guardian* (20 May 2019)

31 Quoted in Fintan O'Toole, *Heroic Failure: Brexit and the Politics of Pain* (Apollo, 2018), loc. 37.3, paragraph 8.21

32 Chris Tighe, 'Pro-Corbyn group challenges "heir of Blair" to be metro mayor', *Financial Times* (19 February 2019)

33 Hannah Graham, 'North-East revealed as having highest number of youngsters with far-right sympathies', *Chronicle* (11 November 2017)

34 Lester Holloway, 'Black & Asian Women Pay Highest Price for Austerity', Runnymede Trust (16 December 2016)

35 Severin Carrell, 'Scotland faces climate "apocalypse" without action to cut emissions', *Guardian* (31 May 2019)

36 India Bourke, 'Climate change will swallow England's coast – taking away not just homes, but memories too', *New Statesman* (26 October 2018)

37 Josh Gabbatiss, 'London under threat of "sinking" as global warming makes sea levels rise, new report finds', *Independent* (5 October 2018); Jack Loughran, 'Climate change to have disastrous impact on London by 2050, report warns', *Engineering and Technology* (19 June 2018)

38 Jennifer Williams, 'Manchester promises to phase out fossil fuels in 20 years in one of the world's toughest climate change pledges', *Manchester Evening News* (14 November 2018)

39 Jonathan Watts, 'Climate and economic risks "threaten 2008-style systemic collapse"', *Guardian* (12 February 2019)

Index